Distribution management: Mathematical modelling and practical analysis

Books on cognate subjects

Elements of linear programming with economic applications
R. C. GEARY & M. D. McCARTHY

Computer simulation models   JOHN SMITH

Mathematical model building in economics and industry
(2 vol.: First and Second Series)   ed. M. G. KENDALL

Econometric techniques and problems   C. E. V. LESER

An introduction to symbolic programming   P. WEGNER

Combinatorial chance   F. N. DAVID & D. E. BARTON

Complete catalogue available from Charles Griffin & Co. Ltd.

Distribution management:

Mathematical modelling and practical analysis

SAMUEL EILON, D.Sc.(Eng.), Ph.D.
Professor of Industrial Management

C. D. T. WATSON-GANDY, M.Phil., M.Sc.(Eng.)

NICOS CHRISTOFIDES, Ph.D., D.I.C.

All of Imperial College of Science and Technology, London

Griffin London

CHARLES GRIFFIN & COMPANY LIMITED
42 DRURY LANE, LONDON, WC2B 5RX

First published   1971

Medium Octavo, viii + 240 pages
69 line illustrations, 41 tables
ISBN 0 85264 191 5

Set by Typesetting Services Ltd, Glasgow C.2
Printed in Great Britain by Compton Printing Ltd, London and Aylesbury

288812

Preface

The distribution function does not seem to have attracted a great deal of attention from management scientists before the 1960's. The need to store and transport goods has always been taken for granted, and it is only in recent years that serious attempts have been made to develop analytical tools in the study of activities in distribution systems. The number, size, and location of depots in a system, the analysis of cost functions of transportation, the design of delivery routes—these are the problems on which attention has been focused recently, and these are the topics discussed in this volume.

Research on distribution systems started in the Management Engineering Section at Imperial College in 1965, and this work was subsequently intensified under a grant from the Science Research Council. The results of the work are summarized in this book. First, an attempt is made to review the literature, which in some fields (as in the depot location problem or the travelling salesman problem) is quite extensive. Secondly, an array of analytical models are described, some well known but many quite new. In certain cases we could not resist the temptation of treating some of the models in a rather general way, because of their possible applications in fields other than distribution—for example, the travelling salesman problem (which has applications in many questions of sequencing) or the loading problem (which has applications in questions of cutting stock). Thirdly, brief references are made to the experience that we have had in the use of these models.

The application of operational research in distribution systems is still in its infancy. There is much to be studied, and many avenues remain to be explored. We hope that this volume will make a modest contribution to this interesting area.

London
December, 1970

S.E.
C.D.T.W.-G.
N.C.

Contents

Chapter 1

Introduction

THE LOGISTICS SYSTEM

Logistics is concerned with the provision of goods and services from a supply point to a demand point. The important role of logistics in warfare has led the armed forces to devote a great deal of attention to the subject, so much so that in people's minds—and in many dictionaries—logistics is associated with the military. But the pro-

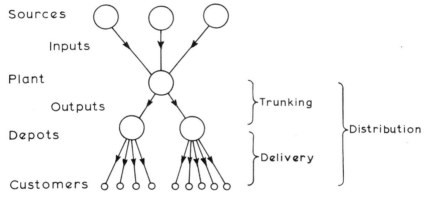

Fig. 1.1   A logistics system

vision of goods and services is also a vital component of commerce and industry, so that in terms of costs and efficiency alone it is a field that merits close examination.

A complete logistics system for an enterprise is shown in Fig. 1.1. A plant is fed with several inputs that come from a variety of sources. The inputs are converted into products (or outputs) by a manufacturing process, and the products are transported to customers through intermediary stores or depots. The shipment of goods to depots is often carried out in bulk (called "trunking"), while the supply to customers generally involves smaller consignments, so that trunking and delivery operations need not always use the same transportation media. The distribution system covers the supply of goods from the factory to customers, and as such it may be regarded as part of the wider logistics system, although the methods of analysis suggested in this book can be extended to cover the supply operations to the factory as well.

The industrial enterprise, which consists of the plant and the depots in the distribution system, occupies a position between the sources of inputs and the market. The enterprise is concerned with the conversion of all these inputs into goods and services that are made available at a point where the customer wishes to use them. Thus, for given locations of the sources and for given requirements of the market, the enterprise needs to plan for effective execution of the various interim operations. It needs, for example, to determine the appropriate location for siting the plant (or plants) and depots, and it is not surprising that the problem of site selection has attracted a great deal of attention from research workers in recent years. In the last decade alone, at least 70 papers have been written on distribution and related topics from a management science viewpoint, and the majority of these papers have been published in the last five years.

There appears at present to be a complete lack of standardization of nomenclature in this field. The terms *plant, depot, warehouse, site* are often used interchangeably, and the choice of terminology is to some extent a function of the nationality of the authors concerned. In this volume we have adopted the following definitions:

A plant is a factory in which some form of production takes place;
A warehouse or *depot* is a centre at which goods are stored and then delivered to customers;
A site is the location of a plant or a warehouse.

We therefore make no distinction between a warehouse and a depot. The characteristics of depots may, of course, vary greatly from one distribution system to another. Some consist of large stores, in which goods are stored for a considerable length of time before delivery; others serve merely as transition points, where large consignments supplied in bulk are broken into smaller consignments for delivery to customers.

In the distribution system the plant supplies one or several depots, and each depot supplies several customers. The flow of goods is usually from the plant to the depot and then to the customer. There are, of course, many distribution systems which do not adhere to this simple model. For example, we often find plants which supply direct to customers, even though there are intermediary depots in the system. In such cases the plant has a dual role as a manufacturing unit and also as a depot. Similarly, there are systems in which some operations on the product are carried out at the depots, such as assembly and finishing operations, packing and labelling, etc. Here the depot combines the dual role of manufacturing unit and distribution centre. Sometimes the depots have a hierarchical structure: a depot supplies several subdepots, and each subdepot then supplies certain customers, while others may be supplied direct from central depots or from the plant.

The flow need not always be confined to the direction of the customer. The postal system, for example, consists of a flow of material from sorting offices to houses, but also a flow from collection boxes to sorting offices; collection of garbage is another example of flow from a large number of scattered points to central points, at which sorting and disposal operations take place. Telephone subscribers may either receive calls from a central exchange, or generate calls to the exchange. In such examples clearly no manufacturing operations in the conventional sense take place, and in considering such systems a wider logistic approach, such as indicated in Fig. 1.1, usually needs to be adopted. Nevertheless, there is in principle no difficulty in adapting the methods discussed in this book to such cases, and the discussion of a distribution system in the context of a hierarchical flow as shown in the diagram (from plant to depots to customers) does not affect the generality of our treatment or its application to the solution of a wide variety of logistic problems.

THE TOTAL COST FUNCTION

In considering the performance of a distribution system we must take account of the total costs incurred in the transportation and storage of goods, and the total cost function C may therefore be described as

$$C = F+G+H \qquad (1.1)$$

where F = cost of the depots in the system,
          G = trunking costs from plants to depots,
          H = local delivery costs from depots to customers.

Not included in this cost function are the conversion or manufacturing costs at the plants and the costs of inputs to the plants, but these costs may be added to the function when a more comprehensive analysis of the logistic system is thought to be desirable. Let us now consider briefly the three cost terms in equation (1.1).

Depot costs

The cost of running a depot in the system consists of the following components:

- depreciation of buildings or rental of premises, maintenance and repairs;
- rates, electricity and other services;
- cost of equipment and personnel for handling the merchandise;
- administration, communication network, invoicing;
- cost of inventories (interest charges, cost of maintenance of goods, deterioration and obsolescence).

These costs may often be combined to yield a total cost for depot i expressed as

$$F_i = a_i + f_i(W_i) \tag{1.2}$$

where $\quad a_i = $ fixed costs for depot i ($i = 1, 2, \ldots, m$),
$\quad\quad f_i(W_i) = $ variable costs which depend on the throughput W_i,

and the cost of all the depots in the system is then

$$F = \sum F_i \tag{1.3}$$

where $\sum$ stands for $\sum_{i=1}^{m}$.

The following comments are appropriate:

(1) The fixed costs a_i may be dependent on the location of the depot, but when it is the same for all depots in the system (i.e. $a_i = a$) then equation (1.3) reduces to

$$F = ma + \sum f_i(W_i) \tag{1.4}$$

(2) For the sake of simplicity, the variable costs are expressed here in terms of the throughput, but in some cases it may be more convenient to use two other important factors, namely either the area of the depot or the level of inventory as indicators for computing variable costs. The use of throughput suggests that we expect the costs to be incurred by the flow and handling of the materials; the area is associated with rental costs of the space required for the depot; the inventory level has implications on carrying charges (including

interest). All three factors should, in fact, be accounted for in the variable cost term in equation (1.2). However, as in a given firm or even industry there is likely to be a close correlation between the three, the choice of a single factor for the variable cost term is probably justified.

(3) The characteristics of the function $f_i(W_i)$ may be different for different depots, for example when handling costs are significant and when they depend on labour costs that differ from one locality to another. If this is not the case then the functions $f_i(W_i)$ may be replaced by a single function $f(W_i)$.

Trunking costs

There are numerous factors that affect trunking costs, and the following is not intended as a comprehensive list:

- the type of the commodity to be transported, the care with which it should be handled and loaded or unloaded;
- the variety of goods involved, and whether some goods impose restrictions on the transportation of others in the system;
- the medium of transportation (rail, road, air, sea or river transport);
- the size of the transportation media;
- the ownership of these media.

The last factor is particularly important. If the means of transportation are owned by the firm, then fixed costs are incurred in addition to the variable costs that arise from the transportation operation itself; but if the organization relies on an outside contractor to move the goods to the depots, then it is more usual to express the trunking costs as directly related to the amount transported for the distances involved.

The main forms of the trunking costs function are as follows:

(1) The costs are weight (or volume) and distance dependent, taking the form

$$G = \beta \sum W_i d_i \qquad (1.5)$$

where β = cost per unit amount per unit distance,
W_i = amount transported from the plant to depot i,
d_i = distance from plant to depot i; this distance may either be the shortest straight-line distance, or the actual distance covered by the transportation medium.

(2) Haulage contractors sometimes quote costs that are weight dependent but not distance dependent:

$$G = \sum \gamma_i W_i \qquad (1.6)$$

where γ_i is the cost per unit amount (say, per ton) transported to depot i and W_i is the amount transported to that depot. The cost parameter γ_i may depend on the location of the depot, so that some sites may be cheaper to transport goods to because of ease of access or because of the possibility of return loads. The implication of such a cost function is that if γ_i is quoted for a given area, then the trunking cost to a depot of a given throughput remains the same for all possible locations of the depot in that area, but the cost function will suddenly assume a new value when the depot is moved across the boundary of the area.

(3) If the trunking is done by containers (say vehicles), each of a given capacity, and if the cost of transporting a container remains the same whether it is full or empty, then the costs may assume the form

$$G = \beta_0 N + \sum \beta_i N_i d_i \qquad (1.7)$$

where $\beta_0 =$ the fixed cost per container (e.g. per vehicle in the case of a company-owned fleet),
  $N =$ the total number of containers (the fleet size),
  $\beta_i =$ the cost per unit distance to transport a container to i,
  $N_i =$ the number of containers transported to depot i.

Equation (1.7) is a general expression for the trunking costs. For the special case $\beta_0 = 0$ and β_i being the same for all locations (say, $\beta_i = \beta$), an equation similar to (1.5) is obtained. For the case when $\beta_0 = 0$ and when the locality rather than the distance travelled is an important factor, equation (1.7) is reduced to one similar to (1.6).

Local delivery costs

A general cost function for local deliveries from depot to customers may be expressed in a form resembling equation (1.7). It is more usual, however, to express this cost as

$$H = \alpha \sum w_j d_{0j} \qquad (1.8)$$

which is similar to (1.5), except that now

  $\alpha =$ delivery costs per unit amount per unit distance,
  $w_j =$ amount delivered to customer j $(j = 1, 2, \ldots, n)$,
  $d_{0j} =$ distance from the depot to customer j,

and $\sum$ stands for $\sum_{j=1}^{n}$. Thus, H is computed for each depot and then summed for all the depots in the system.

The distance d_{0j} in equation (1.8) represents the radial distance between the depot and the customer, which is relevant to the case when a vehicle supplies a customer and then returns to base. In most cases, however, a vehicle may supply several customers in a single tour, and the sum of the lengths of these tours, rather than the sum of the radial distances, needs to be considered.

PROBLEMS IN DISTRIBUTION MANAGEMENT

The management of a distribution system involves the many typical problems that are encountered in the management of any industrial enterprise: there are administrative problems in running the depots, in designing an information and paperwork system, in layout and materials handling, in personnel, in incentives and industrial relations, and so on. All these issues are outside the scope of this volume. We shall mainly devote our attention here to two problems:

(a) the number and location of depots in the system; ·
(b) the routing of vehicles to deliver goods from depots to customers.

The first may be loosely regarded as the *strategic* problem and the second as the *tactical* problem. This distinction is merely a matter of convenience and is associated with the time-span and frequency of the decisions involved. The problem of depot location is not one that the management is likely to consider constantly, and once a decision is made regarding the number and location of the depots, it is not one that will be lightly or frequently altered. The problem of vehicle scheduling, however, needs to be resolved repeatedly, sometimes even every day, and decisions may be altered from one time-period to another, often with impunity.

As we shall see in the next chapter, the depot location problem is not a single problem. The number of depots in the system, their respective sizes, their locations, the allocation of customers to depots – all these are inter-related problems which need to be examined closely. Furthermore, in determining the location of depots it may be necessary to take account of the availability of suitable sites, the proximity of trunk roads (or access to other means of transport), and the availability of labour, as well as numerous other factors.

Furthermore, the vehicle routing problem is not independent of other associated problems, such as the capacity of vehicles used for local delivery, the size and composition of the vehicle fleet, the frequency with which customers should be supplied, and the degree to which the depot should use its own delivery fleet or rely on haulage contractors.

It is also important to realize that problems (a) and (b) cannot always be treated in isolation, since a solution to the one may well affect the other. For example, it is possible to reduce substantially the local delivery costs in equation (1.1) by increasing the number of depots in the system. This will have the effect of shortening the vehicle routes for local deliveries and thereby reduce H in equation (1.8), but the sum of the costs of running depots and trunking is then bound to increase. Similarly, a reduction in F and G in equation (1.1) can be achieved at the expense of H. What we seek, therefore, is a minimum for the overall cost function C through some compromise between depots and trunking costs on the one hand and local delivery costs on the other.

Nevertheless, the distinction between the strategic and the tactical problems is operationally both convenient and valid. In solving the depot location problem we need to take account of the expected local delivery costs and examine the circumstances under which the latter can affect the decision on siting of depots, while on a tactical level the vehicle scheduling problem needs to be analysed for any given location of depots in the distribution system.

THE FRAMEWORK OF THIS BOOK

This book is therefore divided into two parts, the first being devoted to the depot location problem. In Chapter 2 we summarize some of the work which is reported in the literature in this field. In Chapter 3 the single depot problem is discussed and the effect of customer demand on the location of the depot is analysed. Chapter 4 is devoted to the multi-depot problem and various models are suggested, each designed to handle certain assumptions about the cost structure. Chapters 3 and 4 are concerned with deterministic and constant demand from customers, while Chapter 5 examines several cases of variable demand, and Chapter 6 reports a case study on depot location.

The second part of the book deals with distribution from the depot to customers. In Chapter 7 we discuss the travelling salesman problem, namely the problem of designing the shortest route connecting several customers. In many of the problems analysed in the first part of the book it is necessary to feed into the total distribution cost function some estimate of the cost of local deliveries, and these depend on the distances that vehicles have to cover in their travels. Chapter 8 is therefore devoted to estimating these distances. In Chapter 9 the vehicle scheduling problem is analysed, namely the problem of designing vehicle routes, while taking account of distance and capacity constraints on the vehicles. Chapter 10 suggests methods for solving the vehicle loading problem, which is concerned with disposing of a given set of consignments to customers with the smallest number of vehicles, and Chapter 11 discusses methods for determining the optimal size of a vehicle fleet.

PART 1

Chapter 2

Review of the literature on depot location

INTRODUCTION

The father of modern location theory was probably Alfred Weber, who published his book *Uber den Standort der Industrien* in 1909 [46]. Weber examined the location of a plant with the objective of minimizing transportation costs in relation to three points, two of which represented sources of raw materials used for the manufacture of a single product, and the third point represented the market to which the product was supplied. The problem was reduced to finding the possible locations of the plant in order to minimize transportation costs, when the costs of labour and land were assumed to remain the same irrespective of the location. Weber made use of the "weight triangle" which, in conjunction with the locational triangle, permitted the geometrical determination of the resultant of forces. Pick, in his appendix to Weber's book, suggested the use of a force or mechanical analogue, a form of which is the well-known "weights and strings" method for determining the location of a single depot.

In the mathematical sense this problem was considered, in fact, by Cavalieri as early as 1647 [7]. Then Steiner [7, 26, 33] in 1837 solved the problem of finding the point (call it the "centre-point") at which the sum of the distances from it to three given points is a minimum. He subsequently showed that in the case of n points the necessary and sufficient conditions for the optimal centre-point are that the sum of the sines and cosines of the angles between any arbitrary line in the plane and the set of lines connecting the n points with the optimal centre-point must be zero. This result applies only for the special case of finding the location of one centre-point (a depot), when all the other points (customers) to be linked to it have equal weights.

The site selection problem is not one single problem, but a combination of interrelated problems [45], of which four can be identified:

(1) Determine the number of depots.
(2) Determine the location of sites for these depots.
(3) Determine the allocation of customers to these depots.
(4) Determine the size of the depot for each site, taking particular account of the economies of scale inherent in the operating costs of such centres.

Consequently, the general approach has been to treat the problem as a multi-stage decision process in which the parameters are optimized in sequence, each time assuming the other parameters to remain constant. Because of the complexities arising from the inter-relations of these problems, it has often been found necessary to make some simplifying assumptions in the structure of the model and to employ heuristic procedures for finding solutions to these problems.

Despite the seemingly large number of different methods suggested in the literature for the site selection problem, it is possible to distinguish between two basic approaches which authors appear to have taken. The first suggests that a site may be selected anywhere in the area of interest, i.e. there is an infinite number of possible sites. The second approach considers that there is only a finite number of known sites which are feasible. These two approaches will be referred to as the *infinite set* and the *feasible set* approach respectively, and the literature will be discussed under these two headings.

CHARACTERISTICS OF THE TWO APPROACHES

Before examining the various methods in detail it may be useful to enumerate some of the advantages and disadvantages of the two approaches to the problem. The main features of each approach are listed below:

The infinite set approach

(1) It does not require the locations which are selected to be *a priori* attractive.
(2) It is flexible in that it examines a monotonic function.
(3) Alternative solutions are available in multi-site selection problems.
(4) It is possible that the solution will involve a non-feasible location, e.g. a site on a mountain range.
(5) Transport costs must be a monotonic function of distance.

The feasible set approach

(1) It incorporates costs which are related to specific geographical locations.
(2) It does not require transport costs to be any function of distance.
(3) It requires a set of sites which are known to be feasible and for which all cost data are available.
(4) The number of locations must be finite and sufficiently small for computational efficiency.
(5) The set of feasible sites may not include the optimum solution.

One feature that most methods in the literature seem to ignore is the problem of journey planning. Most companies load each lorry with items to be delivered to several different customers in a single round trip. Hence the cost of one journey should be shared amongst many customers. In general both approaches assume that loads are delivered on a "straight there and back" basis. Where cognizance of this problem has been taken in the literature, the methods used rely on simulation, in which a journey-planning algorithm can be incorporated, or on clustering customers into groups, the demand of each group being approximately one lorry load.

THE INFINITE SET APPROACH

This approach is the older of the two, starting with the work of Weber [46]. The models used by the various exponents of the infinite set approach are basically quite similar. They all involve the major assumption that transport costs are a monotonic function of distance, and that this function can be minimized by minimizing the sum of the weighted straight-line distances. Mathematically, in the notation used here, the delivery cost for depot i $(i = 1, 2, \ldots, m)$ may be written as

$$H_i = \sum_{j=1}^{n} \alpha_j w_j d_{ij} \delta_{ij} \quad \text{for } i = 1, 2, \ldots, m \qquad (2.1)$$

where $\alpha_j w_j$ = cost of serving customer j $(j = 1, 2, \ldots, n)$ with the goods w_j that he requires,
d_{ij} = distance between customer j and depot i,
δ_{ij} = 1 or 0, depending on whether customer j is served by depot i or not, respectively.

For the problem of locating more than one depot, the cost is given by summing over all depots. The total cost function can, of course, contain other cost items, such as trunking and operating costs as in equation (1.1). This aspect is covered more fully in Chapter 4.

The problem of determining how many depots are required is usually solved by finding the optimal locations (with respect to transport costs) for 1, 2, 3, . . . depots and adding to each solution the respective costs of the depots; that number which gives the cheapest overall cost is selected as the optimum.

Proofs of the convexity of the model expressed in equation (2.1), showing that for one depot there is a unique minimum when the customer points are not collinear, are given by Palermo [35], Kuhn and Kuenne [26], Tideman [43] and Haley [18]. Haley's proof is quoted in Chapter 3.

As a model based on the infinite set approach is discussed in detail in the next two chapters, the literature will now be reviewed briefly under the heading of the methods used.

Numeric–analytic

The numeric–analytic technique, which is extended in the following chapters, is probably due to Miehle [33], who published his paper "Link-length minimization in networks" in 1958.

Miehle discusses the problem of link-minimization, "when a number of fixed points are to be interconnected through a specified number of junctions". In other words, this is the problem of locating a specified number of depots serving a number of customers when the depots are also interconnected. A special case of this model, i.e. when the depots are linked to the factory, is discussed in Chapter 4. Miehle describes the numeric–analytic technique which has the objective of minimizing the sum of the straight-line distances from the customers to the depots serving them. Briefly, the procedure is to take partial differentials of the objective function with respect to the x and y co-ordinates of each depot; these are set equal to zero and the resultant equations are solved with respect to the depot co-ordinates, thereby giving an improved location for the depot. The improved locations are then substituted back into the objective function, and the procedure is repeated iteratively until no further improvement can be made. The method requires some estimates for the depot locations before the procedure is embarked upon. Miehle also describes the use of Lagrange multipliers to incorporate constraints on the length of the inter-depot links, to cater for cases in which such links are pre-specified.

Wester and Kantner [47] describe a method similar to Miehle's, but which includes a transportation problem due to capacity constraints on the depots. Their method includes the use of the Hitchcock–Koopmans transportation algorithm. In the example problem given, the constraints are arbitrarily assigned and are relaxed and reassigned in the allocation procedure, and this suggests that the algorithm could have been considerably simplified. However, in problems where capacity constraints on depot size are important, this algorithm would prove extremely useful.

Cooper examines the location–allocation problem in a series of papers [7, 8, 9]. He describes a number of heuristic procedures in which the main emphasis is to find suitable starting locations before using a location procedure similar to that described by Miehle. These heuristics are complicated and time-consuming, and they are not suitable for problems in which customers are weighted, as has been noted in [9]. However, some points of interest for the construction of the general model are given. Cooper notes [8] that the objective function is shallow in the region of the optimum. This point, which is discussed further in Chapter 3, is of great importance in practical situations, since it implies that a depot can be moved from the precise optimal location to a more attractive or convenient site without a significant increase to the cost. In [9] Cooper and Drebes examine the problem of capacity constraints and the "limited radius" problem. Their algorithm designed to cater for capacity constraints, although sub-optimal, may prove useful in cases which are too large for the application of the transportation algorithm to be computationally feasible. The latter problem represents the case in which, due to legal or perhaps union restrictions, a lorry driver is not allowed to drive further than some pre-specified distance from base. The algorithm described is divided into two parts, the first for finding the minimum number of depots required to serve the area, the second for finding the best locations for these depots.

Mossman and Morton [34] describe a single depot problem in which the speed of delivery is of paramount importance in determining the order size of each customer. The model presented is essentially the same as those described by Miehle and Cooper, but differs from these two in that the weight delivered to customer j is defined by

$$w_j = w_j^{*-at_j/t_j^*}$$

where w_j = quantity ordered by customer j when the delivery
                time is t_j;
similarly w_j^* = quantity ordered with delivery time t_j^*,
           t_j^* = competitor's delivery time,
           a = proportionality factor for specific demand area and
                product.

The objective function of this model, like those of Miehle and
Cooper, is minimized by an iterative procedure involving improved
locations found from the partial differentials with respect to the depot
co-ordinates. Mossman and Morton also note that this model can be
used to measure the changes in revenue that might occur if com-
petitors speed up their deliveries, or as a guideline in comparing
vehicles, e.g. large and slow lorries versus small and fast ones.

Vergin and Rogers [44] examine the model as expressed in
equation (2.1), and describe a method of solution which involves
moving the depots along the x and y directions by an amount
dependent on the current gradients of the cost function with respect
to x and y. They discuss the choice of initial locations for the single
depot problem and give a proof showing that the centre of gravity
is not necessarily the optimum location for the model. This proof is
quoted in Chapter 3. Vergin and Rogers also discuss and give an
algorithm for what they call the Facilities Location Problem, in
which the distances are rectangular, i.e. movement between points
is restricted to the x and y planes only.

Dynamic programming

Bellman [4] discusses how quasi-linearization may be used to
transform a function such as is expressed in equation (2.1), into a
recursive maximizing form solvable by dynamic programming.
While this formulation is very interesting from an academic point of
view, much simpler algorithms are now available. The problem discussed by Bellman is that examined by Cooper [8], i.e. with equally
weighted customers, and is therefore restricted in character.

Electrical analogue

Electrical analogues are suggested by Brink and de Cani [5], who
use a special-purpose analogue designed to examine problems
involving two-dimensional scalar fields, and Eilon and Deziel [13],
who use a general-purpose machine. Both papers examine essentially

the basic model as in equation (2.1), but reformulated in a form particularly suited to the machine used (Brink and de Cani use a vector formulation while Eilon and Deziel employ a sine wave function).

Brink and de Cani also solve the problem in which the cost is represented by a logarithmic function of distance. They note the effect that heavily weighted (i.e. important) customers can have on the solution by "pulling" the depot closer to them: the more heavily weighted a customer is, relative to other customers, the stronger the effect of this attraction in the optimal solution.

Hitchings [21] also uses an electrical analogue based on the slide-wire principle, in which the distance from depot to customer is proportional to the length of the resistor. Hitchings uses this analogue to solve problems in both two and three dimensions, as well as problems involving discontinuities in the transport costs. These latter problems are analogous to cases in which it is cheaper to change the mode of transport beyond a certain distance.

Mechanical analogue

The mechanical analogue is the well-known "strings-and-weights" method. Since it cannot automatically yield the costs of any particular solution, it must be used in conjunction with some costing procedure, and compared with fast computer-aided methods that are now available it is cumbersome and its use is limited. It is still useful for the solution of the single-depot problem, and its main advantage is its visual appeal in that the effects of making changes to the system can be immediately observed. The method has been used and described by Burstall, Leaver and Sussams [6], Haley [18], Hepburn [19] and Shea [37]. A description of the analogue is given in Chapter 3.

Heuristic methods

Lawrence and Pengilly [27] describe a case study. Most of the effort in this study was apparently spent in developing a realistic cost function, which is quite comprehensive and even includes terms to allow for the reduction of driving speeds through large conurbations (such as London), terms to allow for restricted passage over natural hazards (such as the River Thames), a term to account for the cost of an overnight stay for trips which are longer than one day's drive from base, and differential rentals for depots in different areas. Customers are grouped into sub-areas in such a way that the aggregated demand of each sub-area is an integer number of lorry loads. The assumption is that the cost of making deliveries in any sub-area is constant and that it is only necessary to minimize the cost of travel to the sub-area. The search procedure used is to move each depot to each of the four corners of a square centred on the current depot location. The five locations are costed and the cheapest location is then retained for each depot in turn. When no improvement is found, the size of the square is halved and the process is repeated. The programme is repeated for 1, 2, 3, . . . depots and the cheapest solution is then selected. The authors note that this procedure does not guarantee the optimal solution and that the solution obtained depends on the starting locations (see also Cooper [8] and Chapter 4).

THE FEASIBLE SET APPROACH

The *feasible set approach* has arisen from consideration of two factors which the infinite set approach has not, until just recently, attempted to cater for. The first has to do with the fact that, in general, transportation costs need not be proportional to distance and in particular to straight-line distance; the second is that operating costs of individual depots can vary considerably from town to town and even from location to location in the same town. A further factor is that in many distribution studies the problem is not to set up a completely fresh system, but to select from a system of existing depots those which should be kept open and those which should be closed. The approach implicit in the feasible set method is to select a number of sites which are known to be available and for which actual costs of transportation to each customer and the depot operating costs can be determined. The problem now is to find from this set of locations the subset which minimizes the total distribution costs.

Mixed integer programming

This method of solution has been hampered by the presence of non-linearities in the cost functions, by the presence of fixed costs of the depots and by the problem of capacity constraints on depot size. Although the first and last problems have been largely ignored, some progress has been made to cater for the problem of the fixed costs.

Manne [31] uses the site selection problem to evaluate SAOPMA (the Steepest Ascent One Point Move Algorithm). However, he recognizes that once a choice is made of which sites are open and which are closed at any particular stage in the procedure, it becomes a simple matter to determine the flows from depot to customer. The formulation of this method of solution is in terms of "strategic" variables, indicating which depots are open and which are shut, and "tactical" variables, indicating the flows in the system. Mathematically the cost function is expressed by

$$C = \sum_{i,j} c_{ij} q_{ij} + \sum_{i} F_i \delta_i \qquad (2.2)$$

subject to
$$\sum_{i} q_{ij} = w_j \qquad (2.3)$$

$$q_{ij} \geqslant 0 \qquad (2.4)$$

$$\delta_i = 1 \text{ or } 0 \qquad (2.5)$$

where c_{ij} = the cost of supplying a unit to customer j ($j = 1, 2, \ldots,$ n) from depot i ($i = 1, 2, \ldots, m$); this term may also include the unit operating costs of depot i;
 q_{ij} = the number of units going from i to j;
 F_i = the fixed costs of depot i;
 δ_i = the strategic variable indicating whether depot i is open ($\delta_i = 1$) or closed ($\delta_i = 0$);
 w_j = the demand of customer j.

Constraint (2.3) merely states that the demands of all customers should be met.

An alternative formulation which may be used is that q_{ij} represents the fraction of demand of customer j supplied from depot i. c_{ij} now becomes the cost of serving customer j with the required demand.

The constraint set (2.3) then becomes

$$\sum_{i} q_{ij} = 1 \qquad (2.6)$$

and constraint (2.4) becomes

$$0 \leqslant q_{ij} \leqslant 1 \qquad (2.7)$$

The second formulation has little effect on the method of solution.

SAOPMA, the method evaluated by Manne, starts at an arbitrarily chosen lattice point and then moves to examine other alternative solutions.

Manne concludes that while SAOPMA does not guarantee the

optimum, it works very well. However, he tries the method only on small problems; with larger ones the computer time required is likely to be substantial.

Efroymson and Ray [12] use branch and bound as a method of solution. First they ignore the integer constraints and solve the problem as one in linear programming. The solution forms the first lower bound. If a δ_i in this solution has a fractional value, then the two alternative values of 1 and 0 are considered and the linear programming problem associated with each is solved. Two solutions C_1 and C_2 are thus obtained, and a new lower bound is given by min (C_1, C_2) for the node in the tree represented by the relevant value of δ_i and the values of any other δ_i which have been held at either 1 or 0.

This procedure requires a large number of linear programs to be solved, and the authors therefore proceed to reformulate the problem. In addition to the variables defined earlier, let

M_j = the set of depots that can supply customer j;
P_i = the set of customers that can be supplied from depot i;
n_i = the number of elements in P_i.

The constraint sets become

$$\sum_{i \in M_j} q_{ij} = 1 \quad \text{for } j = 1, 2, \ldots, n \text{ (demand must be satisfied)}$$

$$0 \leqslant \sum_{j \in P_i} q_{ij} \leqslant n_i \delta_i \quad \text{for } i = 1, 2, \ldots, m \tag{2.8}$$

Because of the lack of capacity constraints it is clear that $q_{ij} = 1$ or 0 in the solution, i.e. a depot will serve all or none of the demand of a particular customer.

Efroymson and Ray assert that at any node in the branch-and-bound tree three sets can be identified:

K_0 – includes all the sites at which no depots are located;
K_1 – includes all the sites at which depots are located;
K_2 – includes the "free" sites for which a decision to locate depots has not been made.

Their method is to consider customer j and scan every depot in set K_1 and K_2 and assign the customer to that depot for which we have

$$\min_{i \in K_1 \cup K_2} \left[c_{ij} + g_i/n_i \right] \tag{2.9}$$

where $g_i = \begin{cases} F_i \text{ for } i \in K_2 \\ 0 \text{ for } i \in K_1. \end{cases}$

The depot selected in this way (call it $i*$) leads to $q_{i*j} = 1$ and for all the other depots in $K_1 \cup K_2$ we have to set $q_{i*j} = 0$. If $i* \in K_2$ the value of δ_{i*} is given by

$$\delta_{i*} = \frac{1}{n_{i*}} \sum_{j \in P_i} q_{i*j} \qquad (2.10)$$

This formulation has the advantage that it is now simple and quick to evaluate each node. It has the disadvantage that the number of customers served by depot i is small compared with n_i, which is the potential number it could serve. Hence the amount of the fixed charge absorbed by the depot will be small. To speed up the program the authors have developed three simplifications:

(1) If the minimum net saving obtained by opening a depot exceeds the fixed costs incurred thereby, then it pays to open that depot.
(2) If for any depot i in K_2 it is cheaper to serve customer j from another depot in K_1 then reduce n_i by one. Of course, if this applies to all $j \in P_i$, then $\delta_i = 0$, i.e. that depot can be closed.
(3) If the maximum net saving obtained by opening a depot i in K_2 is negative, then set $\delta_i = 0$ for all branches emanating from that node.

Efroymson and Ray consider three types of depot operating costs. The first is linear with respect to throughput with a fixed charge incurred by opening a depot. The second is concave, composed of two linear segments and with no fixed costs. The third is also composed of two linear segments, but includes fixed costs. The authors state that they solved a number of problems of the order of 50-depot-200-customers with depot costs of the first two types. The computer time on an IBM 7094 was on average about ten minutes. This method was originally written to test the heuristic method of Feldman, Lehrer and Ray [15] (see later).

Gray [16] is mainly concerned with an upper bounded fixed-charge site-selection problem. This problem can be described as that of choosing from a set of warehouses, in which goods can be stock-piled, that subset which satisfies the demand at minimum cost, subject to the constraints on maximum warehouse capacity. The cost function contains a variable cost per unit stored, and a fixed cost associated with each continuous variable. This may be formulated as

$$\text{Minimize } C = \Sigma c_i q_i + \Sigma F_i \delta_i \qquad (2.11)$$

where q_i is the throughput of depot i and c_i is the variable cost per ton at that depot. The constraints are the same as described earlier, except that an additional constraint for warehouse capacity is given by

$$M\delta - q \geqslant 0 \qquad (2.12)$$

where M = a matrix expressing the capacity constraint of depots, and equation (2.3) becomes

$$Aq \geqslant w$$

where A = an $m \times n$ constraint matrix.

Gray uses a version of the Hillier "bound-and-scan" algorithm [20] to generate δ vectors in the form of 0, 1 strings. To reduce the number of 0, 1 strings that must be examined, Gray suggests both upper and lower bounds on the fixed cost $F\delta$.

The initial value for the upper bound F_{max} can be found in the following way. The problem is first solved as a linear program without the integer constraints, and all non-zero δ_i are rounded up to their upper value 1. This problem is simplified by recognizing that at the optimum $\delta_i = q_i/m_i$ (where m_i is the capacity constraint on depot i) is the minimum value of δ_i. Let the value of this solution be L_0. A second linear program is then solved assuming all warehouses open, i.e.

$$\text{Minimize} \quad cq$$

$$\text{subject to} \quad Aq \geqslant w ; \quad 0 \leqslant q \leqslant m$$

which gives a solution C_0. Hence

$$F_{max} = L_0 - C_0$$

This upper bound can be tightened as the program proceeds by substituting a better solution for L_0. The lower bound F_{min} can be found by solving the problem without the integer constraints and with the variable costs set equal to zero, or simply by inspection. This conservative lower bound does not change throughout the program. The Hillier algorithm is then used to generate 0, 1 vectors subject to the constraints $F_{min} \leqslant F\delta \leqslant F_{max}$, and the linear program given below is solved, i.e.

$$\text{Minimize} \quad cq$$

$$\text{subject to} \quad Aq \geqslant w \text{ and to equation } (2.12).$$

Gray extends this approach to three other problems, and algorithms are presented for

- the case for which variable costs are concave or convex (note that these costs should be separable);
- the fixed charge transportation problem, in which fixed costs are associated with the opening of each route;
- the depot location problem where, because of the capacity constraints, variable costs and constraints are of the transportation type and a fixed charge is associated with the opening of each depot.

For this last problem, with which we are most concerned in this book, Gray states there are difficulties in the use of the Hillier algorithm, because of the large number of variables involved. He suggests finding an initial feasible solution by some other method, e.g. the heuristic approach of Kuehn and Hamburger [25] (see later), and then a stripped-down version of the Hillier algorithm, or some other branch-and-bound technique.

Spielberg [40] presents a direct-search mixed integer algorithm for the site-selection problem without capacity constraints. The main objective of his work is to gain computational experience with the mixed-integer programming algorithm of Lemke and Spielberg [28], and to experiment with some devices which may prove useful in similar but more complicated problems. Spielberg uses the second formulation described above, and his procedure falls into three parts:

(1) A search procedure which provides a vector of 0, 1 values for the δ_i. This is in effect a branch-and-bound procedure.

(2) A linear program which, with a given vector of δ, provides lower bounds for the integer problem.

(3) A series of tests designed to cut off branches of the tree.

The transportation method

Baumol and Wolfe [3] describe a case study in some detail. The cost function that they use is the sum of the transportation costs from the factory to depots and from depots to customers. Also included are depot operating costs of the form

$$F\delta + aW^{\alpha}$$

where F is the fixed cost, which does not apply if the depot is not used (i.e. $\delta = 1$ when the depot is used, otherwise $\delta = 0$). The second term of the depot operating costs is a concave function, where

a is a constant;

W = throughput of the depot;

α = an exponent; the authors suggest that the value $\alpha = \frac{1}{2}$ would be in keeping with inventory control practice.

Their procedure is to build a matrix of "transportation" costs from the factory to each customer through that depot that gives the cheapest costs, and then solve the resulting transportation problem. In the first calculation this matrix holds only the pure transport costs, namely the transport costs from factory to depot plus the costs from depot to customer. In subsequent iterations the matrix of costs is built up of transport costs plus the marginal depot operating costs. These transportation problems are constructed and solved until the throughput of the depots does not change from one iteration to the next. The authors point out that this formulation does not take the fixed costs into consideration. They also point out that as a concave function is involved, the method "may take us to the bottom of a ravine" (a local optimum) "and not to the true lowest point".

This point is also stressed by Kuehn and Hamburger [25] (see later) who show that in the small illustrative example given by Baumol and Wolfe, the optimum number of depots is not 4 as suggested, but that each of three of these depots, taken singly, gives a cheaper solution, and this suggests that the method tends to leave too many depots in the final solution. Losch [30] uses a similar approach, but states that in his study there are no fixed costs.

Balinski and Mills [1] consider a concave cost function, which is the sum of the depot and trunking costs, as being piecewise linear and with downward breaks at each point of the change of slope. The authors approximate this function by the average unit depot costs at the appropriate portion of the costs curve, and this enables the problem to be solved by the transportation method within the constraints of depot capacity and of satisfying customer demand. The solution to the transportation problem gives a value λ_Q for the cost function, and this is a lower bound to the optimal solution. If the flows from the transportation solution are substituted back into the original cost equation, a value λ_P is found. The authors prove that the value of the optimal solution lies between the two bounds λ_Q and λ_P. Unfortunately these bounds can sometimes be quite far apart.

Jandy [22] presents an approximate algorithm for the fixed charge, "capacitated" (i.e. having constraints on depot capacity) site location problem. The problem includes linear transport and/or production costs and a fixed charge F_{ki} for a depot at site i

$(i = 1, 2, \ldots, m)$ with capacity k $(k = 1, 2, \ldots, p)$. The problem is formulated as

$$\text{Minimize } C = \sum_{k,i,j} c_{kij} q_{kij} + \sum_{k,i} F_{ki} \delta_{ki} \qquad (2.13)$$

(subject to capacity constraints)

where $c_{kij} =$ production and transport costs from site i of capacity k to customer j $(j = 1, 2, \ldots, n)$;

        $q_{kij} =$ amount delivered from i to j;

        $\delta_{ki} = 1$ or 0 when site i is open or closed at capacity k respectively.

This problem is solved as a transportation problem by imputing a unit investment cost to each plant. Initially this unit cost is based on the assumption that each depot is used to its full capacity. After each iteration, in which the transportation problem is solved optimally, the unit costs are amended, reflecting the changes in the attractiveness of each site. The algorithm also includes a step to allow for the pairwise interchange of cells (i.e. removing under-utilized sites or replacing such sites with other sites), if the objective function shows an improvement.

Simulation methods

Simulation is probably much more widely used in practice than is evident from the literature. This may be due to the understandable reluctance to publish data of a confidential nature.

Shycon and Maffei [39] describe a simulation carried out for the H. J. Heinz Company in America. The model includes production capacities on the factories as a parameter, but there are no constraints on depot size. It also assumes straight-line distances rather than "point-to-point" costs. The simulation includes customer ordering patterns and the transportation rate structure (i.e. bulk loads and depot costs related to geographical areas). The authors point out that once the model is built, it can be used to cost alternative systems, but they stress that the accuracy of the model depends on the availability of suitable data and the capacity of the computer used. They state that the total cost function is shallow in the region of the optimum, and we note that the smaller the number of depots in the solution the less shallow the cost function; but it appears that this point is made for the benefit of the "decision-making executive" (for whom the article is aimed) to indicate that he is not entirely superfluous.

Simulations have also been used by Shea [37] to cost solutions produced by the mechanical analogue.

Heuristic methods

It may be argued that all the methods described earlier involve heuristic procedures of one form or another. However, the three papers mentioned below have no pretensions of including anything else, and they are presented by their authors on the premise that a near-optimal solution may be obtained by determining the location of depots one by one.

Kuehn and Hamburger [25] describe an approach in which depots are added into the solution one at a time. As with all heuristic methods, the cost function is not restricted to any one particular form, and it can be very comprehensive. The function considered by these authors contains trunking and local delivery costs, depot operating costs (both fixed and variable), and also a cost term for delays in delivery. They state that capacity constraints on depots can also be considered, although they do not elaborate on this point.

The procedure developed by Kuehn and Hamburger is composed of two parts. The main program operates by adding that depot which produces the greatest cost saving. The program utilizes two lists of depots, the one holding a list of m potential sites, the other a buffer store of m' especially favoured sites (the value of m' is chosen arbitrarily). At each stage the list of potential sites is examined in relation to local demand only, and those m' sites which give the greatest savings are placed in the buffer store. Each of these m' sites is then evaluated in detail and is either designated as a depot, or returned to the list, or removed from further consideration if no savings are made. When the list of potential sites is exhausted, the program enters the second stage, called the *bump and shift* routine. This routine eliminates any depots which are now uneconomical, because of the proximity of other depots ("bump"). It also attempts to make further savings by relocating each depot at other sites in its neighbourhood ("shift"). The authors have examined several problems using this method, one of which is given, and state that computing time increases at a slower rate with increasing problem size than when linear programming methods are used. They also give an appendix in which the transportation methods of Baumol and Wolfe [3], and Balinski and Mills [1], and the simulation method of Shycon and Maffei [39] are examined.

Feldman, Lehrer and Ray [15] extend the work of Kuehn and

Hamburger [25] in two ways. First, they incorporate a heuristic method to handle concave depot-operating costs; secondly, they introduce a *drop approach* as well as the *add approach* of Kuehn and Hamburger. A *drop approach* is suggested because the *add approach* has an initial rapid drive to achieve feasibility, which may not be the best route to the optimum. The cost function they seek to minimize is similar to that of Kuehn and Hamburger for a single product and without differentials for bulk haulage. They assume that suppliers are unwilling to serve customers more than a certain distance from base, and this takes the form of limiting the number of depots which may serve a particular customer.

The drop approach starts with all depots in the solution, and that depot which achieves the greatest cost saving when removed is then dropped. The add approach utilizes local demand to estimate which portion of the depot operating cost curve is relevant (piecewise linear approximation for this curve is used). The authors note that the solution is sensitive to the shape of the depot cost function, and that making a linear approximation to this function can result in an increased cost solution. They note that as a supplier is unwilling to deliver to customers further than a certain distance from the depot, an insufficient number of depots will mean a loss of sales. However, they do not incorporate an extra term in the cost function to balance this loss against the cost of having an extra depot to serve these customers.

Sussams [42] presents a discursive paper on the location of factory, depot and subdepot. The method is not described in detail, but is partly intuitive. The choice of locations is based on the size of population centres (i.e. it is assumed that demand is related to population) and alternative locations are costed and compared. The method finds the best locations for 1, 2, . . . units up to the point at which the smallest unit remains just economically viable. Sussams also includes a discussion on some marketing considerations which are thrown up by such a study of a distribution system.

Drysdale and Sandiford [10] describe a procedure which incorporates some features of the methods in [15] and [25], and in particular, the drop approach of Feldman, Lehrer and Ray [15]. The method also includes a heuristic procedure whereby the depot fixed costs are incremented stepwise from zero to their final value. The authors state that this procedure is more satisfactory than a single-step increase in that it is less likely to remove depots incorrectly, particularly in the early stages of the program. The authors suggest that 5 per cent step increases are suitable.

The method is designed to solve problems in which the delivery routes have to follow a specified network, and the shortest route algorithm of Shimbel [38] is used. Two tests are performed at each iteration. The first examines whether the depots are justified, namely whether the savings in transport costs by using a depot are greater than the costs of opening it. All depots are tested in pairs for all combinations of pairs. If a depot fails this test, it is removed from the solution. The second test examines whether any depots which have been removed from the system have resulted in an appropriate saving. If this test is negative, the depot is reinstated. A case study is very briefly described; the computer time (on an IBM 360-50) for this study (a 58-node problem) varied between 4 and 30 minutes, depending on the cost parameters used.

Networks

The methods relating to the problem of site selection in a given network are included here in the category of the *feasible set approach* because all nodes in the network are regarded as possible sites, and the assumption is that they are known to be feasible. These methods are particularly suited for site selection in a rail or road network, and account can be taken of the effect of traffic congestion in the network.

Hakimi [17] and Levy [29] use graph theory to show that the optimal locations will always be at the nodes of the network. Hakimi also presents an algorithm for the problem of finding the centre of a graph. This is a min–max problem analogous to that of determining the location of a police station or a hospital with the object of minimizing the maximum distance from the centre of the network.

Maranzana [32] and Surkis [41] use a method similar to the location–allocation method of Cooper [8]. They differ only slightly in approach and in the algorithms they use to find the shortest distance matrix. Their method is to allocate customers to their nearest depot. The procedure then finds amongst the set of customers allocated to a particular depot, that customer location (i.e. node of the network) that minimizes the transport costs defined as the sum of the weighted distances. Mathematically, given P_i, the set of indices of those customers served by depot i, they find the location j_0 ($j_0 \in P_i$) such that

$$\sum_{j \in P_i} w_j d_{jj_0} \leqslant \sum_{j \in P_i} w_j d_{ij} \quad \text{for all } i$$

where w_j = the demand of customer j ($j = 1, 2, \ldots, n$), and

d_{ij} = the shortest distance from customer j to point i (need not be the straight-line distance).

Having found j_0, the depot is then removed to that node; it is re-labelled as i and customers are then re-allocated. This procedure is repeated iteratively until the locations do not change. The optimum number of depots is found by repeating this process for 1, 2, . . . depots and selecting that solution which yields the lowest total cost. Note that trunking costs are not considered in this formulation, but they can be included if required.

A DYNAMIC FORMULATION

All the algorithms described so far, both for the infinite and the feasible set approaches, may be regarded as static in character because they consider the problem only at a given point in time. Let us now turn to two papers which examine the problem of site selection over a planning horizon.

Klein and Klimpel [24] are concerned with developing an algorithm to solve the problem of determining the location and size of a depot over a planning horizon. They adopt the feasible set approach and incorporate economies of scale inherent in depot size. They suggest polynomial expressions for fixed capital requirements, annual working capital (which is assumed recoverable at the end of the project life), fixed and variable annual costs. Given forecasts of demands and of the costs of known sites, the objective function is the sum of the net present values for all depot locations, and this is the function to be maximized, subject to the constraint of satisfying demand and to non-negativity constraints for depot sizes and for shipment sizes. This problem, which has a non-linear objective function and linear constraints, can be solved by the "gradient projection" method of Rosen [36]. The method converges to a solution which may be a local optimum, because of the non-linearity of the objective function, so that several runs may be necessary with different initial feasible solutions. The authors illustrate the method with a single product, "one-shot" plant construction problem, which involves 4 possible sites of which 3 are customers, and consists of 40 variables and 62 constraints. Some 10 runs were required for this problem and each run took approximately 4 minutes on a B-5500 computer.

Ballou [2] employs dynamic programming to determine the depot location strategy over the planning horizon. The method that Ballou proposes is to use a static model to determine the most economic locations for each year of the planning period, from which the best location strategy can be developed. The choice of a static model can be based either on an infinite or a feasible set model, although Ballou uses the infinite set approach of Mossman and Morton [34], which he transforms into a maximizing profit problem by considering the sales at each market. The model requires the costs for each possible location obtained from whichever static model is used, and the costs involved (including the relocation of depots) are then discounted to the present.

CONCLUSIONS

An examination of the literature indicates that in general one of two approaches have been taken. To solve the site selection problem, authors have either adopted a simple cost formulation and developed a complex optimization procedure, or they have built an extremely complex cost model, in which the real world is represented in as much detail as possible, and then used a fairly primitive heuristic method to minimize the cost function. Examples of the former approach are the mixed-integer programming models of Gray [16] and Spielberg [40]; an example of the latter approach is the heuristic search procedure of Lawrence and Pengilly [27].

Considerable effort has gone into the development of these models which are essentially static in nature, but much work still remains to be done on such models before they become "standard" packages for everyday use. Perhaps the main reason for dynamic models not having been vigorously pursued is that most distribution problems are not sufficiently dynamic to warrant the use of far more complex models. This is not to say that no work should be done on these models, but it must be realized that any solutions obtained from such models will be only as good as the forecasts of the demand.

The attitude adopted in this book is a mixture of the two approaches. The method of solution that we suggest in Chapter 4 is basically the numeric–analytic procedure due to Miehle [33], coupled with a location–allocation procedure similar to that described by Cooper [8]. We extend the method to cater for situations which are far more complex than those described by Miehle or by Cooper.

REFERENCES

[1] BALINSKI, M. L. and MILLS, H., A warehouse problem. Prepared for: Veterans Administration, *Mathematica*, Princeton, N.J., 1960.

[2] BALLOU, R. H., Dynamic warehouse location analysis. *J. Marketing Res.*, **5**, 271–6 (1968).

[3] BAUMOL, W. J. and WOLFE, P., A warehouse location problem. *Ops. Res.*, **6**, No. 2, 252–63 (1958).

[4] BELLMAN, R., An application of dynamic programming to location–allocation problems. *S.I.A.M. Rev.*, **7**, No. 1, 126–8 (1965).

[5] BRINK, E. L. and DE CANI, J. S., An analogue solution of the generalized transportation problem. *Proc. 1st Int. Conf. Ops. Res.*, Oxford, 1957.

[6] BURSTALL, R. M., LEAVER, R. A. and SUSSAMS, J. E., Evaluation of transport costs for alternative factory sites. *Opl. Res. Q.*, **13**, No. 4, 345–54 (1962).

[7] COOPER, L., Location–allocation problems. *Ops. Res.*, **11**, No. 3, 331–43 (1963).

[8] COOPER, L., Heuristic methods for location–allocation problems. *S.I.A.M. Rev.*, **6**, No. 1, 37–53 (1964).

[9] COOPER, L. and DREBES, C. B., Formulation and solution of some location–allocation problems. Report No. AM65-3, Department of Applied Mathematics and Computer Sciences, Washington University, St. Louis, Missouri 63130.

[10] DRYSDALE, J. K. and SANDIFORD, P. J., Heuristic warehouse location—a case history using a new method. *J. Canadian Ops. Res. Soc.*, **7**, No. 1, 45–61 (1969).

[11] Economic Development Committee for the Distributive Trades: Planning warehouse locations. National Economic Development Office, Millbank, London, 1967.

[12] EFROYMSON, M. A. and RAY, T. L., A branch-bound algorithm for plant location. *Ops. Res.*, **14**, No. 3, 361–8 (1966).

[13] EILON, S. and DEZIEL, D. P., Siting a distribution centre—an analogue computer application. *Mgmt. Sci.*, **12**, No. 6, B245–B254 (1966).

[14] EILON, S. and WATSON-GANDY, C. D. T., Models for determining depot location. Report No. 69/4, Management Engineering Section, Imperial College, London, 1969.

[15] FELDMAN, E., LEHRER, F. A. and RAY, T. L., Warehouse location under continuous economies of scale. *Mgmt. Sci.*, **12**, No. 9, 670–84 (1966).

[16] GRAY, P., Mixed integer programming algorithms for site selection and other fixed charge problems having capacity constraints. Technical Report No. 6, Department of Operations Research, Stanford University, Stanford, California, 1967.

[17] HAKIMI, S. L., Optimum locations of switching centers and the absolute centers and medians of a graph. *Ops. Res.*, **12**, No. 3, 450–9 (1964).

[18] HALEY, K. B., Siting of depots. *Int. J. Prod. Res.*, **2**, 41–5 (1963).

[19] HEPBURN, J. M., Distribution of blasting explosives. Distribution Systems Session, *Proc. 4th Int. Conf. Ops. Res.*, Boston, 1966.

[20] HILLIER, F. S., An optimal bound-and-scan algorithm for integer linear programming. Technical Report No. 3, Department of Operations Research, Stanford University, Stanford, California, 1966.

[21] HITCHINGS, G. G., Analogue techniques for optimal location of a main facility in relation to ancillary facilities. *Int. J. Prod. Res.*, **7**, No. 3, 189–97 (1969).

[22] JANDY, G., Approximate algorithm for the fixed charge capacitated site location problem. Technical Report No. 67-3, Operations Research House, Stanford University, Stanford, California, 1967.

[23] KEEFER, K. B., Easy way to determine the center of distribution. *Food Industries,* **6**, 450–1 (1934).

[24] KLEIN, M. and KLIMPEL, R. R., Application of linearly constrained non-linear optimization to plant location and sizing. *J. Indus. Eng.* (U.S.), **18**, No. 1, 90–5 (1967).

[25] KUHN, A. A. and HAMBURGER, M. J., A heuristic program for locating warehouses. *Mgmt. Sci.,* **9**, No. 4, 643–66 (1963).

[26] KUHN, H. W. and KUENNE, R. E., An efficient algorithm for the numerical solution of the generalized Weber problem in spatial economics. *J. Reg. Sci.*, **4**, No. 2, 21–33 (1962).

[27] LAWRENCE, R. M. and PENGILLY, P. J., The number and location of depots required for handling products for distribution to retail stores in south-east England. *Opl. Res. Q.*, **20**, No. 1, 23–32 (1969).

[28] LEMKE, C. E. and SPIELBERG, K., Direct zero–one and mixed integer programming. *Ops. Res.*, **15**, No. 5, 872–914 (1967).

[29] LEVY, J., An extended theorem for location on a network. *Opl. Res. Q.*, **18**, No. 4, 433–42 (1967).

[30] LOSCH, E. G., Long-range planning of the distribution system of a brewery. Paper 3, Session 12. I.F.O.R.S. Conference, Venice, 1969.

[31] MANNE, A. S., Plant location under economies-of-scale—decentralization and computation. *Mgmt. Sci.*, **11**, No. 2, 213–35 (1964).

[32] MARANZANA, F. E., On the location of supply points to minimize transport costs. *Opl. Res. Q.*, **15**, No. 3, 261–70 (1964).

[33] MIEHLE, W., Link-length minimization in networks. *Ops. Res.*, **6**, No. 2, 232–43 (1958).

[34] MOSSMAN, F. H. and MORTON, N., *Logistics in Distribution Systems.* Allyn and Bacon Inc., Boston, 1965.

[35] PALERMO, F. P., A network minimization problem. *I.B.M. Journal of Research and Development,* **5**, 335–7 (1961).

[36] ROSEN, J. B., The gradient projection method for non-linear programming – Part 1, Linear constraints. *J. Soc. Ind. Appl. Math.*, **8**, No. 1 (1960).

[37] SHEA, A., Determination of the optimal location of depots. Distributive Systems Session, *Proc. 4th Int. Conf. Ops. Res.*, Boston, 1966.

[38] SHIMBEL, A., Structure in communication networks. *Proc. Symp. Information Networks*, Polytechnic Institute of Brooklyn, Brooklyn, 12th–14th April, 1954.

[39] SHYCON, H. N. and MAFFEI, R. B., Simulation—tool for better distribution. *Harv. Bus. Rev.*, **38**, No. 6, 65–75 (1960).

[40] SPIELBERG, K., Algorithms for the simple plant-location problem with some side conditions. *Ops. Res.*, **17**, No. 1, 85–111 (1969).

[41] SURKIS, J., Optimal warehouse location. 14th Int. Conf., The Institute of Management Sciences, Mexico, 1967.

[42] SUSSAMS, J. E., Some problems associated with the distribution of consumer products. *Opl. Res. Q.*, **19**, No. 2, 161–74 (1968).

[43] TIDEMAN, M., Comment on "A network minimization problem". *I.B.M. Journal of Research and Development,* **6**, No. 2, 259 (1962).

[44] VERGIN, R. C. and ROGERS, J. B., An algorithm and computational procedure for locating economic facilities. *Mgmt. Sci.*, **13**, No. 6, B240–B254 (1967).

[45] WATSON-GANDY, C. D. T., The planning and development of warehousing policies. *Freight Mgmt.*, **3**, No. 6, 37–41 (1969).

[46] WEBER, A., *Uber den Standort der Industrien*. Tübingen, 1909. Translated as *Alfred Weber's Theory of the Location of Industries,* by FRIEDRICH, C. J., Univ. of Chicago Press, 1929.

[47] WESTER, L. and KANTNER, H. H., Optimal location–allocation. *Report of the Armour Research Foundation,* Illinois Institute of Technology; this paper was presented in a condensed form at the 6th Annual Meeting of the Operations Research Society of America, Boston, 1958.

Chapter 3

Single depot location for deterministic demand

INTRODUCTION

In a great number of cases there is no need to examine the entire distribution system, but only parts of it. A problem that is often posed by management is to determine the location of a distribution depot in a single depot system or subsystem. Even in distribution systems which have been in operation for a while and for which well-established working procedures are employed, the need to re-examine the location of a depot may arise, generally for one or several of the following reasons:

- the pattern of demand in terms of customer locations and customer requirements has been subject to significant changes;
- the lease of the existing depot is due to expire, or rental charges have been increased;
- transportation costs to certain customers or localities have changed.

The purpose of this chapter is to examine a simple single depot system and to discuss several methods for solving the problem of determining the optimal location of the depot. A proof will be given to demonstrate that these methods yield a single unique solution to this problem.

THE MODEL

The model consists of one depot, whose location in cartesian co-ordinates is described by (x_0, y_0). This depot is to supply n customers whose locations are known and denoted by (x_j, y_j) (where $j = 1, 2, \ldots, n$). If the cost of transportation of the goods supplied to customer j from the depot is denoted by c_j, then the total local distribution cost is

$$H = \sum_{j=1}^{n} c_j \qquad (3.1)$$

Using the feasible set approach in which the values of c_j from each depot location to each customer j can be found (albeit at the expense of effort and time), the solution can be determined by simply evaluating equation (3.1) for each feasible location. When the transportation cost depends linearly on the weight (or amount) of goods delivered and the distance travelled, then

$$c_j = \alpha_{0j} w_j d_j \qquad (3.2)$$

where $\alpha_{0j} =$ cost per unit weight (or amount) and per unit distance from the depot to customer j;

$\quad\quad w_j =$ weight (or amount) transported to customer j from the depot, henceforth called the customer weight;

$\quad\quad d_j =$ the distance from the depot to customer j.

If the straight-line distance is considered[1] (called the *radial distance*), then d_j is found from

$$d_j = [(x_0 - x_j)^2 + (y_0 - y_j)^2]^{1/2} \qquad (3.3)$$

In the case where α_{0j} depends only on the customer being served and not on the location of the depot, then

$$c_j = \alpha_j w_j d_j \qquad (3.4)$$

resulting in the cost function

$$H = \sum \alpha_j w_j d_j \qquad (3.5)$$

where throughout this chapter the symbol Σ denotes the summation $\sum_{j=1}^{n}$. The problem is to determine the values of (x_0, y_0) such that this cost function is minimized.

Note that because the model does not take account of the direction of the flow of goods, it is possible to consider, without loss of generality, p factories which are replenishing the supplies of items at the depot, as "customers"; each factory will have its own relevant α_j and w_j (where $j = n+1, n+2, \ldots, n+p$) (see also Haley [18])[2].

It is also possible to consider that the parameters in equation (3.4)

---

[1] A further discussion on the use of radial distances is given in Chapter 8.

[2] The reference numbers in this chapter are related to the list of references given at the end of Chapter 2.

are not linear but are represented by some continuous function. Mossman and Morton [34] consider a case in which the speed of delivery is of great significance. By means of market research they develop a function in which the quantity ordered by any customer j is dependent on the delivery time. This function (quoted here with a suitable change of notation) is

$$w_j = w_j^{* \, - a t_j / t_j^*}$$

where w_j = quantity ordered by customer j when the delivery time is t_j;

similarly, w_j^* = quantity ordered with delivery time t_j^*,
         t_j^* = competitor's delivery time,
         a = proportionality factor for specific demand area and product.

In another study Brink and de Cani [5] examine a case in which the cost of delivery to customer j is proportional to the logarithm of the distance to that customer. Brink and de Cani emphasize, however, that any suitable function may be used in a particular case, subject to the condition that the function is continuous.

While all these proposed non-linear cost relationships are interesting, there is not sufficient evidence to suggest that they generally apply in practice, nor is there any indication as to the extent to which the solution to the depot location problem is likely to be sensitive to formulating cost parameters in a linear rather than a non-linear form. For the sake of simplicity, we therefore propose to adhere to the assumption that the total cost function follows the linear relationships implied in equation (3.5).

METHODS OF SOLUTION

In the case of only two customers (i.e. $n = 2$) the solution is obviously trivial in that the depot must lie on a straight line joining the two customers and that the location on that line depends on the ratio of customer weights. This is described in further detail later.

In the special case for which all customer demands are equal, and for whom all α_j are the same, the problem becomes that of minimizing the sum of the radial distances. In this case the solution to the three– and four–customer problems ($n = 3$ and $n = 4$) can be found. In the case of three customers, if the triangle formed by the customers has no angle greater than or equal to $120°$, then the optimum location is the point from which lines drawn radially to each customer form three angles of 120°; if the triangle contains an angle greater than or equal to 120°, then the optimal location of the depot is at that vertex (see Fig. 3.1). These results were shown by Steiner [7, 26, 33].

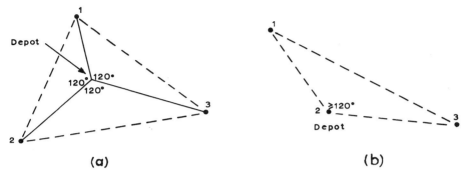

(a)   (b)

Fig. 3.1   Three customers with equal weights
(a) triangle angles < 120
(b) one angle ⩾ 120

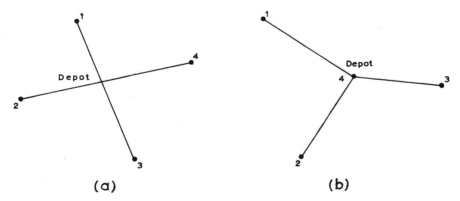

(a)   (b)

Fig. 3.2   Four customers with equal weights
(a) depot at intersection of the two diagonals
(b) diagonals do not intersect

   In the case of four customers, the point of the minimum sum of the radial distances is at the intersection of the diagonals, as shown in (a) in Fig. 3.2. In cases where the customers do not form a convex quadrilateral such as in (b), the optimal position of the depot for equal customers coincides with the "internal" customer, point 4 in (b), namely that customer who is inside the triangle drawn through the remaining customers. The proof of these results is based on simple geometrical relationships: if in either case (a) or (b) a position for the depot is selected at any point other than the one indicated in Fig. 3.2, it can be shown that the resultant total distances from the depot to the customers will be greater than the sum of the distances shown.

Larger problems with unequal customer demands are obviously much more complex and some other method of solution is required.

THE CENTRE OF GRAVITY METHOD

This method of determining the location of a depot has been in use for some time (see Keefer [23], 1934). The method is simply to use the centre of gravity of the customers as the depot location. The co-ordinates of the centre of gravity are found by

$$\bar{x}_0 = \frac{\Sigma w_j x_j}{\Sigma w_j} \quad \text{and} \quad \bar{y}_0 = \frac{\Sigma w_j y_j}{\Sigma w_j} \tag{3.6}$$

An alternative method that has been used, is to employ a weighted centre of gravity, for example, weighted by the costs of transporting goods to customer j as described by Mossman and Morton [34]. This method attempts to account for differentials in transport rates to different customers, and the depot location is then given by

$$\bar{x}'_0 = \frac{\Sigma \eta_j w_j x_j}{\Sigma \eta_j w_j} \quad \text{and} \quad \bar{y}'_0 = \frac{\Sigma \eta_j w_j y_j}{\Sigma \eta_j w_j}$$

where $\eta_{j\bullet} =$ cost per unit weight (or amount).

This method is still often used (see [11], case 7), probably because of the simplicity of the computations which are involved. However, the centre of gravity is not necessarily the optimum solution to the cost function expressed in equation (3.5), as shown by Vergin and Rogers [44].

If the partial differential of equation (3.5) with respect to the depot co-ordinate x_0 is set equal to zero and then solved with respect to x_0, an equation of the form

$$x_0^* = \frac{\Sigma \alpha_j w_j x_j / d_j}{\Sigma \alpha_j w_j / d_j} \tag{3.7}$$

is obtained where x_0^* is the improved x co-ordinate value for the depot (further details of this method are discussed later in the sub-section on the Numeric–Analytic Method). Vergin and Rogers show that in the special case when it is assumed that all customer weights are equal (i.e. $w_j = w$), equation (3.7) can be simplified to

$$x_0^* = \Sigma M_j x_j$$

where

$$M_j = \frac{\displaystyle\prod_{k \neq j}^{n} d_k}{\displaystyle\sum_{\varepsilon = 1}^{n} \left(\prod_{k \neq \varepsilon}^{n} d_k \right)}$$

and, as before, $d_k =$ the distance from the depot to customer k ($k = 1, 2, \ldots, n$).

Now if

$$\sum_{j=1}^{n} M_j = 1 \tag{3.8}$$

then x_0^* is a weighted average of all the x_j's. Further, for the special case,

$$M_j = \frac{1}{n} \quad \text{for all } j \tag{3.9}$$

then

$$x_0^* = \bar{x}_0 = \sum_{j=1}^{n} x_j / n \tag{3.10}$$

which means that the optimal x_0^* co-ordinate is the average value of the x_j's if condition (3.9) holds. However, neither condition (3.8) nor condition (3.9) is true in general. A similar argument holds for the y_0^* co-ordinate. Condition (3.9) is, in fact, only true when the customers lie on the vertices of a regular polygon.

Vergin and Rogers give a three-customer example to illustrate this point. They show that for such an example the centre of gravity yields a solution for which the cost function is 2·25 per cent higher than the optimal solution. This error increases as the relative difference between individual customer weights becomes more disproportionate, and in the example in Fig. 3.9, page 51, the error amounts to 4·5 per cent compared with the optimum.

The reason for this discrepancy, which can be understood more readily by referring to the mechanical analogue described in the next section, is that it is required to find that point at which the moment of the system, provided by the pull exerted by the customers, is minimized. This is, of course, not necessarily at the centre of gravity. This point can be demonstrated by considering the two-customer problem illustrated in Fig. 3.3, where the weights of customers are

Fig. 3.3   A two-customer example

w_1 and w_2 respectively and the two are distance D apart. If the depot is located at a variable distance x measured from customer 1, then the moment of the system with respect to the depot is given by

$$H = w_1 \, x + w_2 \, (D - x)$$

or

$$H = (w_1 - w_2) \, x + w_2 \, D \qquad (3.11)$$

Differentiating with respect to x,

$$\frac{dH}{dx} = (w_1 - w_2)$$

Thus if $w_1 > w_2$, then x must be made as small as possible in order to minimize the value of H; therefore

$$x = 0$$

namely the depot should be located at the site customer 1. Similarly, if $w_1 < w_2$, the depot should be located at customer 2, while for $w_1 = w_2$ any point between the two customers will yield the same result.

Consider now the centre of gravity of this system. The result for $\bar{x}_0$ is given by

$$\bar{x}_0 = \frac{\Sigma \, w_j \, x_j}{\Sigma \, w_j} = \frac{w_2 \, D}{w_1 + w_2}$$

Here the x values are measured from customer 1 and therefore $x_1 = 0$. The moment of the system $H_{\bar{x}_0}$ at the centre of gravity is given by substituting x_0 for x in equation (3.11). Hence,

$$H_{\bar{x}_0} = (w_1 - w_2) \frac{w_2 \, D}{(w_1 + w_2)} + w_2 \, D$$

$$= \frac{2w_1 \, w_2 \, D}{w_1 + w_2} \qquad (3.12)$$

To show that the centre of gravity is not necessarily the best place for the depot, three cases are now examined and the error in each case is calculated.

(1) $w_1 > w_2$

As shown above, the depot location for minimum costs is at the site of customer 1. The moment H_0 of the system at this location is given by

$$H_0 = w_2 D \qquad (3.13)$$

The moment at the centre of gravity is given by equation (3.12); hence the ratio of the moment at $\bar{x}_0$ to the minimum is

$$\frac{H_{x_0}}{H_0} = \frac{2 w_1 w_2 D}{(w_1 + w_2) w_2 D}$$

$$= \frac{2 w_1}{w_1 + w_2} > 1 \qquad (3.14)$$

(2) $w_1 = w_2 =$ say w

As noted earlier, any point x between the two customers will give the minimum value; hence equation (3.11) for H_0 is reduced to (3.13), so that

$$\frac{H_{\bar{x}_0}}{H_0} = \frac{2 w_1}{w_1 + w_2} = 1$$

Thus, when $w_1 = w_2$, the centre of gravity corresponds to the minimum value of the objective function.

(3) $w_1 < w_2$

In a similar manner to (1) above, the result here is given by

$$\frac{H_{\bar{x}_0}}{H_0} = \frac{2 w_2}{w_1 + w_2} > 1$$

To illustrate the error involved in selecting the centre of gravity for depot location, take as an example $w_1 = 2$ and $w_2 = 1$. Substituting these values in equation (3.14) gives $H_{\bar{x}_0}/H_0 = 4/3$. Hence in this case, if the centre of gravity is chosen as the depot location, the error from the optimum is $33\frac{1}{3}$ per cent.

THE MECHANICAL ANALOGUE

The depot location problem has also been solved using a mechanical analogue of the type shown in Fig. 3.4. A map is pasted onto the table, and holes are drilled through the table at the locations of the customers (and/or factories). Strings are passed through these holes with one end carrying a weight proportional to w_j $(j = 1, 2, \ldots, n)$, while the other ends of the strings are tied to a small ring or washer. If the ring is pulled to one side and then released, the weights

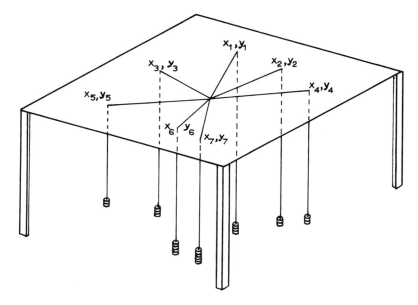

Fig. 3.4   The mechanical analogue

(which represent the customer demands) will pull the ring to the point of minimum potential energy which is the position at which the transport costs are at a minimum. This method has been frequently used and descriptions of case studies are found in the papers by Burstall, Leaver and Sussams [6] and Shea [37].

This is a simple but crude method. The main advantage is, as Shea says in his paper, "that the analogue has a visual impact – people can see and understand what is happening; that it is simple to make amendments to the proposed pattern of distribution, which means that people can try out immediately any ideas that they may have on what should happen; and most important, that it is an excellent method of arousing people's interest".

The method, however, suffers from four principal disadvantages:

(1) Owing to the friction between the strings and the holes, which can become appreciable when a large number of customers are involved, the final position of the ring may become indeterminate.

(2) For problems which involve more than one depot, the dangers of suboptimality may become quite pronounced. Even if friction were to be ignored, the solution will depend on the initial allocation of customers to depots, and it is not always obvious from the data what allocation should be adopted.

(3) As indicated by Burstall *et al.*, the analogue does not distinguish between town and country journeys, in other words it does not take account of α_{0j} in equation (3.2); however, if delivery rates depend only on the location of the customers, as assumed by α_j in equation (3.5), the weights used in the analogue could then be adjusted to represent $\alpha_j w_j$ instead of w_j.

(4) The method does not evaluate the cost function, and this may prove to be the greatest disadvantage.

THE NUMERIC–ANALYTIC METHOD

The numeric–analytic method, first suggested by Miehle [33], is the mathematical equivalent of the mechanical analogue. However, this method can be used with cost functions such as those examined by Mossman and Morton or by Brink and de Cani. It is also possible to incorporate different transport rates for individual customers, should this be necessary. This facility can be seen in the model as expressed in equation (3.5), which is repeated here for convenience:

$$H = \Sigma \, \alpha_j \, w_j \, d_j \qquad (3.5)$$

Equation (3.5) can be minimized by taking partial differentials with respect to the depot co-ordinates x_0 and y_0, and setting these equal to zero:

$$\frac{\partial H}{\partial x_0} = \Sigma \, \alpha_j \, w_j \, (x_0 - x_j)/d_j = 0$$

and

$$\frac{\partial H}{\partial y_0} = \Sigma \, \alpha_j \, w_j \, (y_0 - y_j)/d_j = 0$$

These equations can be solved with respect to x_0 and y_0, and from an initial estimated location the following optimizing solution can thus be obtained:

$$x_0^* = \frac{\Sigma\, \alpha_j\, w_j\, x_j/d_j}{\Sigma\, \alpha_j\, w_j/d_j} \qquad (3.15)$$

$$y_0^* = \frac{\Sigma\, \alpha_j\, w_j\, y_j/d_j}{\Sigma\, \alpha_j\, w_j/d_j} \qquad (3.16)$$

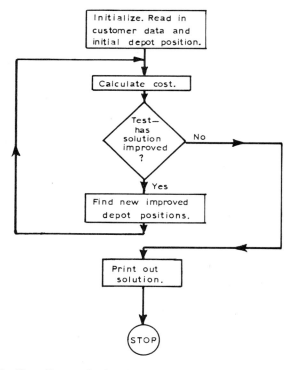

Fig. 3.5   Flow diagram for locating a single depot with radial distances

Using these improved values (x_0^*, y_0^*), the distances to each customer d_j are recalculated, and the method proceeds iteratively until no further improvement can be made. This method easily lends itself to solution on a computer, and a summary of the steps involved is given in the flow diagram, Fig. 3.5.

The algorithm

(1) Choose an initial location for the depot. Some comments on the choice of starting positions are given later.
(2) Calculate the cost according to equation (3.5).
(3) Determine whether the cost function has improved compared with the previous value. If it has, go to 4.
(4) Determine the improved location for the depot from equations (3.15) and (3.16). Go to 2, and repeat until no further improvement can be made in the cost function (3.5).

PROOF OF CONVEXITY

It is necessary now to show that the numeric–analytic method will yield a unique minimum solution, namely that the function in equation (3.5) is convex. A proof is given by Haley [18] and is presented here with a suitable change of notation. Other proofs are given by Palermo [35] and Kuhn and Kuenne [26].

Haley starts by proving the lemma

$$(\Sigma\, a_j)\,(\Sigma\, b_j) > \left(\Sigma\sqrt{a_j b_j}\right)^2 \quad \text{for } a_j > 0,\, b_j > 0$$

A sufficient set of conditions for the function H to be convex is

$$p = \left\{\frac{\partial^2 H}{\partial x^2}\right\}_{x=x_0} > 0$$

$$q = \left\{\frac{\partial^2 H}{\partial y^2}\right\}_{y=y_0} > 0$$

where x_0, y_0 are solutions obtained from equations

$$\frac{\partial H}{\partial x} = 0,\quad \frac{\partial H}{\partial y} = 0$$

and $pq - r^2 > 0$, where

$$r = \left\{\frac{\partial^2 H}{\partial x\,\partial y}\right\}_{x=x_0,\, y=y_0}$$

Now

$$p = \left\{\frac{\partial^2 H}{\partial x^2}\right\}_{x=x_0} = \Sigma\,\alpha_j\, w_j\, \frac{d^2_j - (x_0 - x_j)^2}{d^3_j}$$

$$= \Sigma\,\alpha_j\, w_j\, \frac{(y_0 - y_j)^2}{d^3_j} > 0$$

Similarly, $\quad q = \left\{\dfrac{\partial^2 H}{\partial y^2}\right\}_{y=y_0} = \Sigma\, \alpha_j\, w_j\, \dfrac{(x_0 - x_j)^2}{d_j^3} > 0$

The value of r is: $\quad r = \Sigma\, \alpha_j\, w_j\, \dfrac{(x_0 - x_j)\,(y_0 - y_j)}{d_j^3}$

Denote $\quad a_j = \dfrac{\alpha_j\, w_j}{d_j^3}\,(y_0 - y_j)^2$

and $\quad b_j = \dfrac{\alpha_j\, w_j}{d_j^3}\,(x_0 - x_j)^2\,.$

Hence

$$p = \Sigma\, a_j \qquad q = \Sigma\, b_j \qquad r = \Sigma\, \sqrt{a_j b_j}$$

and using the lemma it now follows that $pq - r^2 > 0$; hence H is convex and has a single unique minimum.

CHOICE OF INITIAL LOCATIONS

In the description of the numeric–analytic method the need for an initial estimate for the depot location was noted. The nature of the objective function makes it possible to choose an initial location for the depot anywhere in the cost space (which is infinitely large). It is logical, however, to choose a point inside the space in which the customers to be served are distributed, as this will reduce the number of iterations and hence the time required for computation.

Vergin and Rogers [44] investigate, in addition to the centre of gravity method, the point of the square weighted mean. This is calculated in the same way as the centre of gravity, but using the square of the weights, i.e.

$$\overline{x_0^2} = \frac{\Sigma\, w_j^2\, x_j}{\Sigma\, w_j^2} \quad\text{and}\quad \overline{y_0^2} = \frac{\Sigma\, w_j^2\, y_j}{\Sigma\, w_j^2}$$

This is designed to give more emphasis to heavily weighted customers. They then examine a point on the extended line joining the centre of gravity (A) and the point of the minimum square weighted mean (B) and situated at a distance from B equal to AB. This new point they find useful in cases where one customer is more heavily weighted than others. After experimentation, however, they conclude that the best policy is to calculate the value of the cost function at each of the three points and select the one with the lowest value as the initial location for further consideration.

The experiments that we have carried out, not only with the locations used by Vergin and Rogers but also with several alternative locations, have indicated that the initial location, if chosen within reason, has very little effect on the number of iterations taken, and hardly any effect on computing time. Table 3.1 shows some of these results for a 20-customer problem. The data for this problem are given under the head of Case 1 in the Appendix to this chapter.

Table 3.1   Effect of initial location of depot in a 20-customer problem

No.	Starting location x_0	y_0	Number of iterations	Comments
1	5·60	4·51	10	Centre of gravity*
2	4·30	5·00	11	Intersection of diagonals†
3	6·00	4·50	13	Approximate centre selected visually
4	0·00	0·00	12	Corner of area
5	0·00	10·00	11	Corner of area
6	5·98	1·24	16	Chosen at random
7	8·25	6·70	12	Chosen at random
8	4·50	7·30	12	Chosen at random
9	3·00	8·00	12	Chosen at random

* Note that as customers are of equal weighting, this is also the location of square weighted mean.
† The intersection of the diagonals of the quadrilateral formed by the four outermost customers, i.e. those nearest the boundaries of the area, $x = 0$, $y = 0$; $x = 10$, $y = 10$.

The computing time for solving the nine problems on an IBM 7094 computer was 0·37 min.

These results were obtained with accuracy to the third decimal place in the cost function. For those who may wish to solve this problem by hand, it would be necessary to have only 5 or 6 iterations to obtain the optimal location to an accuracy of two decimal places. The reason for this phenomenon is discussed more fully below.

SOME ATTRIBUTES OF THE MODEL

In order to illustrate the behaviour of the model and to show some of its attributes, four examples are given here. These examples illustrate a 20-customer problem. The same customers are used (and $\alpha_j = \alpha = 1$) in all cases, but the demands in each case vary. For case 1 the weights are all equal, i.e. $w_j = w$ for all j; in case 2 the weights lie between 1 and 10 units; in case 3 the weights range

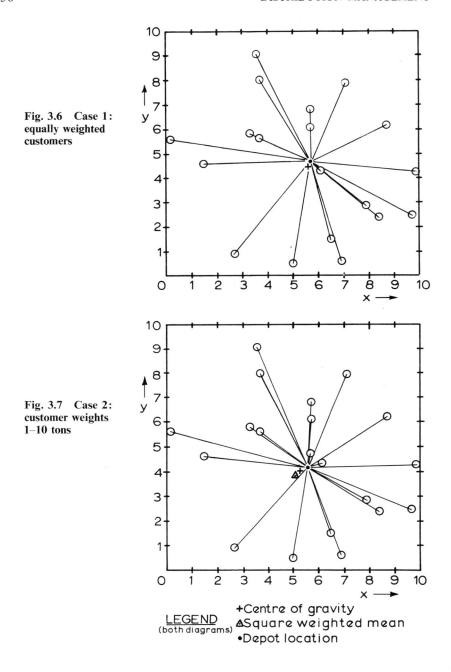

Fig. 3.6 Case 1: equally weighted customers

Fig. 3.7 Case 2: customer weights 1–10 tons

LEGEND
(both diagrams)

+Centre of gravity
△Square weighted mean
•Depot location

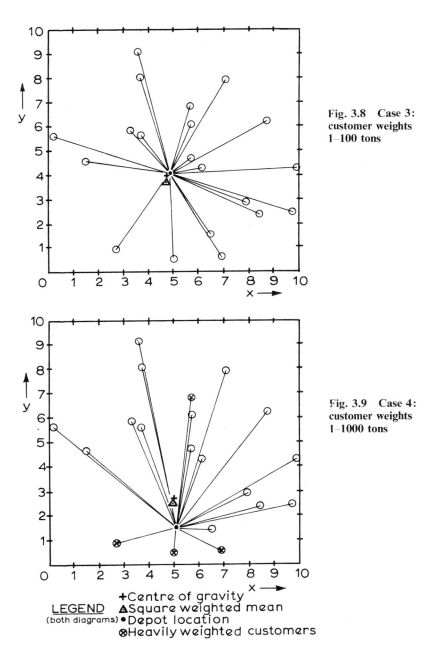

Fig. 3.8   Case 3:
customer weights
1–100 tons

Fig. 3.9   Case 4:
customer weights
1–1000 tons

LEGEND
(both diagrams)
+Centre of gravity
△Square weighted mean
•Depot location
⊗Heavily weighted customers

from 1 to 100, and in case 4 from 1 to 1000. The data for these problems are given in the Appendix to this chapter; the results are shown in Table 3.2 and illustrated graphically in Fig. 3.6 to 3.9.

Table 3.2   Results for four cases of a 20-customer problem

Case No.	Optimum location x_0	y_0	Cost	% deviation from the optimum A	B
1	5·70	4·70	66·097	0·49	0·49
2	5·57	4·15	288·665	0·39	1·10
3	4·84	4·03	2038·923	0·03	0·23
4	5·07	1·43	10129·262	4·46	3·80

A – Centre of gravity
B – Point of minimum square weighted mean

(1) It can be seen from Table 3.2 that the centre of gravity is not necessarily the optimal location for the depot, although the errors in the cases shown here are not very large, being never more than $4\frac{1}{2}$ per cent and being almost negligible in Case 3. The centre of gravity can produce large errors when one customer is heavily weighted compared with the others. This was demonstrated in the two-customer example discussed earlier.

(2) It is interesting to examine the effect of heavily weighted or important customers, which can be seen by comparing Fig. 3.8 and 3.9. In Fig. 3.8, illustrating Case 3, the customer demands are roughly even, but in Fig. 3.9, illustrating Case 4, there are four customers (no. 2, 15, 16 and 17) who are much more heavily weighted than the others. Three of these customers (no. 2, 15 and 16) are close together at the bottom of the area, and the pattern shown in Fig. 3.9 is very different from the other three cases. It is also interesting to note that the optimal depot location shown in Fig. 3.9 is very close to the intersection of the diagonals of the quadrilateral formed by these four customers. The error in locating at this intersection rather than the optimal location is only 1·85 per cent. This attribute may be of some advantage for solving problems manually, when the most heavily weighted customers can be easily identified.

(3) The speed at which the algorithm converges is dependent on the gradient of the cost function at each iteration. From Table 3.3 it would appear that in practice the function converges very rapidly when the depot is some distance away from the optimal location but rather slowly when it is close to the final position. Note also that

the value of the cost function at the third iteration is less than 5 per cent above the optimal value. This attribute has been noticed in many of the single depot cases that we have examined. These experiments confirm that a relatively large change in the location of the depot in the vicinity of the optimal position results in a relatively small change in the value of the cost function. This indicates that in the region of the optimum the cost space is very shallow, and this conclusion is supported by similar findings of Cooper [8].

**Table 3.3   Values at each iteration for Case 1
with a random starting position**

Cost	x_0	y_0
101·468	3·00	8·00
72·928	4·61	6·09
68·119	5·14	5·33
66·852	5·45	5·03
66·359	5·62	4·85
66·151	5·69	4·74
66·103	5·71	4·70
66·100	5·70	4·70
66·098	5·70	4·70
66·098	5·70	4·70
66·097	5·70	4·70
66·097	5·70	4·70

Table 3.3 further illustrates the remarks made earlier about the number of iterations that are required to arrive at a solution. It was noted earlier that it is not necessary to carry out all these iterations when the solution has to be calculated manually to two decimal places, and in Table 3.3 the last five iterations could then be dispensed with.

As a further illustration of the shallowness of the cost function, Fig. 3.10 shows the iso-cost curves for a fifty-customer-one-depot problem (the data for this problem are given in the Appendix to this chapter). The curves are drawn at approximately 5·6 per cent intervals. Notice that the curves are wide apart near the centre, and get closer together when they are far away from the optimal location.

Two useful conclusions may be drawn from this property of the cost function. First, in a practical situation the depot may be moved from the optimum location a fair distance away to an otherwise more attractive or feasible site without appreciably increasing the transportation costs. Secondly, if the depot is already located at a given site near the optimum, fluctuations in demand are not likely to have an appreciable effect on the transportation costs.

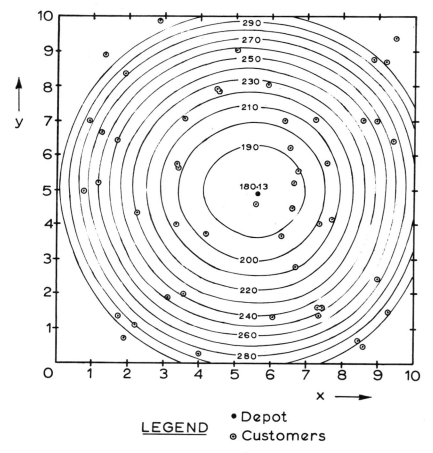

LEGEND   • Depot
              ⊙ Customers

Fig. 3.10   Iso-cost curves for one depot

CONCLUSIONS

The conclusions reached in this chapter are summarized here, for convenience, as they are also applicable to some of the more complex models described in the following chapter.

(1) The centre of gravity is not necessarily the best location for a

depot, and this position is exacerbated when some customers are heavily weighted in relation to others.

(2) The model as expressed by equation (3.5) can be minimized using the new values x_0^* and y_0^* given by equations (3.15) and (3.16).

(3) This method of solution can handle non-linear cost functions, provided that the cost functions are monotonic and continuous.

(4) The function expressed in equation (3.5) is convex and has a unique minimum.

(5) The attraction of very heavily weighted customers can be quite marked and it can have a significant effect on the location of the depot.

(6) The cost function is shallow near the optimum location, but gets steeper as one moves away from it. This property gives added flexibility in a practical situation when considerations other than minimum transportation costs are of some importance.

APPENDIX 3.1

Data for 20-customer problem

Customer No.	Co-ordinates		Weights			
	x	y	Case 1	Case 2	Case 3	Case 4
1	0·2	5·6	1·0	1·0	10·0	1·0
2	2·7	0·9	1·0	8·0	80·0	800·0
3	6·1	4·3	1·0	5·0	5·0	5·0
4	7·1	7·9	1·0	2·0	2·0	1·0
5	8·4	2·4	1·0	5·0	50·0	50·0
6	5·7	6·1	1·0	2·0	2·0	1·0
7	8·7	6·2	1·0	1·0	1·0	1·0
8	1·5	4·6	1·0	5·0	50·0	50·0
9	9·9	4·3	1·0	1·0	1·0	1·0
10	7·9	2·9	1·0	7·0	7·0	70·0
11	9·7	2·5	1·0	1·0	1·0	1·0
12	6·5	1·5	1·0	7·0	7·0	70·0
13	3·3	5·8	1·0	9·0	9·0	90·0
14	3·6	9·1	1·0	6·0	60·0	60·0
15	6·9	0·6	1·0	7·0	70·0	700·0
16	5·0	0·5	1·0	6·0	60·0	600·0
17	5·7	6·8	1·0	8·0	80·0	800·0
18	3·7	8·0	1·0	3·0	30·0	30·0
19	3·7	5·6	1·0	2·0	20·0	2·0
20	5·7	4·7	1·0	2·0	20·0	2·0

Cost of transport $\alpha_j = \alpha = 1$ per unit weight and per unit distance for all cases.

Data for 50-customer problem

Cust. No.	Co-ordinates x	y	Cust. No.	Co-ordinates x	y	Cust. No.	Co-ordinates x	y
1	1·33	8·89	21	2·22	4·35	41	3·57	1·99
2	1·89	0·77	22	0·88	7·02	42	7·34	1·38
3	9·27	1·49	23	8·53	7·04	43	6·58	4·49
4	9·46	9·36	24	6·49	6·22	44	5·00	9·00
5	9·20	8·69	25	4·53	7·87	45	6·63	5·23
6	7·43	1·61	26	4·46	7·91	46	5·89	8·06
7	6·08	1·34	27	2·83	9·88	47	1·13	5·25
8	5·57	4·60	28	3·39	5·65	48	1·90	8·35
9	6·70	2·77	29	0·75	4·98	49	1·74	1·37
10	8·99	2·45	30	7·55	5·79	50	9·39	6·44
11	8·93	7·00	31	8·45	0·69			
12	8·60	0·53	32	3·33	5·78			
13	4·01	0·31	33	6·27	3·66			
14	3·34	4·01	34	7·31	1·61			
15	6·75	5·57	35	6·37	7·02			
16	7·36	4·03	36	7·23	7·05			
17	1·24	6·69	37	1·68	6·45			
18	3·13	1·92	38	3·54	7·06			
19	8·86	8·74	39	7·67	4·17			
20	4·18	3·74	40	2·20	1·12			

Demand of all customers = 1 unit,
Cost of transport $\alpha = 1$ per unit weight and per unit distance.

Chapter 4

Multi-depot location for deterministic demand

INTRODUCTION

In the previous chapter we examined several methods for solving the problem of locating a single depot. In this chapter we extend the *numeric–analytic method* to enable a solution to be obtained for those cases in which it is necessary to examine the location of more than one depot. The methods described here are also applicable to the problem of locating a single depot in a multi-depot distribution system and in which it is necessary to examine the interactions of the single depot with those already located.

As indicated in Chapter 2, there are two approaches to the depot location problem in a multi-depot system. These are the *infinite set approach*, which allows the depots to be located anywhere in the region under consideration, and the *feasible set approach*, which has a finite set of given sites where depots may be located.

In a practical situation it is clearly useful to compare several alternative locations, and this is ostensibly what the feasible set approach is designed to do. Rather than ignore the depot overhead costs until a solution for its location is considered, as required by the infinite set approach, the feasible set approach ensures that undesirable and impractical locations need not be considered and real operating costs are accounted for from the beginning.

Our own view is that these arguments are oversimplified; there are certain real practical difficulties in defining a feasible set, and some are briefly discussed below.

(1) Undesirable or impractical locations can often be easily identified; for example, it is generally impractical to consider mountains, lakes, waterways, and many city centres as possible locations. But after these locations are eliminated, a vast geographical area usually remains. In view of the fact that the feasible set puts an initial important constraint on the problem—so important that the decision on what to include in the set may be more crucial than the

subsequent analysis—it is necessary to define a fairly large feasible set. In one practical example, where the solution for the distribution system involved three depots, the initial feasible set consisted of some 250 locations. Even so, there is no assurance that other sites would not have proved to yield better solutions had they been included in the feasible set.

(2) The data collection problem then becomes immense. The time and the cost required to assemble information on expected operating costs are quite substantial. Many of the operating cost parameters can only be estimated within wide ranges, so wide in fact that they render any comparison between the expected costs of two possible depots meaningless. In addition, any cost data that may be regarded as at all reliable mainly relate to prevailing conditions at each feasible site, whereas data that depend on predictions of future conditions are usually extremely difficult to determine without extensive investigations.

(3) A problem based on the feasible set is usually a very large problem. For example, a distance matrix for 200 depots and 5000 customers consists of one million items of information and this has serious implications on computer storage requirements.

For these reasons we have decided to discard the feasible set approach and to develop models following the infinite set approach. These models are designed to handle a number of problems with varying degrees of complexity associated with the size of the problem and with the way in which transportation costs are formulated. If the distribution system is considered as a hierarchy which consists of factories supplying depots, which in turn supply an array of customers, then two distinct types of transportation costs may be identified:

(a) Trunking costs from factories to depots,

(b) Local distribution costs from depots to customers.

Because trunking often involves transportation in bulk, it is usually cheaper than local distribution and its cost function may fit several alternative formats. In addition, there are costs associated with the operating of the depots; some of these costs are fixed and others are a function of the throughput. The six models presented here take account of this distinction between the cost parameters and some of the forms in which they can be expressed (see also Eilon and Watson-Gandy [14]).[1] These models are:

---

[1] The reference numbers in this chapter are related to the list of references given at the end of Chapter 2.

(1) The basic model, in which only local distribution costs are included.

(2) A model in which trunking costs are linear with respect to distance.

(3) A model in which the trunking cost function is linear, but has discontinuities.

(4) A model for trunking costs which are unrelated to distance.

(5) A model for overall cost optimization, which takes account of economies of scale in warehousing operations.

(6) A model similar to (5), but in which the depot operating-cost parameters are dependent on the geographical location.

MODEL 1 (THE BASIC MODEL)

Model 1 is based on the work of Miehle [33] and Wester and Kantner [47] (these publications appeared almost at the same time). The same problem was also investigated (although from a slightly different angle) by Cooper [7, 8] and by Cooper and Drebes [9].

The model consists of m depots, the location in cartesian co-ordinates of depot i (where $i = 1, 2, \ldots, m$) being given as (x_i, y_i). These depots supply n customers, the co-ordinates of customer j (where $j = 1, 2, \ldots, n$) being (x_j, y_j). If the cost of transportation of the goods supplied to customer j from depot i is denoted by c_{ij} then the total local distribution cost is:

$$H = \sum_{i=1}^{m} \sum_{j=1}^{n} c_{ij} \qquad (4.1)$$

When the transportation cost depends linearly on the weight (or amount) of goods delivered and the distance travelled, then

$$c_{ij} = \alpha_{ij} w_{ij} d_{ij} \qquad (4.2)$$

where　α_{ij} = cost per unit weight (or amount) and distance;
　　　　w_{ij} = weight (or amount) transported from depot i to customer j;
　　　　d_{ij} = the distance from i to j; if straight-line distances are considered, d_{ij} is found from

$$d_{ij} = \left[(x_i - x_j)^2 + (y_i - y_j)^2\right]^{1/2} \qquad (4.3)$$

For a given set of customers and depots, the cost matrix $[\alpha_{ij}]$ and the distance matrix $[d_{ij}]$ are known and the problem can be formulated as a standard transportation model with the object of determining w_{ij} to minimize the total cost function. If, however, there are no capacity constraints on the depots, the problem is reduced to an assignment model in which each customer is served by one depot, the amount w_{ij} delivered to customer j being identical to the demand of that customer. In the case where α_{ij} depends only on the customer being served and not on the depot serving it, then

$$c_{ij} = \alpha_j w_j d_{ij} \tag{4.4}$$

resulting in the cost function

$$H \equiv C(1) = \sum_{i=1}^{m} \sum_{j=1}^{n} \alpha_j w_j d_{ij} \delta_{ij} \tag{4.5}$$

where $\delta_{ij} = 1$ when customer j is served from depot i, otherwise $\delta_{ij} = 0$. The problem is to determine the values of (x_i, y_i) such that the cost function in this equation becomes a minimum. The notation $C(1)$ indicates that this function refers to Model 1, in which the local distribution costs are assumed to follow equation (4.4)

Model 1 represents a simple distribution system, in which customers are served by several depots, but no account is taken of how the goods arrive at the depots. Clearly this model can be valid only for a system in which direct distribution to customers is undertaken without other intermediate storage points. As the models that are discussed later incorporate important features of Model 1, it is useful to study its attributes in some detail, even though the model itself has only limited application.

Solution to Model 1

An iterative procedure for finding a minimum solution to cost functions such as the one given in equation (4.5) is described by Miehle [33]: first, it is necessary to choose a set of initial locations for the depots, and customers are then allocated to depots in a way that minimizes the cost function. For this simple model, in which there are no capacity constraints on the depots, this allocation is determined on the basis of distance, namely each customer is allocated to the nearest depot. If there are no capacity or other constraints, the solution to equation (4.5) can be found through partial differentials with respect to x_i and y_i as follows:

$$\frac{\partial C(1)}{\partial x_i} = \sum_{j=1}^{n} \alpha_j w_j (x_i - x_j) \delta_{ij}/d_{ij} = 0$$

$$\frac{\partial C(1)}{\partial y_i} = \sum_{j=1}^{n} \alpha_j w_j (y_i - y_j) \delta_{ij}/d_{ij} = 0$$

from which the optimizing solutions, denoted by x_i^* and y_i^*, are found:

$$x_i^* = \frac{\sum_{j=1}^{n} \alpha_j w_j x_j \delta_{ij}/d_{ij}}{\sum_{j=1}^{n} \alpha_j w_j \delta_{ij}/d_{ij}} \qquad (4.6)$$

$$y_i^* = \frac{\sum_{j=1}^{n} \alpha_j w_j y_j \delta_{ij}/d_{ij}}{\sum_{j=1}^{n} \alpha_j w_j \delta_{ij}/d_{ij}} \qquad (4.7)$$

These solutions are improved locations for the depots compared with the original locations. The customers are then reallocated to their nearest depot and the program proceeds iteratively until no further improvement can be obtained.

Algorithm for determining the optimal solution

The algorithm proceeds, therefore, in the following steps:

(1) Choose an initial starting location for each depot.

(2) Allocate each customer to the nearest depot, and calculate the value of the resultant function.

(3) Calculate new depot locations using equations (4.6) and (4.7).

(4) Go to (2) and repeat until no further reduction in costs can be made.

This procedure, which we have termed the *adaptive location–allocation method,* is similar to the *alternate location–allocation method* of Cooper [8]. The adaptive method is, however, a true iterative decision process in that first a reallocation and then a relocation decision is made at each iteration, whereas Cooper's method optimally locates depots before testing the allocation. Some results that we have obtained in order to compare the two methods suggest that the adaptive method is an improvement on Cooper's algorithm, particularly in the number of iterations required to reach a solution. The method is also similar to the location–allocation approach described by Surkis [41].

Some attributes of Model 1

(1) That, for this iterative procedure, equation (4.5) is convergent in the case of a single depot (i.e. for $m = 1$), has been shown by Haley [18], Kuhn and Kuenne [26] and Palermo [35]; the cost function being convex has a single unique optimal solution. The proof by Haley is given in Chapter 3. As equation (4.5) is the sum of m convergent equations, it is also convergent for the multi-depot case.

Thus, in the case of a single depot, in which the problem of assigning customers to depots does not arise, the iterative procedure yields a single unique optimal solution, irrespective of the initial location chosen for the depot. In multi-depot systems, however, the allocation of customers to depots depends on the locations of the depots, and as their positions change, so may the assignment change. For any given allocation the procedure for Model 1 results in a unique solution, but as many allocation configurations are possible, there are many such final solutions and the emergence of each depends on the initial positions chosen for depot locations.

This phenomenon is illustrated in the results shown in Table 4.1, which involves a system of 50 customers and $m = 1, 2, \ldots, 5$ depots.

Table 4.1   Results for a 50-customer problem*

Number of depots	Best solution $C(1)$	Number of trials	Number of local optima found	% deviation worst solution from $C(1)$	Time for 20 trials† (min)
1	180·13	2	1	—	0·6
2	135·52	230	18	6·9	0·8
3	105·21	200	26	25·8	1·3
4	84·15	185	37	15·2	2·1
5	72·24	200	61	40·9	2·4

* Details on the customer locations and solutions to this problem are given in Appendix 4.1.
† Time on an IBM 7090 computer and including compilation time. For $m = 1$ the time is for 2 trials only and for $m = 2$ the time is for 15 trials only.

For each value of m (except for $m = 1$) the problem was solved many times, and as m was increased, the number of different solutions that were found also increased. That some of the solutions can deviate substantially from the overall optimum is shown in the fifth column,

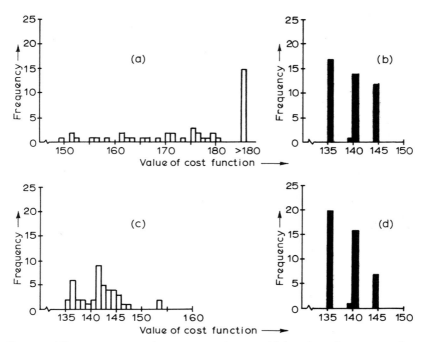

Fig. 4.1 Histograms comparing student estimates with locations chosen at random before and after minimization for two depots

(a) random locations (initial values)   (b) random locations (final values)
(c) student estimates (initial values)   (d) student estimates (final values)

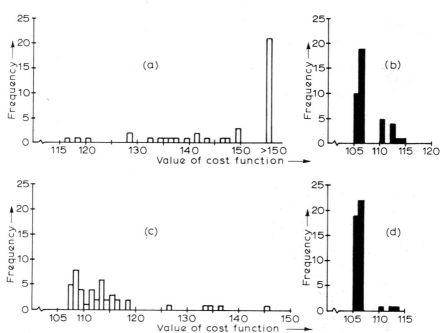

Fig. 4.2 Histograms comparing student estimates with locations chosen at random before and after minimization for three depots

(a) random locations (initial values)   (b) random locations (final values)
(c) student estimates (initial values)   (d) student estimates (final values)

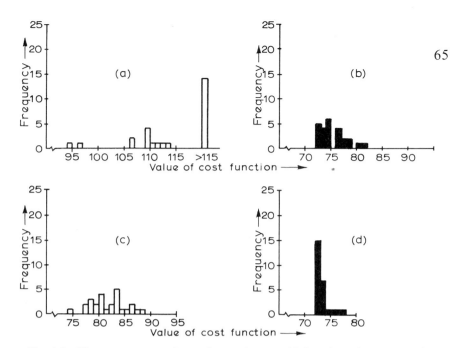

Fig. 4.3   Histograms comparing student estimates with locations chosen at random
before and after minimization for five depots

(a) random locations (initial values)   (b) random locations (final values)
(c) student estimates (initial values)   (d) student estimates (final values)

Table 4.2   Initial and final solutions for the 50-customer problem ($m = 3$)

Initial	Final
128·311	114·030
134·587	110·548
135·090	106·039
137·151	106·003
139·185	106·359
141·158	106·359
141·900	105·214
146·496	105·214
149·057	110·716
149·227	105·214
151·410	105·214
152·665	105·214
154·467	106·353
157·923	110·548
167·447	106·003
175·673	110·548
184·106	106·003
185·161	106·003
212·421	106·003
233·833	112·271

in which the worst and the best solutions that were found are compared for any given value of m.

(2) There is currently no efficient method that will guarantee that the optimal solution is obtained. For each trial, a corresponding solution is derived, which may be regarded as a suboptimum. After several trials, a set of suboptima is obtained (note that some of these solutions may be identical, although the starting conditions are different) and the best solution from this set is selected.

The question arises whether the initial locations of depots at the beginning of each trial should be chosen in any particular way, namely whether a good initial set of locations (which corresponds to a comparatively low cost function) will yield a good final solution (which is comparatively superior to others in the set of suboptima). An obvious method is to assign initial co-ordinate positions to depots at random, and in view of the fact that the algorithm suggested here is very fast in terms of computing time (see Table 4.1) a large number of trials can easily be undertaken.

Cooper [7, 8, 9] suggests some heuristic procedures for determining the initial depot locations, but his methods tend to be rather involved and not readily adaptable to cases where customer demand is unevenly distributed.

To test whether "intelligent" guesses for initial depot locations are preferable to random guesses, the following experiment was carried out. The 50-customer problem (for details see Appendix 4.1) was given to a number of people who were asked to suggest depot locations for given values of m. These locations were then fed into the algorithm as initial locations and the corresponding suboptima were obtained. These results are compared in Fig. 4.1, 4.2 and 4.3 with the results obtained from random initial locations. While there was no statistically significant difference in the final results for $m = 2$ or for $m = 3$, the results were found to be significantly different for $m = 4$ and for $m = 5$, where the set of suboptimal solutions derived from the initial "random" locations was much more widely spread than the other set. The best solution in both sets was, however, the same in all cases. Our conclusion is that "intelligent" guesses for initial locations may improve the chances of obtaining a good solution for each trial and may, therefore, be useful.

The lack of correlation between good starting solutions and their corresponding final solutions is demonstrated in Table 4.2 which is concerned with the same 50-customer problem for $m = 3$. The first entry in this table is the best of all initial solutions in the 20 trials, yet the corresponding final solution in this case is the worst.

These results suggest that it is undesirable to rely on too small a number of trials, even if their initial solutions appear to be very promising.

(3) An important attribute of the model is the attraction effect

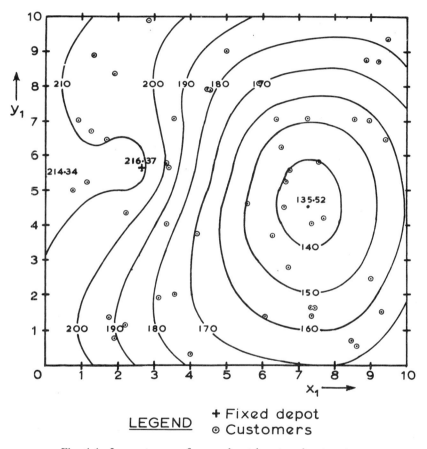

LEGEND   + Fixed depot
           ⊙ Customers

Fig. 4.4   Iso-cost curves for one depot in a two-depot system

of heavily weighted customers. This was illustrated for the single depot case described in Chapter 3 and is still applicable to the multi-depot model described here.

(4) As was also described in Chapter 3, the cost function is shallow in the region of the optimum (see also Cooper [8]). Fig. 4.4

illustrates the iso-cost curves for one depot in a two-depot problem (the other depot being considered fixed). The rings in this diagram are drawn at approximately 7·4 per cent intervals (but the 140 cost ring gives an increase in cost of approximately 3·3 per cent, hence the 150 ring gives a cost increase of approximately 10 per cent, and so on). Note that although the depot can be moved some distance from the optimum before the cost increases by more than 5 per cent, the actual distance depends on the direction in which the depot is moved.

(5) As the cost function is continuous, the infinite set approach has great flexibility: it can be used to determine the optimum locations of all the depots in the system, to obtain comparative costs for any combination of known fixed sites, or to determine the best locations for some of the depots while the position of others remains fixed. It is also comparatively simple to find for any solution the effect of different demand patterns and customer locations, or the effect of changes in the cost parameters. All these tests form an indispensable part of a sensitivity analysis to examine the robustness of the solution to the distribution model.

MODEL 2 (LINEAR TRUNKING COST)

In this model, the local distribution from depots to customers is as described in Model 1. A factory which supplies the depots is situated at (x_0, y_0) and the trunking cost from the factory to depot i is β_i per unit amount and distance. As supply to the depot is often carried out in bulk, the trunking cost parameter β is usually smaller than the local distribution cost parameter α.

The total cost function for Model 2 becomes:

$$C(2) = \sum_{i=1}^{m} \beta_i W_i d_{0i} + \sum_{i=1}^{m} \sum_{j=1}^{n} \alpha_j w_j d_{ij} \delta_{ij}$$

$$= \sum_{i=1}^{m} \beta_i W_i d_{0i} + C(1) \qquad (4.8)$$

where W_i = amount transported to depot i,
d_{0i} = distance from factory to depot i.

The first term in this equation represents the trunking cost in the system, the second term is the local distribution cost function shown in equation (4.5).

Again, if there are no capacity or other constraints on the

depots, the optimal locations of the depots can be found in the same way as shown in equations (4.6) and (4.7), except that now:

$$x_i^* = \frac{\beta_i \, W_i \, x_0/d_{0i} + \sum_{j=1}^{n} \alpha_j w_j x_j \delta_{ij}/d_{ij}}{\beta_i \, W_i/d_{0i} + \sum_{j=1}^{n} \alpha_j w_j \delta_{ij}/d_{ij}} \tag{4.9}$$

$$y_i^* = \frac{\beta_i \, W_i \, y_0/d_{0i} + \sum_{j=1}^{n} \alpha_j w_j y_j \delta_{ij}/d_{ij}}{\beta_i \, W_i/d_{0i} + \sum_{j=1}^{n} \alpha_j w_j \delta_{ij}/d_{ij}} \tag{4.10}$$

These equations are similar to equations (4.6) and (4.7) with the addition of an extra term to the numerator and denominator to cater for the trunking costs. This is equivalent to considering the trunking process in reverse, namely that the factory is a special type of customer which is served by all the depots. Like equation (4.5), equation (4.8) is the sum of m convergent expressions and is therefore also convergent.

Model 2 is, in fact, a simple extension of Model 1. The introduction of the factory and the trunking cost parameter β_i are equivalent to increasing the size of the customer matrix covered in Model 1, but otherwise the structure of the problem is unaffected. The algorithm suggested for solving Model 1 is, therefore, applicable for solving Model 2 as well.

Notice that α_j in this model is defined in relation to customer j whose location is known, so that different cost rates that depend on the position of customers are automatically incorporated. On the other hand, the parameter β_i refers to depot i, the final location of which is unknown, and for any given problem the value of β_i is assumed to remain constant throughout the solution procedure. In cases where the identity of the depot does not affect the cost rate, the trunking cost parameter is reduced to a single value $\beta_i = \beta$. A further possibility is that this parameter β is dependent on the location of the factory (or factories) serving depot i, and this is taken into account in Models 3 and 4 which are described later.

The method of allocation of customers to depots is based on the minimum unit costs of transportation from the factory to the customer, when depot costs are ignored. Thus, for customer j the cost of supplying one unit through each of the m depots is computed (as the sum of trunking and delivery costs) and the customer is allocated to that depot which involves the lowest costs.

Although Model 2 considers a single factory supplying all depots, a multi-factory system can be handled in very much the same way. The cost function in equation (4.8) will still apply, except that the first term must then be replaced with one that accounts for the trunking costs from all factories to all the depots. An additional procedure may be required to allocate depots to factories in the case of capacity constraints on the factories.

MODEL 3
(DISCONTINUOUS LINEAR TRUNKING COSTS)

In some cases, such as the one reported by Shea [37], the trunking costs are found to be linearly related to distance, but the parameter β is dependent on the district in which a depot is situated. Thus, the region under consideration is divided into r districts, and the rate β_k is quoted for bulk transportation to depots in district k (where $k = 1, 2, \ldots, r$). Unlike Model 2, where β is fixed for each depot irrespective of its geographic position, in Model 3 the parameter β_k changes when depots cross district boundaries. The trunking cost from the factory to depot i is then expressed as

$$\beta_k \, W_i \, d_{0i} \, \delta_{ik}$$

where $\beta_k =$ cost per unit amount and unit distance when the destination is in district k, and

$\delta_{ik} = 1$ if depot i is situated in district k, otherwise $\delta_{ik} = 0$.

The total cost function is

$$C(3) = \sum_{i=1}^{m} \sum_{k=1}^{r} \beta_k \, W_i \, d_{0i} \, \delta_{ik} + C(1) \qquad (4.11)$$

The problem is to find the locations of the depots such that this cost function is minimized.

Method of solution

Assuming for a moment that each depot remains in the district in which it is initially located, and that there are no capacity or other constraints on depots, then equation (4.11) can be minimized in exactly the same way as in Model 2, yielding results similar to equations (4.9) and (4.10).

If during the iteration process a depot crosses a district boundary, and the value of the cost function is below or equal to the previous value, the depot continues to move towards an optimal solution, and

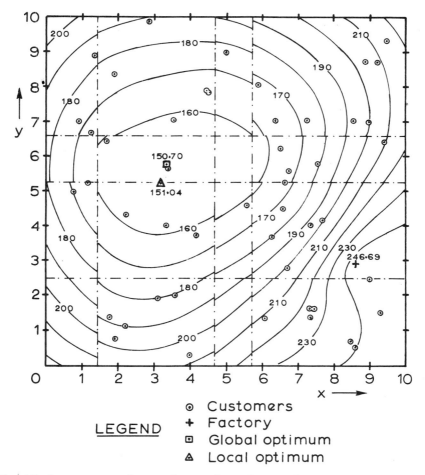

Fig. 4.5   Iso-cost curves for one depot and one factory when the trunking cost is a function of distance and district

Dotted lines are district boundaries for trunking costs

the procedure suggested for Model 2 remains unaltered, except that the appropriate values of β_k need to be substituted in equation (4.11). If, on the other hand, the cost function increases when a depot crosses a boundary, then that depot must be confined to remain in

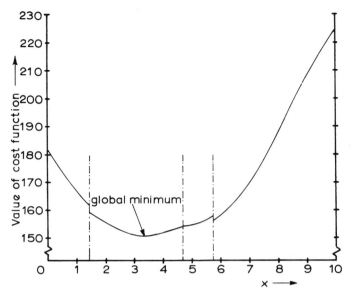

Fig. 4.6   Total cost function (section through $y = 5\cdot80$, see Fig. 4.5)

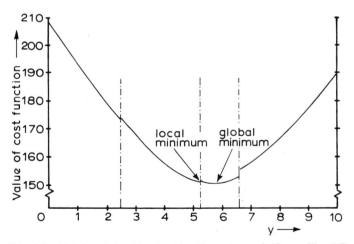

Fig. 4.7   Total cost function (section through $x = 3\cdot40$, see Fig. 4.5)

its old district and to move along the boundary, until a point may be reached when it is cheaper to cross the boundary. Hence, with the introduction of constraints on depot movement, equation (4.11) remains convergent.

The effect of this algorithm is to produce some solutions with depots constrained on district boundaries, and these solutions are additional to those obtained in Model 2. Here, too, it is felt that choosing initial depot locations at random is probably a satisfactory procedure to follow.

An example of discontinuous cost functions is illustrated in Fig. 4.5 where iso-cost curves are given for a distribution system involving 50 customers, one factory, one depot and 16 trunking districts. (The locations of the customers are given in Appendix 4.1, and the location of the factory and the 16 values of β_k in Appendix 4.2.) Fig. 4.6 and 4.7 show two cross-sections taken across the iso-cost map in Fig. 4.5 and demonstrate the effects of piece-wise linear trunking costs. Notice that not all the valleys created on district boundaries are local optima.

MODEL 4
(DISTRICT-DEPENDENT TRUNKING COSTS)

In our studies of distribution problems we have encountered cases in which the trunking rate is dependent on the amount delivered and on the district in which the depot is situated, but not on the distance between the factory and the depot.

Model 4 is similar to Model 3, except that the trunking cost parameter β_k is replaced by a new parameter γ_k which is not related to distance. As in Model 3, the region is divided into r districts, each district having its own parameter γ_k. The trunking cost from the factory to depot is then expressed as

$$\gamma_k \, W_i \, \delta_{ik}$$

where γ_k = cost per unit weight (or amount) delivered when the destination is in district k $(k = 1, 2,..., r)$;
   W_i = weight (or amount) delivered to depot i;
   $\delta_{ik} = 1$ if depot i is situated in district k, otherwise $\delta_{ik} = 0$.

The total function cost function then becomes

$$C(4) = \sum_{i=1}^{m} \sum_{k=1}^{r} \gamma_k \, W_i \, \delta_{ik} + C(1) \tag{4.12}$$

where, as before, the first term represents the total trunking costs, while the second term is the local distribution costs as expressed in equation (4.5) (Model 1).

Method of solution

The first term in equation (4.12) remains constant as long as a depot does not move from one district to another, and the optimizing solution in equations (4.6) and (4.7) for Model 1 is, therefore, valid for this model. Model 4, however, involves discontinuities in the cost function when a depot crosses a district boundary. The following heuristic procedure is therefore designed to solve this problem:

(1) Choose an initial location for each depot.

(2) Allocate each customer to a depot. This allocation is done, as in the previous models, in a way that minimizes the cost function. In Model 4, where the trunking cost parameter γ_k is a cost per unit weight, the allocation must be made with respect to the lowest g_{ij}, where

$$g_{ij} = \alpha_j d_{ij} + \sum_{k=1}^{r} \gamma_k \delta_{ik} \tag{4.13}$$

g_{ij} being the cost to deliver a unit weight to customer j through depot i.

(3) Find the value of this solution from equation (4.12).

(4) Calculate the depot locations using equations (4.6) and (4.7).

(5) Go to (2) and repeat until no further improvement can be made. Note that as in Model 3, depots may be constrained to remain in their previous districts if they cross a boundary into a more expensive district.

(6) The above algorithm will lead to a local optimal solution which may be improved by the following search procedure. For each depot examine the values of the trunking rates in the neighbouring districts. If a cheaper neighbouring district is found (in terms of the trunking rate γ_k), move the depot across the boundary and find the value of the new solution. This procedure is repeated for all depots until no further improvement can be made.

(7) Return to (2) and repeat until the cost function cannot be further reduced.

It can be seen that equation (4.12) is similar to equation (4.5) for Model 1, with the addition of a constant trunking-cost term. Hence, bearing in mind the possible constraints on depot movement and the necessity of allocating customers to the cheapest depot (to ensure that equation (4.12) is being minimized and not equation (4.5)), equation (4.12) is also convergent.

It should be noted that this heuristic solution procedure does not

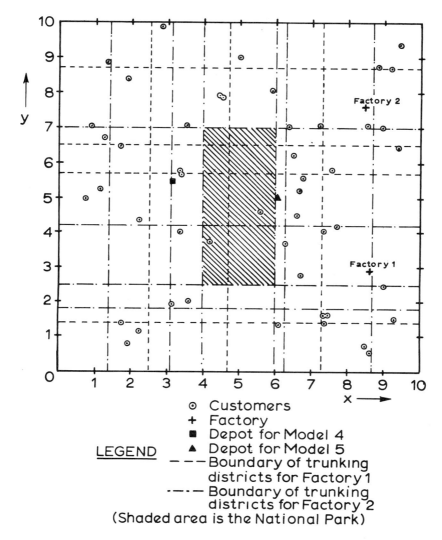

Fig. 4.8   An example of district-dependent trunking rates for Models 4 and 5

necessarily yield the optimal solution. In the first instance, the initial solution derived from steps 1 to 5 depends on the starting locations given to the depots. Secondly, the final solution may well depend on the order in which depots are examined in step 6, and, so far, there is no evidence that any particular order will guarantee that the optimal solution is obtained. As is to be expected, the search procedure described in step 6 does reduce the number of local optima, but even so, as in Model 1, the suggested procedure yields a suboptimum, and after performing several trials, the best solution is selected. An example of this method is shown in Fig. 4.8. This illustrates a solution to a 50-customer, two-factory, two-product and one-depot case (details are given in Appendix 4.3). Notice that the values of γ_k depend on which factory the goods are being trunked from, i.e. there are two sets of γ_k's, one associated with each factory. There are, in fact, 42 trunking districts associated with factory 1 and 35 trunking districts associated with factory 2. Notice also that although the example is a 2-product case, factory 2 only manufactures product 1. It is assumed that there are no capacity constraints on either factories or depots. The solutions for this problem, assuming 0, 1, 2 and 3 depots, are given in Appendix 4.3.

This example illustrates not only the use of Model 4, showing a case in which breaks in trunking rates may influence the location of a depot, but also the way in which district-dependent trunking rates can be handled. Notice that in Fig. 4.8 the shaded area bounded by $x = 4.0$, $x = 6.0$, $y = 2.5$ and $y = 7.0$ is assumed to be a forbidden area for depot location (say, because of an existing national park). This situation can be accommodated by making the trunking costs for delivery into this area prohibitively high, so that it will never be an economical proposition to site a depot there.

MODEL 5 (TOTAL COST FUNCTION)

Model 5 is not merely an extension of Model 4; account is now taken of the cost of running the depots. The cost function, therefore, consists of three terms, as discussed in Chapter 1:

(1) Warehousing costs, denoted as F_i for depot i.
(2) District-dependent trunking costs for transportation from factory to depots.
(3) Costs for local distribution from depots to customers.

The last two terms are covered by equation (4.12). The first term is assumed to take the form

$$F_i = a + bW_i + c\sqrt{W_i} \qquad (4.14)$$

where a, b and c are constants.

This is a continuous concave function with a fixed cost term a and variable costs that depend on the throughput W_i. The last term takes account of the effect of economies of scale on unit handling and storage costs.

The total cost function for Model 5 is:

$$C(5) = \sum_{i=1}^{m} F_i \delta_i + C(4) \qquad (4.15)$$

where $\delta_i = 1$ if $W_i > 0$, but $\delta_i = 0$ if $W_i = 0$.

In addition to providing a solution for the depot location problem, Model 5 highlights the need to provide an answer to the question: "How many depots should there be in the system?".

Method of solution

As the first term in equation (4.15) is not affected by depot locations, the solution procedure for Model 4 may be used here. Starting with random or selected positions for the depots, an allocation of customers to depots is made based on the criterion of serving a customer from the cheapest depot rather than the nearest. Following the arguments propounded in connection with Model 4, the marginal cost per unit amount delivered to customer j, including trunking costs to depot i and unit warehousing costs, is

$$g_{ij} = \alpha_j d_{ij} + \sum_{k=1}^{r} \gamma_k \delta_{ik} + b + c/(2\sqrt{W_i}) \qquad (4.16)$$

The coefficient b is constant for all depots and may be disregarded. In the initial allocation the throughput values W_i are unknown and the allocation proceeds according to the sum of the first two terms (as in Model 4). In any subsequent iterations the values of W_i are taken from the results of the previous iteration.

This procedure implies that initially W_i is assumed to be the same for all depots. Alternative initial conditions could be considered whereby the initial amount W_i for depot i is taken at random (provided that $\Sigma W_i = \Sigma w_j$) and is then fed into (4.16) to produce the marginal cost per unit of supplying customer j through depot i.

This method of allocation favours large depots over small ones, because of the economies of scale inherent in the last term of equation (4.16), but this tendency is tempered by increases in local distribution costs. It should be pointed out that the method of allocation suggested does not necessarily guarantee convergence to a local optimum, because of the last term in equation (4.16), but in our experience the method has worked satisfactorily.

The allocation procedure is based on the marginal unit cost of transportation and warehousing, and disregards the fixed cost a in the warehousing cost function (4.14). For any given solution that emerges from this allocation method, it is possible that if a depot is made to close down, thereby increasing the local distribution costs to the customers served from that depot, the total cost function would still decrease, owing to the saving in fixed costs. To investigate these possibilities a *drop routine* is incorporated in the solution procedure. A drop routine is adopted rather than an *add routine,* which calls for a depot to be added to an existing solution, because the add routine involves the additional problem of deciding where to locate the new depot and thereby substantially increases the amount of computations.

The solution procedure for Model 5 is summarized below:

(1) Select a value for m which exceeds the number of depots expected in the final solution and assign random initial locations to the depots.
(2) Allocate customers to depots according to the lowest marginal unit cost in equation (4.16), either when the initial W_i's are the same or chosen randomly.
(3) Find the resultant depot throughput values W_i and the improved depot locations from equations (4.6) and (4.7).
(4) Allocate customers to depots according to equation (4.16) and calculate the total cost function (4.15). Return to (3) and repeat until no further improvement in the cost function is obtained.
(5) Apply the drop routine:
– remove the smallest depot in the system;
– allocate the customers served by this depot to other depots according to equation (4.16);
– cost this solution;
– if the cost is lower than that obtained in step 4, go to step 3 and repeat 3 and 4 until the cost function cannot be reduced any further;
– repeat the drop routine until no improved solution is found.

Although Model 5 is based on the assumption that trunking costs are district-dependent, there is no difficulty in extending Models 2 and 3 to cover warehousing costs in very much the same way.

A numerical example for Model 5 (see Fig. 4.8) is based on the 50-customer, 2-factory, 2-product problem used to illustrate Model 4 (the data are given in Appendix 4.3). It should be noted that this solution calls for factory 2 to be closed down and for all customers to be served from a single depot. The cost of the solution of Model 4 is more expensive by 7·7 per cent than that derived from Model 5, and the depot positions derived by the two models are quite different. One reason for the difference in the results for the two models is that in Model 4 it is assumed that neither of the factories can be closed; the other reason lies in the economies of scale of the warehousing cost function, in which a reduction in the number of distribution centres leads to substantial savings.

MODEL 6
(DISTRICT-DEPENDENT WAREHOUSE COSTS – THE TOTAL COST FUNCTION)

In Model 5 the assumption was made that the cost coefficients a, b and c in the warehousing cost function are the same for all warehouses. This is clearly a limiting assumption in that factors such as the cost of depot space, wages, accessibility, proximity to main roads and other amenities are likely to vary perhaps considerably from one vicinity to another. One way to overcome this shortcoming is to make the coefficients a, b and c district dependent.

This is incorporated in Model 6. The region under consideration is divided into s districts, in a similar manner to the district-dependent trunking costs, and in each district l $(l = 1, 2, \ldots, s)$ the cost coefficients a_l, b_l and c_l represent the prevailing warehousing costs in that district.

The warehousing cost function now becomes

$$F_i = \sum_{l=1}^{s} \delta_{il} \, (a_l + b_l \, W_i + c_l \sqrt{W_i}) \qquad (4.17)$$

where $\delta_{il} = 1$ if warehouse i is situated in district l $(l = 1, 2, \ldots, s)$, otherwise $\delta_{il} = 0$.

The total cost function now becomes as in equation (4.15), where F_i takes the form of equation (4.17). If, for example, the trunking costs are linear with respect to distance (Model 2), the total cost function becomes

$$C(6) = \sum_{i=1}^{m} \delta_i \, F_i + C(2) \qquad (4.18)$$

where $\delta_i = 1$ if $W_i > 0$, but $\delta_i = 0$ if $W_i = 0$.

Method of solution

The method of solution for Model 6 is a combination of the methods for Models 4 and 5. A search routine, which is used to improve on local optima, is borrowed from Model 4, and from Model 5 we take the drop routine and the solution procedure for the relevant trunking cost. Starting with random or selected locations for the depots, the allocation of customers is made such that the total cost function is minimized (namely each customer is served from the cheapest rather than the nearest depot). The marginal unit costs follow equation (4.16), except that now the coefficients b and c are replaced by b_l and c_l. For example, if the trunking costs follow Model 2 (linear with respect to distance), the allocation of customer j is made to that depot which minimizes for any given i

$$g_{ij} = \alpha_j d_{ij} + \beta_i d_{0i} + \sum_{l=1}^{s} \delta_{il} (b_l + c_l/2\sqrt{W_i})$$ (4.19)

Note that the fixed cost term a_l in the warehousing cost equation has been ignored. We found, as did Drysdale and Sandiford [10], that including the unit cost equivalent of the fixed costs in the allocation equation, i.e. the term

$$\sum_{l=1}^{s} \delta_{il} a_l / W_i$$ (4.20)

tended to remove depots, which should not have been removed, at the early stages of the program.

Some experiments were carried out in which only a proportion of the term (4.20) was added to the allocation equation (4.19). These indicated that the larger the percentage included, the faster the program was, but the final solution became more suboptimal. We achieved a balance when the term (4.20) was multiplied by a factor of 0·3. More work, however, needs to be done to find the value of this factor for a large number of problems.

The solution procedure for Model 6 is summarized below:

(1) Select a value for m which exceeds the number of depots expected in the final solution, and assign random initial locations to the m depots.

(2) Allocate customers to depots according to the lowest marginal unit cost. Initially, as the throughputs of the depots are unknown in the first iteration, use the first three terms of equation (4.19) (or its equivalent). Alternatively, allocate the total throughput randomly, as explained earlier.

(3) Find the resultant depot throughput values W_i and the improved depot locations from the appropriate equations.

(4) Allocate customers to depots according to (4.19) or the appropriate equivalent, and calculate the total cost function. Return to (3) and repeat until no further improvement in the cost function is obtained.

(5) Apply the search procedure:
- for each warehouse examine the neighbouring districts for a cheaper warehousing cost;
- if a district is found in which any part of the warehousing is cheaper than that in which the depot is currently sited, move the depot into that district and cost that solution;
- repeat for all districts and all depots in turn; keep the cheapest solution;
- if a cheaper solution is found, go to (3); otherwise go to (6).

(6) Apply the drop routine.

By the time the program has reached this stage the depots will be in the best possible warehousing cost districts (because of the action of the search procedure). Generally, the smallest depot will also incur the higher unit costs and would therefore be the first candidate to eliminate from the solution. It may sometimes be useful to consider whether the second smallest depot, rather than the smallest, should be eliminated, particularly when there are wide variations in the fixed costs.

An important assumption in this model is that the costs of a warehouse are likely to be similar in a given area. We feel that this assumption is not unreasonable in that the price of land for warehousing (given planning restrictions) or the rental of a warehouse with the required facilities is likely to be comparable within a given area. The grid can, of course, be drawn as fine as we wish and, as illustrated by the numerical example for Model 5, infeasible areas can be forbidden by giving the relevant coefficients a very high value.

CONCLUSIONS

All these models have been tested not only with theoretical problems but also with several case studies, one of which is described in Chapter 6. It has been found that the method of locating warehouses suggested in Model 5, which is based on the total cost function, gives cheaper solutions than the methods advocated by Haley [18], Surkis [41] and others, which are based on minimizing the transportation costs and then adding the respective warehousing costs. Although in many cases the cost difference between the two approaches may not be substantial, the latter approach clearly suffers from the disadvantage that it takes no account of the economies of scale in the warehousing cost function, a feature that can be of some significance, as indicated in the example shown in Fig. 4.8.

The models described here should not be regarded as rigid tools for eliciting the precise co-ordinate dimensions for the depots in the system, but rather as pointing out the areas in which to look for possible sites. The fact that the cost function is shallow in the region of the optimum gives a certain amount of flexibility, so that the solution to the appropriate model can be followed up by a meticulous study of the merits of alternative sites in any one locality. The value of the models lies in limiting the vast amount of time and effort which is otherwise needed in identifying and investigating a very large number of feasible sites, if one follows the feasible set approach.

Although the models described in this chapter are discussed with reference to particular forms of transportation and warehousing cost functions, the methods of analysis are applicable to a wide variety of other cost functions.

APPENDIX 4.1

(a) Data for the 50-customer problem

Cust. No.	Co-ordinates x	y	Cust. No.	Co-ordinates x	y	Cust. No.	Co-ordinates x	y
1	1·33	8·89	18	3·13	1·92	35	6·37	7·02
2	1·89	0·77	19	8·86	8·74	36	7·23	7·05
3	9·27	1·49	20	4·18	3·74	37	1·68	6·45
4	9·46	9·36	21	2·22	4·35	38	3·54	7·06
5	9·20	8·69	22	0·88	7·02	39	7·67	4·17
6	7·43	1·61	23	8·53	7·04	40	2·20	1·12
7	6·08	1·34	24	6·49	6·22	41	3·57	1·99
8	5·57	4·60	25	4·53	7·87	42	7·34	1·38
9	6·70	2·77	26	4·46	7·91	43	6·58	4·49
10	8·99	2·45	27	2·83	9·88	44	5·00	9·00
11	8·93	7·00	28	3·39	5·65	45	6·63	5·23
12	8·60	0·53	29	0·75	4·98	46	5·89	8·06
13	4·01	0·31	30	7·55	5·79	47	1·13	5·25
14	3·34	4·01	31	8·45	0·69	48	1·90	8·35
15	6·75	5·57	32	3·33	5·78	49	1·74	1·37
16	7·36	4·03	33	6·27	3·66	50	9·39	6·44
17	1·24	6·69	34	7·31	1·61			

Cost of local distribution $\alpha_j = 1$ unit per ton-mile
Demand of customers = 1 ton for all customers

(b) Solutions to the 50-customer problem for Model 1

m	Cost	Co-ordinates of final depot locations
1	180·128	5·62, 4·90
2	135·522	2·67, 5·65; 7·24, 4·54
3	105·214	2·33, 5·15; 7·40, 1·65; 7·06, 6·84
4	84·154	3·13, 1·92; 2·46, 7·05; 7·43, 1·61; 7·35, 6·22
5	72·238	3·13, 1·92; 7·44, 1·58; 2·46, 7·05; 8·63, 7·52; 6·66, 5·21

APPENDIX 4.2

Data and results for the example of Model 3 shown in Fig. 4.5

Customer data   The locations of the customers are given in Appendix 4.1. Demand of customers $w_j = 1$ ton for all customers. Cost of local distribution $\alpha_j = 1$ unit per ton-mile.

Factory location   (8·61, 2·91)

District trunking rates per ton-mile and district boundary co-ordinates

x boundary — y boundary	1·44	4·69	5·73	10·00
2·47	·786	·317	·088	·026
5·26	·755	·433	·099	·059
6·60	·873	·568	·626	·284
10·00	·928	·899	·901	·426

Results for 1-*depot,* 1-*factory*

Objective function C(3)	Location	
	x_i	y_i
150·70	3·33	5·78
151·04	3·21	5·26

N.B. For those who wish to repeat this experiment the allocation was, for simplicity, to the nearest depot and not the cheapest; also, the factory acted as a depot serving customers nearest to it.

APPENDIX 4.3

Data and results for the 50-customer, 2-factory, 2-product example of Model 4 illustrated in Fig. 4.8

Customer data The locations of the customers are given in Appendix 4.1.

Customer demand (tons)

Customer No.	Product 1	Product 2	Customer No.	Product 1	Product 2	Customer No.	Product 1	Product 2
1	27	27	18	175	110	35	110	38
2	18	81	19	177	80	36	139	113
3	78	43	20	22	69	37	74	125
4	114	122	21	200	62	38	175	0
5	67	15	22	218	19	39	135	124
6	200	19	23	117	0	40	130	7
7	81	68	24	47	67	41	119	40
8	211	105	25	108	55	42	216	43
9	56	18	26	198	67	43	121	102
10	24	9	27	105	21	44	60	31
11	0	113	28	186	83	45	216	83
12	40	71	29	175	128	46	168	108
13	103	2	30	171	15	47	69	108
14	94	60	31	42	33	48	121	3
15	157	39	32	202	72	49	205	79
16	9	125	33	94	108	50	126	93
17	166	43	34	4	121			
						Totals	5870	3167

Factory data

No.	Location x_0	y_0	Manufacturers 1	Product 2
1	8·61	2·91	yes	yes
2	8·46	7·62	yes	no

APPENDIX 4.3 (*cont.*)

Transport costs   Local distribution $\alpha = £0.05$ per ton-mile. The district trunking costs γ_k (£ per ton) are for given district boundary co-ordinates.

Trunking from factory 1

y boundary \ x boundary	2·5	4·0	4·7	6·0	7·3	10·0
1·4	·290	·160	·125	·125	·115	·080
2·5	·275	·160	·125	·095	·095	·050
5·7	·275	·200	∞	∞	·075	·050
6·5	·275	·215	∞	∞	·075	·075
7·0	·275	·215	∞	∞	·105	·170
8·7	·290	·235	·235	·200	·170	·170
10·0	·325	·290	·325	·290	·290	·325

Trunking from factory 2

y boundary \ x boundary	1·4	3·1	4·0	6·0	6·3	8·7	10·0
1·8	·350	·325	·275	·225	·225	·200	·200
2·5	·325	·290	·275	∞	·200	·170	·200
4·2	·325	·275	·235	∞	·170	·170	·170
7·0	·290	·235	·175	∞	·150	·125	·150
10·0	·275	·200	·175	·150	·150	·050	·050

Warehousing costs (£)

$$F_i = 500 + 3W_i + 100 \sqrt{W_i} \qquad (A.4.1)$$

where W_i = total output of depot i.

It is assumed that both factories will serve customers direct when it is economical to do so. Therefore, both factories will act as depots and be charged the appropriate amount according to equation (A.4.1).

Further it is assumed that factory 1 can manufacture sufficient quantities of both products to serve the demand for the whole area, i.e. there are no capacity constraints. However, should factory 2 require any amount of product 2, which it does not manufacture itself, this must be trunked from factory 1 at the relevant rate (£0·17 per ton).

Scaling factor   All distances should be multiplied by a scaling factor equal to 6·154 to convert the map scale to miles.

APPENDIX 4.3 (*concluded*)

Results for the 50-customer, 2-factory, 2-product example

Solutions to Model 4

No. of depots	Total transportation costs (£)	Total cost (£)	Time for 10 trials*
0	11,269	52,824	—
1	7,292	52,171	1·00
2	6,169	54,114	1·46
3	5,333	55,978	2·03

Location of depots

No. of depots	Location (x_i, y_i)
0	—
1	3·10, 5·46
2	3·10, 6·24 : 3·13, 1·92
3	3·10, 6·30 : 3·13, 1·92; 6·63, 5·23

Solutions to Model 5

Distribution centre	Total cost (£) †
1 depot only located at (6·00, 5·07)	48,414
Factory 1 only	51,652
Factory 2 only	52,139

The time for 10 trials starting with 2 depots equals 2·08*.

---

* Time in minutes on an IBM 7094 computer.
† Includes fixed costs for each factory which has zero throughput. This can be regarded as a penalty for not distributing direct from the factory.

Chapter 5

Depot location for variable demand

One of the fundamental assumptions made in all published treatises on the depot siting problem is that the geographical locations of the customers in the system are known and that their demands remain static. Clearly, such an assumption does not always apply in practice, and we therefore propose to discuss briefly in this chapter several cases in which the demand on the depot varies from one time-period to another. These variations can come about in a number of ways. The requirements of customers are such that they generate orders of different magnitude; also, the set of customers in the system constantly changes with the addition of new customers and the deletion of old ones from the list.

In all such cases it is necessary to examine the effect of this variable demand on the local delivery costs and to feed this cost into the total cost function. While in many cases the local variable demand is unlikely to affect the pattern of transportation in bulk from factories to depots and the number of depots needed in the system, it is nevertheless a problem that needs to be examined.

CASE 1: DETERMINISTIC DEMAND

Let the distribution system consist of a single depot and n customers at given locations (x_j, y_j) where $j = 1, \ldots, n$. The demand pattern is described by the following matrix:

	Period 1	$\ldots$ t $\ldots$	T	Total
Customer 1	w_{11}	w_{1t}	w_{1T}	w_1
$\vdots$				
j	w_{j1}	w_{jt}	w_{jT}	w_j
$\vdots$				
n	w_{n1}	w_{nt}	w_{nT}	w_n

Customer j demands a delivery of w_{jt} in time-period t ($t = 1, \ldots, T$) and the planning horizon consists of T periods. This is a situation that may occur in the retail trade when the requirements of a customer vary from day to day but his demand adheres to a given weekly pattern.

If a single depot is located at (x_0, y_0) and the distance between customer j and the depot is given by d_j (expressed as a straight-line distance as in Chapter 3, or as a corrected radial distance), and if we are only concerned with radial distances, then the local delivery cost is obtained by

$$H = \alpha \sum_{j=1}^{n} \sum_{t=1}^{T} w_{jt} \, d_j \qquad (5.1)$$

where α is the cost per unit of demand per unit of distance (such as ton-mile). This expression is an extension of equation (3.5), except that in Chapter 3 the time-periods were assumed to be identical, whereas here the requirements of each customer in terms of ton-miles are summed over the cycle time T. If we substitute

$$w_j = \sum_{t=1}^{T} w_{jt} \qquad (5.2)$$

where w_j is now the total demand of customer j over the whole cycle T, we have

$$H = \alpha \sum_{j=1}^{n} w_j \, d_j \qquad (5.3)$$

which is the same expression as was used in Chapter 3, and hence the methods used in that chapter to determine the optimal location of the depot to minimize H apply here.

The problem becomes more complex when we do not consider radial distances but "travelling salesman" distances, namely when we wish to take account of the fact that a vehicle may visit several customers in a single tour before returning to the depot. Here it is convenient to differentiate between two cases:

    (a) it is assumed that the same set of customers is always allocated to the same vehicle;

    (b) because of the capacity constraints for vehicles, the allocation of customers to each vehicle may change from one period to another.

In case (a) the number of vehicles required to meet the demand remains unchanged. Indeed, for any given position of the depot the route of each vehicle remains the same throughout the T time-periods, and this route will obviously be designed in such a way as to minimize the distance covered in order to visit the customers involved. However, if the location of the depot is moved, it is necessary to verify that the route designed for the previous location still applies.

Take the example given in Fig. 5.1, where a vehicle is scheduled to start from the depot situated at point P, visit four customers, and

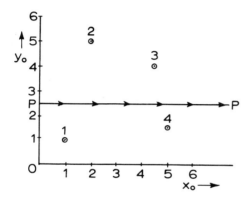

Fig. 5.1   A four-customer problem

return to P. The number of possible sequences (each sequence being a possible tour) in which n customers can be visited from a depot is $\frac{1}{2}n!$ or 12 in this example:

Tour	Sequence
1	$P-1-2-3-4-P$
2	$P-1-2-4-3-P$
3	$P-1-3-2-4-P$
4	$P-1-3-4-2-P$
5	$P-1-4-2-3-P$
6	$P-1-4-3-2-P$
7	$P-2-1-3-4-P$
8	$P-2-1-4-3-P$
9	$P-2-3-1-4-P$
10	$P-2-4-1-3-P$
11	$P-3-1-2-4-P$
12	$P-4-1-2-3-P$

Let the depot P now move along the x-axis as shown in Fig. 5.1, thereby affecting the length of each possible tour. The values of four tours are plotted in Fig. 5.2, from which we find that tour 6 remained the shortest up to $x_0 \approx 2\cdot7$, and beyond that point tour 1 becomes shorter; while when x_0 exceeds approximately $3\cdot8$, tour 12 is the shortest. Other tours, such as tour 3, need never be considered at all,

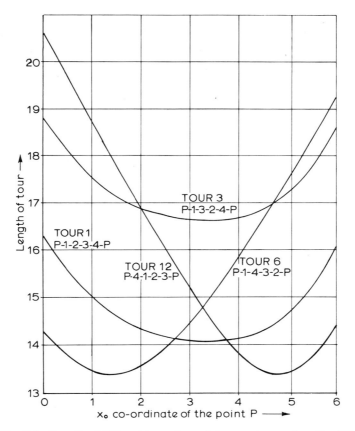

Fig. 5.2   Length of different tours through four customers (see Fig. 5.1)

as long as the movement of P is confined to the path shown in Fig. 5.1. In considering the local delivery cost for such a case, the length of the best tour (shown by the lower-bound line in Fig. 5.2) should be fed into the cost function for any given value of x_0.

The problem remains essentially the same as stated in equation

(5.3), except that now, instead of considering each customer, we need to consider each tour, so that

$$H = \alpha \sum_k u_k D_k \qquad (5.4)$$

where u_k is the total requirements of all customers supplied by vehicle k, and D_k is the length of the tour k.

Strictly, u_k is the amount that a vehicle carries at the beginning of the tour, but the actual load on the vehicle decreases along the route as consignments are delivered to customers, so that u_k is not carried for the whole distance D_k, but an allowance for this difference can generally be made by adjusting the value of α. In the special case where the delivery costs depend on the distance travelled and not on the amount carried, equation (5.4) reduces to $\alpha \sum_k D_k$.

The method of solution may proceed along the lines suggested in Chapter 3, but while the function (5.3) has a unique optimal value, the function (5.4) may have several optimum points, and the solution obtained by the method suggested in Chapter 3 may depend on the starting values of x_0, y_0. It is therefore necessary to repeat the procedure for several initial depot locations in a similar fashion to the solution method for the multi-depot problem, as discussed in Chapter 4.

Case (b) represents a more complicated situation. Here the capacity constraints for vehicles may be such that a vehicle cannot serve the same set of customers throughout the cycle T. It is therefore necessary for each period and for each given location of the depot to allocate customers to vehicles and design their routes, as described in Chapters 9 and 10, and these calculations need to be repeated for new values of x_0 and y_0, before the optimal location of the depot can be determined.

CASE 2:   RANDOM CUSTOMER SET

Here it is assumed that when a customer puts in an order he does so for a given consignment and the size of the order is time-independent. The pattern of ordering is assumed to be binomial, with p_j describing the probability that customer j will order his consignment in any one period. Thus the number of customers to generate orders in one period is, say, n, and this number may vary from period to period. In the extreme case where $p_j = 1$ we have the deterministic case discussed in Chapter 3.

There are two methods of constructing a cost function for this case.

(1) Simulation

For each time-period the probability that customer j puts in an order is p_j and the probability that he does not is $1 - p_j$. Thus the orders of customers may be simulated for each time-period and the corresponding values of u_k and D_k in equation (5.4) can then be calculated. The delivery costs vary, of course, from period to period, depending on n and on the locations of the n customers, but if the simulation is repeated many times, the expected costs per period can be obtained. The cost is thus computed for various depot positions until no further reduction in the cost function is obtained by a shift in the depot location. As the result is likely to be affected by the initial position of the depot, the exercise needs to be repeated for several initial conditions. This method is equally valid for the assumption that all n customers are served by a vehicle in one single tour and for the case where several tours need to be designed for each period (following the algorithm proposed in Chapter 10).

(2) Approximation

Let $p(n)$ be the probability of there being n customers requiring service in any one time-period, and let D_0 be the expected distance involved in supplying n customers and $w(n)$ the expected total demand for that period. The cost of delivery is then

$$C = \alpha \sum_{n=0}^{n_0} p(n)\, w(n)\, D_0 \qquad (5.5)$$

where n_0 is the total customer population from which n customers are drawn and

$$\sum_{n=0}^{n_0} p(n) = 1$$

The larger n_0 and the smaller p_j, the more random the demand matrix seems for each time-period. In the special case where the cost is independent of the demand w_j, the function (5.5) is reduced to

$$C = \alpha \Sigma p(n) D_0$$

It now remains to estimate D_0, namely the expected length of the tour through n customers. This problem is discussed at some length in Chapter 8 and the expected value of D_0 can be derived from Fig. 8.22, and where appropriate from Fig. 8.20.

CASE 3: RANDOM DEMAND

If the customers to be supplied in any time-period are drawn from a very large population and if there are no dominant regular customers and customer demand varies widely, then it is convenient to describe the situation by two probability density functions: $p(n)$, being the probability that n customers need to be served, and $g(w)$, being the probability that the amount w needs to be supplied to the customer. In the absence of important regular customers, or densely populated pockets of customers, the n customers may be assumed to be randomly distributed in the region.

This problem may be analysed by simulation. The distributions $p(n)$ and $g(w)$ are used to generate demand patterns and the delivery costs are then computed for each time-period, so that after an adequately long simulation the expected cost can be computed for any given depot location.

To use an approximation, it is convenient to compute the average demand per customer (denoted by w_0), so that the expected requirements for n customers are nw_0. If the capacity of vehicles is known, and if the distance constraint on vehicles is not dominant, then the number of tours involved in supplying the n customers can be computed. Using the results in Chapter 8, we can then find the approximate value of the delivery costs.

Chapter 6

A case study

THE COMPANY AND THE PROBLEM

The case study given here serves several purposes. First, it illustrates how models such as those described in Chapter 4 can be used in practice, and secondly it highlights some of the characteristics of these models.

The case study concerns a British manufacturing company for engineering products; the customers were in the main industrial, but some deliveries were made to wholesalers as the product can be be used by "do-it-yourself" enthusiasts. The company manufactured several products, but an analysis of its sales revealed that one product accounted for more than 80 per cent of the total and it was felt, therefore, that the study could be confined to the distribution of the main product.

The problem arose initially in that the lease of the depot currently used by the company in Birmingham was shortly due to expire. The management felt that this provided an excellent opportunity to examine the distribution of their product in that region and, in particular, to determine the most economic number and location of depots to serve the region.

The region in question can loosely be described as consisting of Wales and the West Midlands. As can be seen from the map shown in Fig. 6.1, it covers the whole of Wales and extends as far east as Peterborough. In the north it includes Derby and Nottingham, but not Crewe or Stoke-on-Trent, and in the south it includes Worcester, but not Gloucester or Cheltenham.

Practice prior to the study

Prior to the study the company leased one depot in Birmingham and also rented space in a public warehouse in Cardiff. Replenishment loads were trunked from the factory on the outskirts of London

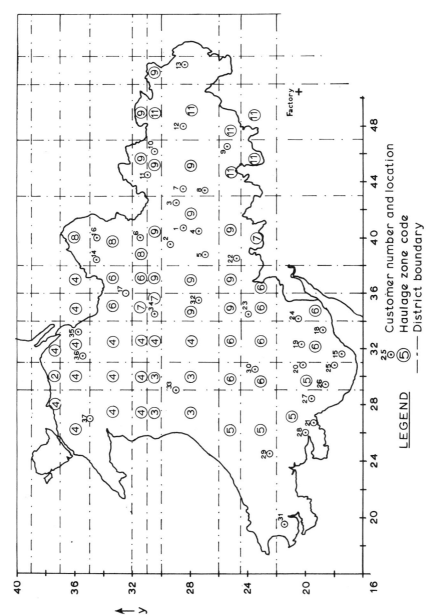

LEGEND

⊙ Customer number and location

⑤ Haulage zone code

—·— District boundary

Fig. 6.1 Map of area showing customer locations and haulage zones

to these depots by a haulage contractor on a regular basis (at least once a week in the case of the Birmingham depot). Delivery from the depots was done in part by haulage contractors and in part by company-owned vehicles, depending on which mode was the most convenient at the time. Company policy stated that all deliveries should be made within 24 hours of receipt of the order; however, in practice it was found that this was not strictly adhered to and deliveries were made within a maximum of 72 hours of the order being received. The actual time taken depended on the location of the customer and on how his order could best be fitted in.

Customer locations

Even with such a relatively small problem it was impossible to account for each individual customer, and this for two reasons. First, the number of customers was rather large, thereby raising problems of adequate computer storage capacity. Secondly – and this was a more fundamental reason – most of the orders were essentially of the "one-off" type, namely orders for any one customer were so infrequent that an order pattern for each customer could not be established without a rather lengthy analysis based on limited information. It was thus found easier to forecast future demand for an area rather than for individual customers and it was, therefore, decided to group customers into areas, and to consider each area as a single customer.

The total region was divided into 37 customer areas. This was done by aggregating salesman territories in a fairly arbitrary manner. We tried to keep the customer areas as compact as possible, while attempting to smooth the demand per area by making areas with a large demand density comparatively small and areas with a low demand density comparatively large. For this reason, and because of the boundaries of the original sales territories, the resultant customer areas were not particularly regular in shape. The demand for each customer area was aggregated and was considered to originate from a single point in the appropriate area. These points were assumed to be approximately at the centre of gravity of the corresponding customer areas, and these 37 locations are shown on the map in Fig. 6.1.

Demand data

Several analyses were carried out on the demand data for the whole region. In particular, the orders for one year were examined. This examination revealed the following interesting characteristics:

(1) The very high proportion of small orders: the distribution of order size, given in Fig. 6.2, showed that almost 50 per cent of all orders were worth £10 or less.
(2) The value to the company of the few, but very large orders: although only 10 per cent of all orders were worth more than £100, these large orders accounted for 70 per cent of the turnover.
(3) No seasonality: no significant seasonal variations were observed.

The high proportion of small orders led to a cost analysis of

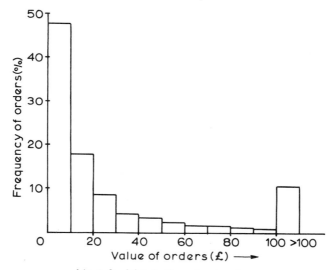

Fig. 6.2   Distribution of order size

deliveries. It became clear that it was cheaper to deliver all orders greater in value than £100 direct from the factory rather than channel them through the depot. It was necessary, therefore, to examine the number and location of depots to handle most economically the remaining orders.

These orders were then summed for each customer area and multiplied by a trend figure obtained from historical data to give a forecast measure of customer demand, assuming that the then present trend in sales and pattern of order size would continue in the future. The figures thus obtained were used as the demand data to determine the number and location of depots required to serve the region.

Cost of warehousing

Naturally, at the outset of the analysis the ultimate sizes of the depots were not known. It was therefore necessary to develop a cost function of a depot in terms of its size or (more conveniently) its annual throughput. An examination of the costs involved in running a depot led to the construction of an annual cost function F of the form

$$F = A + BW + (C + VI) \left(\frac{W}{104} + 2\sigma \right) \qquad (6.1)$$

where W = annual throughput of the depot (in tons),
A = annual fixed costs of the depot,
B = handling cost per ton-throughput,
C = depot cost per average ton of stock per annum,
V = factory cost of product per ton,
I = interest rate on capital tied in stock,
σ = standard deviation of weekly demand (in tons), estimated by

$$\sigma = \sigma_Q \sqrt{\frac{W}{Q}} \qquad (6.2)$$

where Q = total annual sales through all the depots,
σ_Q = standard deviation of total annual sales.

The first two terms in expression (6.1) are self-explanatory; they include the fixed and the handling costs of the depot. The third term accounts for the average costs of storage (C) and the costs of the inventory (VI) held in the depot. The company operated an inventory control policy in which the goods sold during one week were replenished in the following week. Hence the term in the final set of brackets represents the average amount of stock held. σ in the third term in equation (6.1) accounts for the variability in weekly demand, and is assumed to be related to the standard deviation of the total annual sales according to the simple expression (6.2).

If W is considered as the main variable in the cost function, then equation (6.1) may be reduced to

$$F = a + bW + c\sqrt{W} \qquad (6.3)$$

where a, b and c are constants. Several tests on actual costs were carried out and it was found that the cost function (6.3) represented very well the actual cost of depots then currently in use in the company's distribution system. The function assumes weekly replenishment loads, which was the company's current practice. This assumption was examined further and it was found that it was cheaper to deliver in bulk on a weekly basis rather than any other time-span.

Trunking costs

Current company practice was to use haulage contractors to deliver stock replenishment loads to the depots. Management response to questions and an examination of the costs involved

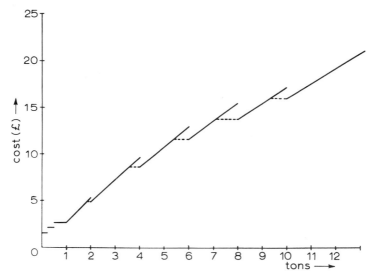

Fig. 6.3   Haulier charges for a typical district against tons carried

indicated that this practice would continue in the future. Alternative modes of transport could be company-owned vehicles and rail transportation.

An examination of the rates quoted by hauliers revealed that they charged a rate which was piece-wise linear with tonnage carried. These rates varied according to the district to which the load was destined. It appeared that each haulage contractor had better contacts in some districts, which made it easier for him to obtain return loads and thus make the operating of his vehicles more economical. In part these economies were passed on to the customer to encourage him to send more goods to these districts, and hence the rates per district were not necessarily related to distance. The rates for a typical district are illustrated in Fig. 6.3.

This form of trunking cost fits well the format given in Model 4, which is described in Chapter 4. In fact, Model 4 is specifically designed to cope with haulage contractor charges which may vary from one destination to another.

It was then necessary to divide the whole region into appropriate districts, each having its own trunking rate. This was accomplished simply by obtaining quotations from the haulier about his trunking rates to various towns and locations in the region. The rates were then plotted on a map of the region, and horizontal and vertical lines were drawn dividing the districts with different haulage rates. In this way the area was covered by a 9×9 grid and each district was labelled with the appropriate trunking rate code, following the haulage contractors' practice. The districts and codes are marked on the map, Fig. 6.1. Districts which fall outside the region have been given a very high rate, so as to encourage depots to be located only inside the region.

Local delivery costs

The company's practice for local deliveries in the region prior to the study was as follows. In Cardiff, where the company rented space in a warehouse run by a haulage contractor, the local deliveries were made entirely by the haulage contractor's vehicles. At the Birmingham depot, deliveries were made both by company-owned vehicles and by haulage contractors. Because of the large proportion of small orders which could be handled more economically by the haulage contractors (who could fit in these orders with other drops) it was felt that the system employed in Birmingham was likely to continue in the future.

A detailed examination was carried out on a sample of orders to determine an average rate for the local deliveries for both the haulage contractors and for company-owned vehicles. Following this study it was decided to examine two delivery rates of 5p (5 new pence) per ton-mile and 10p per ton-mile, as this would also give some indication of the sensitivity of the model to changes in the local delivery rate.

THE MODEL AND THE COMPUTATION METHOD

The total cost must clearly account for both warehousing and transportation costs. As we saw earlier, the warehousing cost is concave, consisting of continuous and fixed cost elements. The trunking costs on the other hand are composed of discrete trunking rates per ton and vary from district to district, while the local delivery rates are linear with respect to both distance and weight carried. The problem is to determine the number and location of depots to minimize the total distribution-cost function, which may be expressed mathematically as follows:

$$C = \sum_{i=1}^{m} \left(F_i \, \delta_i + \sum_{k=1}^{r} \gamma_k \, W_i \, \delta_{ik} + \sum_{j=1}^{n} \alpha_j \, w_j \, d_{ij} \, \delta_{ij} \right) \qquad (6.4)$$

where

m = number of depots;
r = number of trunking cost districts;
n = number of customers;
F_i = warehousing cost of warehouse i, as expressed in equation (6.3), $i = 1, \ldots, m$;
δ_i = 1 or 0 if warehouse i is open or closed, respectively;
γ_k = trunking rate in district k per ton, $k = 1, \ldots, r$;
W_i = annual throughput of warehouse i;
δ_{ik} = 1 or 0 if warehouse i is in district k or not, respectively;
α_j = cost of local delivery to customer j per ton-mile, $j = 1, \ldots, n$; in the case study the delivery rate is assumed to be uniform for all customers, namely $\alpha_j = \alpha$;
w_j = forecast demand of customer j in tons;
d_{ij} = straight-line distance from i to j;
δ_{ij} = 1 or 0 if customer j is served by warehouse i or not, respectively.

The solution method used was that described in Chapter 4 for solving Model 5 with district-dependent trunking costs. The method is described in detail in that chapter and, briefly, the solution procedure is:

– allocate customers to the cheapest depot, i.e. allocate customer j to

$$\min_i \left[\alpha_j \, d_{ij} + \sum_{k=1}^{r} \gamma_k \, \delta_{ik} + c/(2\sqrt{W_i}) \right] \quad \text{for all } j \qquad (6.5)$$

– find the optimal locations for the current number of depots, given their initial locations;
– apply the drop routine and repeat until no further improvement can be made.

RESULTS[1]

Several computer runs were made using the algorithm described in Chapter 4 with initial depot locations chosen at random, and these runs were repeated for the two local delivery rates $\alpha_j = \alpha = 5p$ and 10p per ton-mile, respectively. The optimal solution in both cases proved to be the same, namely that there should be only one depot located at the co-ordinates (40·5, 28·5), the difference in cost between the two local rates being just over £1000.

The actual solutions were: with $\alpha = 5p$, one depot was required located at (40·5, 28·5) for a cost of £7,280; with $\alpha = 10p$, one depot was required located at (40·6, 28·6) for a cost of £8,330.

The optimal location is on the outskirts of Birmingham, but the final choice of the actual location should be made with reference to other considerations, such as site availability or ease of access to the M5 (the South Wales motorway).

To test the effect of using a model other than Model 5, further runs were carried out using the algorithm for Model 4 (that is, the model without warehousing costs and with a fixed number of depots). Computations were performed for twelve cases, i.e. for 0 to 5 depots and for the two local delivery rates. The results of these runs are summarized in Fig. 6.4, and are listed in Table 6.1 following.

As expected, there is a difference between the results of the two models. For Model 4 with the local rate of 5p per ton-mile, the whole region should be served direct from the factory, the difference in cost being about £200 or 3 per cent above the solution for Model 5. With the local rate at 10p per ton-mile the cheapest solution from Model 4 suggested that the region be served by the factory plus one depot in Birmingham rather than by one depot alone as given by the results for Model 5, the cost for Model 4 being about £500 or $5\frac{1}{2}$ per cent higher than that for Model 5.

One striking point of interest about these results is not only the proximity in the locations of corresponding depots for the two values of the local delivery rate, but the property of "additivity". At any given situation described in Table 6.1, moving from any value of m to $m+1$—namely adding a depot to the system—does not affect the locations of the previously located depots. If this result proves to be generally true, it would be of great practical significance. It implies that in an expanding market where the relative demand of consuming areas remains static, a company can expand its distribution system by

---

[1] The costs associated with this case study have been suitably disguised.

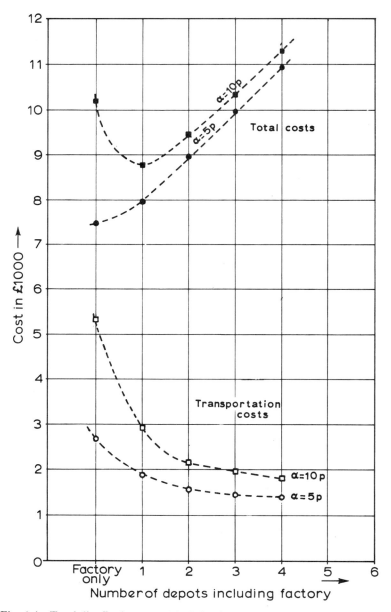

Fig. 6.4 Total distribution costs (shaded points) and transportation costs (clear points) for Model 4. α = local delivery rate

Table 6.1   Results using Model 4

Local rate α (p)	No. of depots m	Cost $C(£)$	Depot locations (x, y)
5	0	7,490	—
5	1	7,940	(40, 29)
5	2	8,960	(40, 29); (31, 19)
5	3	9,970	(40, 29); (31, 19); (44, 29)
5	4	11,030	(40, 29); (31, 19); (46, 31); (41, 28)
5	5	11,950	(40, 29); (31, 19); (46, 31); (41, 28); (32, 36)
10	0	10,170	—
10	1	8.780	(40, 29)
10	2	9,390	(41, 29); (31, 19)
10	3	10,390	(40, 29); (31, 19); (45, 29)
10	4	11,250	(40, 29); (31, 19); (45, 29); (32, 36)
10	5	12,280	(40, 29); (31, 19); (46, 31); (32, 36); (41, 28)

adding depots without having to resite existing depots, since the optimal locations of the latter remain unaffected.

This hypothesis is supported by Sussams [42],[1] in a paper on the distribution of consumer products in Britain, and some of his results for a factory location problem are listed in Table 6.2.

Table 6.2   Results for a factory location problem (*from Sussams* [42])
(Approximate capacity as percentage of total demand)

Site \ Number of factories	1	2	3	4	5	6	7
Birmingham	100					16	16
London		50	50	33	33	33	29
Manchester		50	33	33	33	22	22
Glasgow			17	17	11	11	11
Cardiff or Bristol				17	17	12	11
Newcastle						6	6	6
Southampton							5

---

[1] See references at the end of Chapter 2.

This table shows that, with the exception of the change from 1 to 2 factories, the hypothesis of "additivity" holds for the particular problem that Sussams examined. In view of these two interesting results, it was decided to test the hypothesis further. Solutions for depot locations were derived for several problems:

(1) The problem described in the case study, but only local delivery costs were accounted for.
(2) As (1), but the most important customers 1 and 2 were excluded from the demand matrix.
(3) As (1), but the customers were divided into two groups east and west of the line $x = 40$, the location problem being solved for each group separately.

The results showed that most of the depot locations were remarkably stationary, but that they were often added to the distribution system in a different order. It was concluded that the resultant preference for certain locations was due to the customer demand pattern and not to the effect of the trunking rates or the number of depots in the system.

A further series of tests was carried out to examine the effect of changes in costs, in particular the trunking costs, and changes in customer demands. It was found that the effect of additivity is not necessarily general and that if this effect is found in a particular case it may not be stable with time, unless the trends in demand and/or the changes in transport costs are evenly spread over the whole region.

Sensitivity analyses

Before making any recommendation to the company, it was decided to examine the robustness of the model to changes in the local delivery rate (α), and runs were carried with α ranging from 2·5 to 25p. The results of these tests are listed in Tables 6.3 and 6.4 below and shown graphically in Fig. 6.5.

Fig. 6.5 reveals the value of the local delivery rate at which it is desirable to change the number of depots to maintain minimum total distribution costs. Thus it is cheapest to use the factory only when the local rate varies from 0 to about 4p per ton-mile. With α ranging from 4p to about 17p it is cheapest to use one depot only, but when the local rate exceeds 17p, it is desirable to add another depot. It also appears that for any given value of α, having a distribution system based on the factory plus a depot is not as effective as one of

Table 6.3   Optimal costs (in £) for different values of the local delivery rate α

α (new pence)	Factory only	One depot only	Factory + 1 depot	Two depots only
2·5	6,150	6,760	(7,340)	—
5	7,490	7,280	(7,940)	—
10	10,170	8,330	—	8,930
15	12,850	9,360	(9,810)	9,540
20	15,530	10,400	(10,840)	10,140
25	18,210	11,610	—	10,750

Table 6.4   Optimal depot locations for different values of α

Location of factory (50·5, 20·5)

α (new pence)	Total cost	Depot location	Comments
2·5	6,150	—	Factory only
5	7,280	(40·5, 28·5)	1 depot only
10	8,330	(40·6, 28·6)	1 depot only
15	9,360	(40·7, 28·5)	1 depot only
20	10,140	(40·6, 28·6); (31·0, 19·0)	2 depots only
25	10,750	(40·6, 28·6); (31·0, 19·1)	2 depots only

the other solutions. Fig. 6.5 shows that the costs of serving the region are linearly dependent on α, the slope of the cost line decreasing when a depot is added to the system. The reason for this linear relationship is that the locations of the depots remain virtually unchanged, as shown in Table 6.4. We can see from the cost function in equation (6.4) that only the last term, the local delivery cost, is a linear function of α, whereas the other terms are unaffected by α. Thus, if the allocation of customers to depots does not change, then the whole cost function becomes a linear function of the local delivery rate α.

Let us now turn to the sensitivity of the model to changes in other cost parameters in the distribution system.

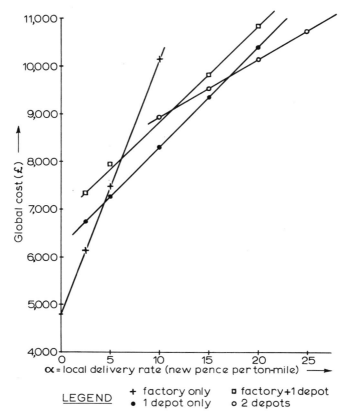

Fig. 6.5   Sensitivity of the optimum solution to changes in local delivery rate
(Model 5)

Warehousing costs

Assuming that the form of the warehousing cost function does
not change, an increase in the warehousing costs results in an overall
increase in costs. This tends to decrease the number of depots in the
optimal solution, so that, as depots become more expensive, one or
more depots may need to be closed down. The effect of changes
in the various constituents of the warehousing cost function can also
be easily examined; for example, it is not difficult to ascertain that an
increase of 10 per cent in the handling cost in equation (6.1) leads to
an increase of about $1\frac{1}{2}$ per cent in the total distribution costs.

Trunking rates

Similarly, the effect of an overall increase in the trunking rates also causes a general increase in costs and, therefore, tends to decrease the number of depots in the final solution. For example, if prior to the increase there is a choice between using either the factory or one depot, it may be more economical after the increase to serve all customers direct from the factory.

An increase in delivery rates to certain districts can affect the system in two ways. First, it can affect the location of the depot directly by making it worthwhile to move a depot from its current optimal location into a new district, for which a cheaper haulage rate prevails. Such a move results in an increase in local delivery costs, but the new location of the depot may be justified if this increase is more than offset by savings in trunking costs. Naturally, if the local delivery rate is sufficiently high, the location of the depot may become independent of trunking rates.

The second way in which the trunking costs can affect the system is indirectly through the allocation of customers to depots. The formula for allocating customers to depots is given in expression (6.5). Here the ratio of αd_{ij} to the appropriate γ_k is important. The greater the latter, the more likely it is that the larger depots are sited in a district with low haulage costs. This also affects the number of local optima that are obtained.

Location and number of customers

In the case study described in this chapter, a possible change in the number of customers is unlikely to lead to serious problems because the customers have been grouped into customer areas. The loss of a whole customer area implies that all the customers in that area are lost, and this is unlikely, but of course not impossible (for example, the introduction of a new competitive product can cause a switch of customer allegiance). A change in the location or in the number of customers may have a direct effect on the location of the depots, and the magnitude of such an effect naturally depends on the size of the change. The loss (or gain) of a small customer can have very little effect on the system, whereas the loss (or gain) of a large customer may be quite significant.

Customer demand

The effect of a change in individual customer demand is

essentially the same as that of a change in the number and location of customers. However, an overall moderate increase or decrease across the board in customer demand generally has no effect on the optimal solution, primarily because the solution is largely determined by the relative values of w_j in equation (6.4). As demand continues to increase, a point is eventually reached where an increase in the number of required depots is indicated.

CONCLUSION

The results of the analysis for this case study suggested that management had a choice between two solutions: the first was to deliver to all customers direct from the factory, the second to have a distribution system with a single depot from which all small orders would be supplied.

Owing to insufficient data it was felt that in the analysis of the model the possible economies of scale expected from concentrating all supplies from the factory were not adequately accounted for. At the same time fresh negotiations with the haulier were embarked upon, resulting in somewhat more favourable rates to the company, so that a decision was made to adopt the first solution, namely the supplying of all customers in the region by the haulier direct from the factory.

PART 2

Chapter 7

The travelling salesman problem

INTRODUCTION

Imagine a travelling salesman having to visit n customers or cities. He starts from city 1 and needs to visit each of the other $n-1$ cities only once and then return to city 1. The cost of travelling between any pair of cities (expressed in terms of distance, time or monetary expenditure), say from city i to city j, is given as c_{ij} in a cost matrix C. The problem is to design such a route through the n cities that would minimize the total cost of the tour. This is known as *the travelling salesman problem*.

We distinguish between two types of travelling salesman problems. The first has a symmetrical cost matrix, namely the cost of travelling from i to j is the same as travelling from j to i ($c_{ij} = c_{ji}$); the second has an asymmetrical cost matrix ($c_{ij} \neq c_{ji}$).

The travelling salesman problem is not confined to situations which involve physical travelling, but has an application in the wider context of sequencing problems. Take, for example, the cost of loading n jobs on a machine, where a changeover cost (in terms of set-up time or in monetary units) is involved whenever a new job is loaded, so that c_{ij} is the cost of changing from job i to job j. If the changeover cost is dependent not only on which job is loaded on the machine but also on which job is taken off, then the cost matrix $[c_{ij}]$ is asymmetrical. The problem of determining the sequence in which the jobs should be loaded in order to minimize the overall cost of changeovers is equivalent to finding the lowest cost tour in a travelling salesman problem with a cost matrix $[c_{ij}]$.

THEORETICAL ASPECTS

The travelling salesman problem has become famous because of its ease of statement and great difficulty of solution. With n cities and an asymmetrical cost matrix, there are $(n-1)!$ possible tours that the salesman can traverse, and therefore the optimal solution to the problem can always be found (at least in principle) by enumerating all the possible tours and calculating their values, thus determining which tour is the optimal. However, even for a comparatively small number of cities, the complete enumeration of all tours becomes a computationally impossible task (note, for example, that 10! is about $3 \cdot 5 \times 10^6$, whereas 15! jumps to approximately $1 \cdot 3 \times 10^{12}$); therefore, by a "solution" to the travelling salesman problem is meant a "reasonably efficient" algorithm for determining the optimal tour.

The present theory for the travelling salesman problem is not at all adequate in the sense that a solution to the problem cannot, in general, be found as efficiently as it can be derived for, say, an assignment problem. Nevertheless, there exist certain theorems for the travelling salesman problem that make it possible to construct some algorithms which are vastly superior to complete enumeration, even though they may not be "efficient" in the above-mentioned sense.

It may be useful to introduce here the following definitions. Given n points and m lines joining them,

a link is a line joining two points;

a chain is a sequence of links such that the end-point of the first link is the beginning of the second link, etc., except for the first and the last links; every point and every link in a chain appears only once;

a hamiltonian chain is a chain that passes through all the n points;

a hamiltonian circuit is a chain which passes through all the n points and in which the first and the last points coincide;

a tour is a hamiltonian circuit (the term "tour" is more commonly used in distribution problems);

a subtour is a hamiltonian circuit through a subset of the n points;

the travelling salesman tour is the shortest hamiltonian circuit;

a spanning tree is a collection of $n-1$ links joining the n points, so that any point can be reached from any other point;

the shortest spanning tree (denoted by SST) is the shortest of all spanning trees.

These definitions are not necessarily confined to the assumption that the n points are distributed in a Euclidean space.

Some theorems

We start by listing the main theorems, most of which are rather obvious, but which reveal exploitable properties of the problem structure.

Let a tour be denoted by $t = (i_1, i_2, \ldots, i_n, i_1)$ and the cost of this tour be

$$z(t) = \sum_{j=1}^{n-1} c_{i_j\, i_{j+1}} + c_{i_n\, i_1}.$$

Here $(i_1, i_2, \ldots, i_n)$ is a permutation of the integers from 1 to n, giving the order in which the cities are visited.

Theorem 7.1 If the cost matrix C represents Euclidean distances, then the optimal tour does not intersect itself [7].[1] This theorem is obvious from geometrical considerations, since any two intersecting links can be replaced by two non-intersecting links of a shorter total distance.

Theorem 7.2 If H is the convex hull of the points representing the travelling salesman problem in a two-dimensional Euclidean space, then the order in which the cities which form the vertices of H appear in the optimal tour is the same as the order in which these cities appear on H [9]. This theorem is a direct consequence of Theorem 7.1.

If m cities out of the total number n lie on a convex hull, then Theorem 7.2 reduces the total number of tours that need be investigated from $\frac{1}{2}(n-1)!$ to $(n-1)!/(m-1)!$ (for the symmetrical problem). Thus, Theorems 7.1 and 7.2 together can serve to exclude from consideration those tours (which constitute the vast majority of all possible tours) that do not satisfy the above conditions. Almost all algorithms can be improved by taking advantage of the properties of the optimal tour which are implied in these theorems, and some approximate algorithms, such as the one due to Croes [4], are in fact based entirely on Theorem 7.1.

Theorem 7.3 If a constant e_i is subtracted from all entries in row i of the cost matrix C and a constant f_j subtracted from all entries in column j of the resulting matrix, then the optimal tour under the final matrix

$$C' = [c_{ij} - e_i - f_j]$$

is the same as the optimal tour under the original matrix. Also, if

---

[1] See list of references at end of this chapter.

$z(t)$ is the cost of any tour t under the original matrix and $z'(t)$ the cost of the same tour under the final matrix, then

$$z'(t) = z(t) - \Sigma\, e_i - \Sigma f_j$$

Again this theorem becomes obvious when one remembers that exactly one link must "go-to" and "come-from" every city in the tour. The theorem allows one to work with "reduced" matrices with many zero elements, which is very convenient [14]. The numbers e_i and f_j are called the "reducing constants".

Theorem 7.4   If a certain tour t does not contain the link (a, b), then

$$z(t) \geqslant \min_{j \neq b} c_{aj} + \min_{i \neq a} c_{ib} \equiv p_{ab} \quad \text{(say)}. \qquad (7.1)$$

This theorem is a direct consequence of the fact that if the tour is not allowed to contain the link (a, b) then it must contain links (a, x) and (y, b), where $x \neq b$ and $y \neq a$. The smallest possible values for these two links are

$$\min_{j \neq b} c_{aj} \quad \text{and} \quad \min_{i \neq a} c_{ib} \quad \text{respectively,}$$

hence the theorem. The quantity p_{ab} defined by equation (7.1) is called the "penalty" for not including the link (a, b).

In their branch-and-bound algorithm (described later), Little *et al.* [14] use Theorem 7.3 to produce lower bounds and Theorem 7.4 to choose the next branching in the tree search.

METHODS OF SOLUTION

There are many ways of obtaining "solutions" to the travelling salesman problem, and these can be divided into four fundamentally different groups. Some of these methods are "exact" (in the sense that they guarantee the optimal solution when the algorithm is pursued to the end) whilst others are "approximate", giving only a near-optimal solution at the termination of the computation. The four different ways of generating solutions are discussed below.

(A)   Sequential tour-building

With this method one starts from any one city (say city i_1) and builds up the sequence $(i_1, i_2, \ldots, i_n, i_1)$, bringing in sequentially one city at a time, until a tour is obtained. This way of generating solutions includes both exact and approximate methods. The simplest approximate method gives rise to the crudest of all possible algorithms in which the nearest unvisited neighbour city is the next city to be included in the sequence. When the last city has been visited, one returns to city i_1. Exact algorithms belonging to this category of sequential tour-building are the algorithms of Held and Karp [10] (using dynamic programming) and Little, Murty, Sweeney and Karel [14] (the branch-and-bound method).

(B) Tour-to-tour improvements

With this method one starts with an initial tour (say, an arbitrary or a random one), which one subsequently attempts to improve' upon by following some specific rule. For example, one might try to interchange the position of two cities in the original sequence, or to replace two links by another couple of links. A termination rule would then be applied when no further improvement can be made under the original set of "improvement rules". The final tour that is obtained in this way represents an approximate solution, and this is the case for all the procedures of tour-to-tour improvement that have been suggested to date.

Having obtained a "final" tour in this way, one may then repeat the process several times (each time starting from a different initial tour) and eventually select the best of the various "final" tours. Iterative schemes within this category have proved very effective, giving excellent quality solutions. Particularly noteworthy are the algorithms of Croes [4], Lin [13] and Reiter and Sherman [15].

(C)   Enumerative method

As mentioned earlier, a complete enumeration of all the possible tours is not feasible on computational grounds. However, partial enumeration is possible, and one could then choose the best tour from the subset of tours that have been enumerated. Since the total number of tours in a reasonable size problem is enormous, and since the large majority of these consist of very "bad" (i.e. high cost) tours, it is not surprising that this method does not generally produce very good results. However, if some simple tests are included in the computation procedure in order to exclude from enumeration obviously bad tours, then the performance of this simple method is greatly improved.

The algorithm of Roberts and Flores [16] essentially falls into this category. However, instead of partially enumerating the tours for the complete problem, Roberts and Flores reduce the size of the problem by excluding links that they consider very unlikely to be in the final solution. They then completely enumerate all the hamiltonian circuits (i.e. tours) in the reduced network and finally select the best of these as the solution to the problem.

(D) Subtour contraction

This method starts with an optimal solution to the assignment problem for the cost matrix C with all diagonal elements set to infinity. The cost c_{ij} is interpreted as the cost of assigning city i to city j, namely linking i to j in the tour; and once i is assigned to j it cannot be assigned to any other city. The solution to the assignment problem reveals the best linkages that can be designed, and the purpose of putting $c_{ii} = \infty$ is to prevent single link loops.

If the solution to the assignment problem is a tour (namely, all the linkages combine into a route that passes through all the cities) then this is the optimal travelling salesman tour. If the solution to the assignment problem is not a tour, then it must consist of several subtours, in which case special methods are used to eliminate the subtours by joining them to form one tour that passes through all the n points.

Exact algorithms using this method are the branch-and-bound algorithms of Eastman [6] and Shapiro [17], the linear integer programming approach of Dantzig, Fulkerson and Johnson [5], and the Gilmore–Gomory method for travelling salesman problems which have a cost matrix of a special structure [8].

DESCRIPTION OF SOME ALGORITHMS

This section describes some algorithms that have been successful in handling the travelling salesman problem. At least one algorithm from each of the four classes of solution methods is included here. The list is by no means exhaustive and many interesting algorithms are not mentioned. A short description of most of the available algorithms and a comparison of results obtained by using some of them can be found in reference [2], which also includes an extensive bibliography for the travelling salesman problem.

(A) Dynamic programming

Dynamic programming models of the travelling salesman problem have been developed by Held and Karp [10], Bellman [1] and Gonzales [9]. The various approaches are essentially the same and are as follows:

Let S be a subset of m elements which belong to the set of integers $S_0 = \{2, 3, \ldots, n\}$ and let x be an element of S. Let us consider the chain that connects all the cities in set S.

Let the shortest (or lowest-cost) distance travelled, starting from an arbitrary city (city 1), then visiting all the cities in the set S and ending with city x, be denoted by $C(S, x)$. Thus,

$$\text{for} \quad m = 1, \quad C(\{x\}, x) = c_{1x} \quad \text{for all } x \tag{7.2}$$

$$\text{for} \quad m > 1, \quad C(S, x) = \min_{y \in S - \{x\}} \left[C(S - \{x\}, y) + c_{yx} \right] \tag{7.3}$$

The cost of a chain drawn through the cities in set S can therefore be described as the sum of two cost terms: the first is the cost of a chain connecting all the cities in the set $S - \{x\}$ (i.e. the set S from which the city x is removed) and ending in city y, and the second is the cost of the link between x and y.

The $C(S, x)$ can now be computed for all subsets S of S_0, and for all cities x, by starting from equation (7.2) and using equation (7.3) recursively. Finally, the minimum cost of a complete tour (including the return to city 1) is derived as

$$C_* = \min_{x \in S_0} \left[C(S_0, x) + c_{x1} \right] \tag{7.4}$$

The optimal tour itself can also be obtained from the principle of optimality. Thus, for any integer value of p $(2 \leqslant p \leqslant n-1)$ we have:

$$C\left(\{i_2, i_3, \ldots, i_{p+1}\}, i_{p+1} \right) = C\left(\{i_2, i_3, \ldots, i_p\}, i_p \right) + c_{i_p i_{p+1}} \tag{7.5}$$

if the tour $(i_2, i_3, \ldots, i_n)$ is to be the optimal tour.

The last city i_n in the optimal permutation is that value of x in equation (7.4) which gives the minimum cost. Knowing this value of i_n, equation (7.5) can then be used recursively to obtain $(i_{n-1}, i_{n-2}, \ldots, i_2)$ which is the optimal tour.

This formulation of the travelling salesman problem by dynamic programming can be simplified for the case of symmetrical cost matrices as follows [13]:

If the total number of cities n is odd, then it can be expressed as $2u+1$; if it is even then it can be expressed as $2u$.

Suppose n is odd. We can compute $C(S, x)$ for all subsets S of S_0 from $m = 1$ to $m = u+1$ from equations (7.2) and (7.3). When $m = u+1$ we can denote a set S' which includes all the cities in $S_0 - S$ and a city $x \in S$ (see Fig. 7.1). At this stage the $C(S', x)$ would have already been computed.

Thus the cost of the optimal tour can be found from

$$C_* = \min_{S} \left[\min_{x \in S} [C(S, x) + C(S', x)] \right] \qquad (7.6)$$

where S ranges over all subsets of S_0 containing $u + 1$ cities. Fig. 7.1 shows diagrammatically the principle of the simplification that is possible with symmetrical cost matrices. If n is even, the procedure remains exactly the same, except that $C(S, x)$ need be computed only up to $m = u$.

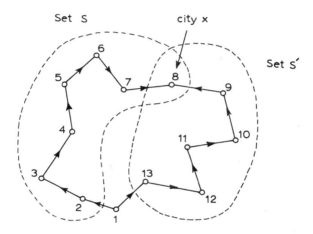

Fig. 7.1   Dynamic programming formulation for symmetrical matrices
$$C(S, x) = \text{cost of chain } 1, 2, \ldots, 8)$$
$$C(S', x) = \text{cost of chain } 1, 13, \ldots, 8)$$

Once the cost of the optimal tour is known, the sequence of cities that form this tour can be found from the principle of optimality as follows:

The "middle" city x and the sets S_* and S_*' which give the optimal value C_* are known from equation (7.6). We first find a city $x_1 \in S_* - \{x\}$ such that

$$C(S_* - \{x\}, x_1) + c_{x_1 x} = C(S_*, x)$$

then a city $x_2 \in S_* - \{x, x_1\}$ such that

$$C(S_* - \{x, x_1\}, x_2) + c_{x_2 x_1} = C(S_* - \{x\}, x_1),$$

and so on until the set S_* is exhausted.

Similarly, for the set S'_* we find the sequence $x'_1, x'_2, \ldots,$ etc., until S'_* is exhausted. The final optimal tour is then

$$1, \ldots\ldots, x_2, x_1, x, x'_1, x'_2, \ldots\ldots\ldots, 1 \, .$$

The dynamic programming approach is illustrated by the following example.

Example 7.1 Consider the 5-city travelling salesman problem, the cost matrix of which is:

$$[c_{ij}] =$$

	1	2	3	4	5
1	—	6	11	3	4
2	7	—	14	8	10
3	12	5	—	10	2
4	6	15	7	—	5
5	4	9	8	13	—

From equation (7.2) we can write immediately (for $m = 1$):

$$C(\{2\}, 2) = 6 \, ; \quad C(\{3\}, 3) = 11 \, ; \quad C(\{4\}, 4) = 3 \, ; \quad C(\{5\}, 5) = 4 \, .$$

Now applying equation (7.3) recursively for $m = 2$, we can write

$$C(\{2, 3\}, 2) = \min_{y \in \{3\}} \left[C(\{3\}, y) + c_{y2} \right] \, ,$$

and using the values of $C(S, x)$ for $m = 1$ found earlier, we get:

$$C(\{2, 3\}, 2) = \min \left[11 + 5 \right] = 16 \, .$$

Similarly,

$$C(\{2, 3\}, 3) = 20$$
$$C(\{2, 4\}, 2) = 18$$
$$C(\{2, 4\}, 4) = 14$$
$$C(\{2, 5\}, 2) = 13$$
$$C(\{2, 5\}, 5) = 16$$
$$C(\{3, 4\}, 3) = 10$$
$$C(\{3, 4\}, 4) = 21$$

$$C(\{3, 5\}, 3) = 12$$
$$C(\{3, 5\}, 5) = 13$$
$$C(\{4, 5\}, 4) = 17$$
$$C(\{4, 5\}, 5) = 8$$

Applying equation (7.3) recursively for $m = 3$, we get

$$C(\{2, 3, 4\}, 2) = \min_{y \in \{3, 4\}} \left[C(\{3, 4\}, y) + c_{y2} \right]$$

Using the values of $C(S, x)$ for $m = 2$ which were calculated earlier, we obtain

$$C(\{2, 3, 4\}, 2) = \min \left[\underbrace{10+5}_{y=3}, \underbrace{21+15}_{y=4} \right] = 15 .$$

Similarly,

$$C(\{2, 3, 4\}, 3) = 21$$
$$C(\{2, 3, 4\}, 4) = 24$$
$$C(\{2, 3, 5\}, 2) = 17$$
$$C(\{2, 3, 5\}, 3) = 24$$
$$C(\{2, 3, 5\}, 5) = 22$$
$$C(\{2, 4, 5\}, 2) = 17$$
$$C(\{2, 4, 5\}, 4) = 21$$
$$C(\{2, 4, 5\}, 5) = 19$$
$$C(\{3, 4, 5\}, 3) = 16$$
$$C(\{3, 4, 5\}, 4) = 22$$
$$C(\{3, 4, 5\}, 5) = 12$$

Applying equation (7.3) recursively for $m = 4$, we get

$$C(\{2, 3, 4, 5\}, 2) = \min_{y \in \{3, 4, 5\}} \left[C(\{3, 4, 5\}, y) + c_{y2} \right]$$

Again using the values of $C(S, x)$ for $m = 3$ found earlier, we have

$$C(\{2, 3, 4, 5\}, 2) = \min \left[\underbrace{16+5}_{y=3}, \underbrace{22+15}_{y=4}, \underbrace{12+9}_{y=5} \right] = 21$$

Similarly,

$$C\left(\{2, 3, 4, 5\}, 3\right) = 27$$
$$C\left(\{2, 3, 4, 5\}, 4\right) = 25$$
$$C\left(\{2, 3, 4, 5\}, 5\right) = 23$$

The cost of the optimal tour can now be found using equation (7.4) as

$$C_* = \min_{y \in \{2, 3, 4, 5\}} \left[C\left(\{2, 3, 4, 5\}, y\right) + c_{y1} \right]$$

which after substitution of the costs found earlier becomes

$$C_* = \min \left[\underbrace{21 + 7}_{y=2}, \underbrace{27 + 12}_{y=3}, \underbrace{25 + 6}_{y=4}, \underbrace{23 + 4}_{y=5} \right] = 27 .$$

The value of $C_* = 27$ is the cost of the optimal tour.

In order to identify this tour we proceed as follows:

The cost $C_* = 27$ is obtained using the value $y = 5$; hence 5 is the last city (city i_5) to be visited in the optimal tour. Applying now equation (7.5), we find the cities in reverse order to that in which they appear in the optimal sequence. Thus,

$$23 = C\left(\{2, 3, 4\}, i_4\right) + c_{i_4 5}$$

The value of $i_4 \in \{2, 3, 4\}$ which satisfies this equation is $i_4 = 3$; hence city 3 is the one immediately preceding city 5. Similarly we find $i_3 = 4$, and $i_2 = 2$. The optimal tour is therefore given by

$$1 - 2 - 4 - 3 - 5 - 1 .$$

(B) Branch and bound

Branch and bound, or tree-search techniques, have been used to solve the travelling salesman problem, and tree-search algorithms have been written based on both the sequential tour-building method (Little *et al.* [14] and the subtour contraction method (Eastman [6] and Shapiro [17]). Although Shapiro's algorithm is slightly more efficient that Little's, we describe Little's method here because of its other advantages. This method can be extended to include constraints not present in the pure form of the travelling salesman problem, but which appear in real distribution problems. Also, an important property of Little's method not present in Shapiro's algorithm is that if, for any reason, the tree search is stopped before the end, a good (and quite often the unproven optimal) solution has been obtained.

The basis of Little's algorithm is to divide the set of all the possible tours into smaller and smaller subsets and to calculate for each subset a lower bound on the cost of the best tour therein. The object of calculating bounds is twofold:

(i) they may be used as guidance for the partitioning of the subsets, and

(ii) they limit the search and also identify the optimal tour. (The optimal tour is a tour whose cost is less than or equal to the lower bounds on all the unsearched subsets.)

The algorithm is explained below. It is convenient to represent the partitioning as branchings of a tree, where the nodes represent the subsets of tours.

We start with the original cost matrix C (in which all diagonal elements are set to infinity) and apply Theorem 7.3. First, we subtract from every entry of each row the smallest element (e_i) of that row and repeat this process for all the rows. We then subtract from every entry of each column of the resulting matrix the smallest element (f_j) of that column and repeat the operation for all the columns. The resulting matrix C' is then said to be "reduced" (contains at least one zero in every row and column), and the sum of the reducing constants is

$$h_0 = \sum_i e_i + \sum_j f_j$$

From Theorem 7.3 we then have $z'(t) = z(t) - h_0$, where $z'(t)$ refers to the tour cost for the reduced matrix C' and $z(t)$ to the tour cost for the original matrix. Since all the elements in the reduced matrix are non-negative, therefore $z'(t) \geqslant 0$, and hence $z(t) \geqslant h_0$, i.e. h_0 is a lower bound on the cost of any tour for the original matrix.

We can now start to form a tour by selecting (as a first link to be committed) one of the links (in the reduced matrix) which has a zero cost. Instead of selecting any one of these links at random, a criterion may be formulated which would make some of them preferable to others. Little suggests calculating, for each zero element ($c'_{x_1 x_2}$) of the reduced matrix, a minimum penalty that would have to be incurred if link ($x_1 \ x_2$) is not selected. This penalty ($p_{x_1 x_2}$ say) could be calculated according to Theorem 7.4. We would then select that link whose cost under the reduced matrix is zero and whose penalty is the largest.

Suppose link ($x_1 \ x_2$) is chosen in this way. The total number of tours is now divided into two subsets, those that include link ($x_1 \ x_2$) and those that do not. This division is shown diagrammatically as nodes $(x_1 x_2)$ and $(\overline{x_1 x_2})$ in Fig. 7.2. The bound for all tours contained in a node is shown marked at the node. Thus, since $p_{x_1 x_2}$ is the minimum penalty that has to be paid for not including link $(x_1 x_2)$, the bound on node $(\overline{x_1 x_2})$ is $h_0 + p_{x_1 x_2}$.

Now, if link $(x_1 x_2)$ is included, no other link can emanate from city x_1 or finish at city x_2. Thus row x_1 and column x_2 of the matrix can now be crossed out as they will no longer be needed. Also, link $(x_2 x_1)$ is no longer possible as it would create a small subtour, and hence the cost element in cell $(x_2 x_1)$ is set to infinity, thereby preventing it from being subsequently selected.

The crossing out of row x_1 and column x_2 produces an $(n-1)$ by $(n-1)$ matrix, which it may be possible or impossible to "reduce". If it can be reduced in the same way as the original matrix, the sum

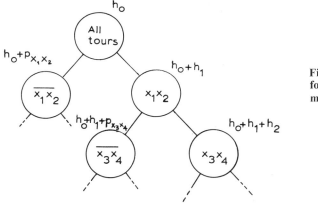

Fig. 7.2 **Decision tree for branch-and-bound method**

of the reducing constants is denoted as h_1. If the matrix cannot be reduced then $h_1 = 0$. Theorem 7.3 would then give the lower bound of all tours containing link $(x_1 x_2)$ as $h_0 + h_1$.

We are now ready for a new branching. Again, the new penalties of all the zero elements of the new matrix are calculated and a link, say $(x_3 x_4)$, is selected to branch to. The lower bound for node $(\overline{x_3 x_4})$ is then $h_0 + h_1 + p_{x_3 x_4}$ and that for node $(x_3 x_4)$ is $h_0 + h_1 + h_2$, where h_2 is the sum of the reducing constants of the $(n-2)$ by $(n-2)$ matrix formed by crossing out row x_3 and column x_4 (in addition to row x_1 and column x_2 which have already been crossed out).

Infinities are again inserted in the appropriate places in the matrix to prevent subloops from ever being formed. Thus, for example, if link $(x_3 x_4)$ does not join with link $(x_1 x_2)$, element $(x_4 x_3)$ is set to infinity. On the other hand if $x_3 = x_2$ (i.e. the two links together form a chain $x_1 x_2 x_4$), then element $(x_4 x_1)$ is set to infinity.

The branching can be continued until the selected links $(x_1 x_2)$, $(x_3 x_4), \dots$, etc. form a tour of cost, say, z_0. If the lower bounds on all the nodes from where branching is possible (i.e. the "free" nodes that have not been branched from) are greater than or equal to z_0, then this is the optimal tour. If not, then any one of the nodes with a bound less than z_0 can be chosen for further branching. If, for example, the bound on node $(\overline{x_3 x_4})$ is less than z_0, then branching can be continued from there. Before this is possible, however, the cost matrix must be reset to correspond to node $(\overline{x_3 x_4})$. Thus, starting from the top of the tree with the original reduced matrix, link $(x_1 x_2)$ must be included (row x_1 and column x_2 are crossed out) and link $(x_3 x_4)$ must be excluded (the element in cell $(x_3 x_4)$ is set to infinity). Further infinities to prevent subloops are also inserted in the appropriate cells in the matrix.

While resetting the matrix to correspond to the node from which the branching is to continue, a new bound B for this node is also calculated as the sum of the lengths of the links included in the tour so far, plus the sum of the reducing constants. It should be noted that, in general, B is not the same as the lower bound previously assigned to the node. The value of B is no longer just a lower bound but represents the real length of the tour constructed so far.

The branching proceeds with the value z_0 being continuously updated, until the lower bounds on all the "free" nodes become greater than z_0. When that happens, the tour whose cost is z_0 is the optimum tour and the search is terminated. Fig. 7.3 shows a flow diagram of the method, using branching-strategy (i) (see later).

The functions of the various boxes in this figure are explained further below.

(1)   Read in the cost matrix C, set z_0 (the cost of the best tour so far) to infinity, and number the node X from which branching will continue.

(2)   Reduce C, set $h_0 = $ sum of reducing constants. Set $w(X)$ (the lower bound on node X) $= h_0$.

(3)   Choose node (k, l)—called node Y—to branch to, so that p_{kl} is the largest of all the penalties.

(4)   Branch to the negative node $\bar{Y}$ and set its bound $w(\bar{Y}) = w(X) + p_{kl}$.

(5)   Branch to Y. Cross out row k and column l. Insert infinities in C to prevent subloops from possibly being formed. Reduce C

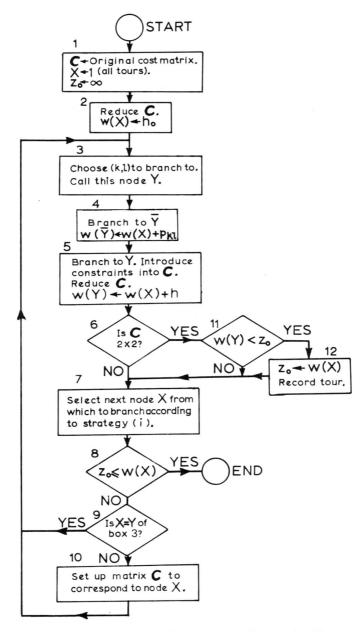

Fig. 7.3 Flow diagram of the branch-and-bound algorithm

and find h (the sum of the reducing constants). Set bound on node Y as $w(Y) = w(X)+h$.

(6), (11) and (12)   If C is now a 2×2 matrix, a tour has been obtained, and if the cost of this tour $w(Y)$ is less than z_0 record it, update z_0 and continue; otherwise just continue.

(7)   Select the next node X to branch from, as that node with the lowest bound $w(X)$.

(8)   If all the bounds are greater than z_0 the branching is finished, the tour in the store is optimal, and its cost is z_0; otherwise continue.

(9)   If the branching is to continue from node Y which we have just branched to (i.e. if $X = Y$ as determined at step 3), go to step 3 without updating C; otherwise continue.

(10)   The matrix C must be updated and set up to correspond to node X as follows. Read the original cost matrix into C. Find $G = \Sigma c_{ij}$ for all the elements c_{ij} which have been committed in the chain, going from the top of the tree to node X. For each such c_{ij} delete row i and column j of C, and set infinities into the appropriate cells in C to prevent subloops. For each negative node in the chain from the top of the tree to node X set the corresponding element in C to infinity. Reduce C and set a new bound on X as $w(X) = G + $ the sum of the reducing constants. Go to step 3.

The choice of which node to branch from was assumed so far to be made at random, provided the bound of that node is less than z_0. In fact, this choice affects both computing time and computer storage requirements to a very great extent. Two alternative strategies for choosing the node can be used:

(i) Branch from the "free" node which has the least bound.
(ii) Branch from the "free" node nearest to the present node, proceeding upwards in the tree and throwing away branches that have been searched.

Strategy (i) solves the problem in less time, but it is not useful for large problems because information for all the nodes has to be stored, thereby quickly exhausting computer storage space. Strategy (ii) takes slightly longer to compute than strategy (i), but it can solve much larger problems since the same part of the computer store can be used several times, namely it can be reassigned to store information about new parts of the tree as branches are thrown away.

The branch-and-bound method is illustrated by the following example.

Example 7.2 Consider the 5-city travelling salesman problem of Example 7.1, where the cost matrix is given on page 121.

We start by reducing the cost matrix which produces the following relative cost matrix:

	1	2	3	4	5	Reducing constants for rows e_i ↓
1	—	0	6	0	1	3
2	0	—	5	1	3	7
3	10	0	—	8	0	2
4	1	7	0	—	0	5
5	0	2	2	9	—	4
Reducing → constants for columns f_j	0	3	2	0	0	26 ← Sum of reducing constants $= h_0$

The penalties of the elements whose values in the above matrix are zero are calculated as:

$$p_{1,2} = 0; \quad p_{1,4} = 1; \quad p_{2,1} = 1; \quad p_{3,2} = 0;$$
$$p_{3,5} = 0; \quad p_{4,3} = 2; \quad p_{4,5} = 0; \quad p_{5,1} = 2.$$

The largest of these penalties is $p_{4,3}$ or $p_{5,1}$, both having value 2. Let us choose any one of these arbitrarily, say $p_{4,3}$, and branch to node (4, 3) of the tree, as shown in Fig. 7.4.

The bound on node $\overline{(4,3)}$ is then $h_0 + p_{4,3} = 26 + 2 = 28$. We now cross out row 4 and column 3, place an infinity in position (3, 4) in the relative cost matrix, and again reduce this matrix (in this case the matrix is already reduced and $h_1 = 0$). The matrix then becomes:

	1	2	4	5	e_i ↓
1	—	0	0	1	0
2	0	—	1	3	0
3	0	0	∞	0	0
5	0	2	9	—	0
f_j →	0	0	0	0	0 ← h_1

The penalties of the elements whose values in this matrix are zero are:

$$p_{1,\,2} = 0\,; \quad p_{1,\,4} = 1\,; \quad p_{2,\,1} = 1\,; \quad p_{3,\,1} = 0\,;$$
$$p_{3,\,2} = 0\,; \quad p_{3,\,5} = 1\,; \quad p_{5,\,1} = 2\,.$$

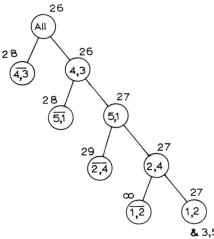

Fig. 7.4   Tree-search for Example 2

The largest of these penalties is $p_{5,1}$, as shown in Fig. 7.4. The bound on node $(\overline{5,1})$ is then $26 + p_{5,1} = 28$.

We now cross out row 5 and column 1, place an infinity in position $(1, 5)$ and reduce the matrix, which then becomes:

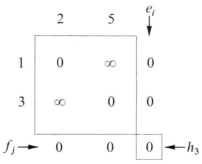

The sum of the reducing constants is $h_2 = 1$, and hence the bound on node $(5, 1)$ becomes $26 + 1 = 27$. The penalties of the zero elements in this matrix are:

$$p_{1,2} = 0 \, ; \quad p_{1,4} = 0 \, ; \quad p_{2,4} = 2 \, ; \quad p_{3,2} = 0 \, ; \quad p_{3,5} = 2 \, .$$

The largest penalty is $p_{2,4}$ or $p_{3,5}$. Let us choose to branch to node $(2, 4)$. The bound on node $(\overline{2,4})$ becomes $27 + p_{2,4} = 29$.

We now cross out row 2 and column 4 and place an infinity in position $(3, 2)$ of the matrix to prevent subloop $(2, 4, 3, 2)$ from being formed. The matrix is now 2×2; it is already reduced and is shown below:

The bound on node $(2, 4)$ is $27 + h_3 = 27$. With this 2×2 matrix the only non-infinite links are (1, 2) and (3, 5). These links complete the tour, as shown in Fig. 7.4.

Having obtained a tour with cost 27 we now check the bounds on the "free" nodes. We see that the lowest of these is 28 and therefore no more branching is necessary. The tour obtained, which is made up of links (4, 3), (5, 1), (2, 4), (1, 2) and (3, 5) (i.e. tour 1–2–4–3–5–1), is therefore the optimal tour, and is the same as that obtained from the dynamic program.

(C) Local optimization algorithms (tour-to-tour improvement)

The last two methods for solving the travelling salesman problem are exact since they guarantee an optimal answer, if carried to their final conclusion. The technique described here is an approximate method, but it has significant advantages over other methods, some of which are discussed in the next section.

The method suggested by Theorem 7.1 was first exploited by Croes [4]. His method, which starts from some arbitrary tour, produces an intersectionless tour by an iterative application of a simple transformation which he calls inversion. Inversion is simply a replacement of two links in a tour by two other links to form a new tour. Reiter and Sherman [15] carry the idea of local optimization further and produce an algorithm which they call ALGO IV (r).

ALGO IV (1) starts with a random tour, say $t = (i_1, i_2, \ldots, i_n, i_1)$, and tries to find the best way of inserting every city in the sequence remaining after that city is removed from the tour—for example the best way of inserting i_1 in the sequence $(i_2, i_3, \ldots, i_n)$—and likewise for all the other cities, until no improvement in the tour is possible. ALGO IV (2) then tries to find the best way of inserting a link of two cities in the remaining sequence, for example the chain (i_1, i_2), (or its reverse (i_2, i_1)), in the sequence $(i_3, i_4, \ldots, i_n)$, and so on for all other chains of two cities until no further improvement is possible. When neither ALGO IV (1) nor ALGO IV (2) can give any improvement, one then proceeds to ALGO IV (3) which is similar to the previous algorithms, except that it checks chains of three cities.

Fig. 7.5 shows diagrammatically the local optimization procedure of Reiter and Sherman's algorithms.

At about the same time, Lin [13] published a method which is very similar to Reiter and Sherman's. Lin defines a tour to be r-optimal if no improvement can be obtained by replacing any r of its links by any other set of r links.

In this context the intersectionless tours produced by the method of Croes would be called 2-optimal, since a tour is always inter-sectionless if no improvement can be obtained by interchanging any two links by another set of two links. Also, Reiter and Sherman's algorithms would classify as an attempt to find 3-optimal tours, as Fig. 7.5 illustrates. Thus in Fig. 7.5(b), for example, the three links (i_9, i_2), (i_2, i_3) and (i_6, i_7) are replaced by the three links (i_9, i_3), (i_6, i_2) and (i_1, i_7). Further work on the 3-optimal tour has been done by Christofides and Eilon [3].

Fig. 7.6(a) and 7.6(b) illustrate the search for a 2-optimal and a 3-optimal tour, respectively. For 2-optimality only two alternative tours (for every choice of a set of two links) need be tested, as shown in (a), whereas for 3-optimality, eight alternative tours (for every choice of a set of three links) should be examined, as shown in (b).

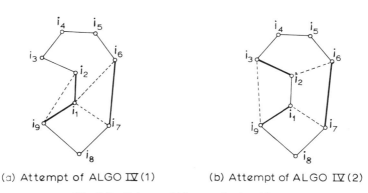

(a) Attempt of ALGO IV (1)   (b) Attempt of ALGO IV (2)

Fig. 7.5   Reiter and Sherman's algorithms

——— old links
– – – new links

From what has been said above, it is obvious that for a tour of an n city travelling-salesman problem to be optimal, a necessary and sufficient condition is that it should be an n-optimal tour.

Consider any arbitrary tour. The number of ways in which r links can be chosen from this tour is $\binom{n}{r}$. The removal of r links from the tour will result in r disconnected chains of cities, some of which may consist of single cities. Of the $\binom{n}{r}$ ways of choosing r links a pro-portion p_0 will lead to no single cities, a proportion p_1 to one single city, etc., and a proportion p_r to r single cities. The number of ways that r chains of cities, of which x, say, are single cities, can be joined together to form tours is

$$2^{r-x-1}(r-1)!$$

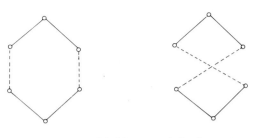

(a) Two ways of linking two chains into a tour

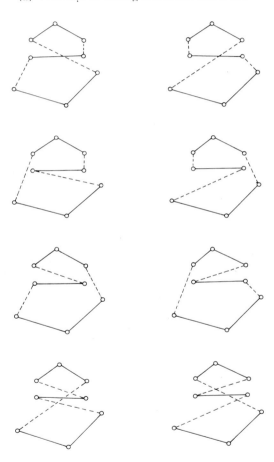

(b) Eight ways of linking three chains into a tour

Fig. 7.6

Thus, starting from an arbitrary tour, the minimum number of checks necessary to ensure that an r-optimal tour is obtained is given by

$$T(n, r) = \tfrac{1}{2} \binom{n}{r} (r-1)! \{p_0 2^r + p_1 2^{r-1} + \ldots + p_r\} \qquad (7.7)$$

For example, in the limiting case, when the optimal tour is to be obtained by this method ($r = n$, $p_0 = p_1 = \ldots = p_{r-1} = 0$ and $p_r = 1$), equation (7.7) gives the required number of checks as $T(n, n) = \tfrac{1}{2}(n-1)!$ which is the total number of all possible tours, and this is equivalent to complete enumeration.

When r is reasonably small compared with n, the process of removing r links to produce r disconnected chains largely results in no chain consisting of a single city, and only a small proportion of the total number of ways of choosing the r links will produce any single cities. Thus, for $r \ll n$, $p_0 \approx 1$ and $p_1 \approx p_2 \approx \ldots \approx p_r \approx 0$. Hence equation (7.7) reduces to

$$T(n, r) \approx \binom{n}{r} (r-1)! \, 2^{r-1}. \qquad (7.8)$$

For large n (say, a few tens) and $r = 2$, the number of checks necessary to ensure 2-optimality becomes

$$T(n, 2) \approx n(n-1) \approx n^2 \qquad (7.9)$$

and the number of checks necessary to ensure 3-optimality is

$$T(n, 3) \approx \frac{4}{3} n(n-1)(n-2) \approx \frac{4}{3} n^3 \qquad (7.10)$$

Hence, although in order to guarantee an optimal tour (i.e. to find an n-optimal tour) a prohibitive amount of computing work is involved, a 2-optimal or 3-optimal tour can be found quite easily with a reasonable amount of computing time, as suggested by equations (7.9) and (7.10). Moreover, experiments have shown (some details are given later) that 2- or 3-optimal tours have a high probability of being optimal, and when they are not optimal their costs are only slightly greater than the cost of the optimal tour.

(D) Partial enumeration

The algorithm of Roberts and Flores [16], which is an approximate method of solution, consists of the following sequence of operations:

(1)   Find good starting tours.

(2)   Improve these tours.

(3)   Extract sufficient information from the improved tours to determine links or chains of cities likely to appear in the conjectured optimal tour.

(4)   With certain cities paired off, develop the graph of the network and enumerate all hamiltonian circuits.

Further comments are given below:

(1) From the original cost matrix an *ordered cost matrix* and an *ordered row index matrix* are formed in the following way. In the ordered cost matrix the element in cell (i, j) is the *cost* between the city j and its ith nearest neighbour. In the ordered row index matrix the element (i, j) is the *number* of the city which is the ith nearest to city j.

The ordered row index matrix is then used to generate feasible and potentially good tours through the following procedure. Start with any element e_{ix} (say, equal to k) in the ordered row index matrix. This will commit link (k, x). Now scan rows $i = 1, 2, ...$ successively until an element (say, e_{iy}) with value x is found. Commit link (x, y) to form the chain (k, x, y). If any subloops are formed, reject e_{iy} and continue scanning the rows until the next element whose value is equal to x is found and tried. Start scanning the rows from the top again, until an element (e_{iz}, say) with value equal to y is found. Commit link (y, z) to form chain (k, x, y, z). If subloops result, reject e_{iz} and continue scanning as previously. Again, start scanning the rows from the top until an element e_{iw} with the value equal to z is found to form the chain (k, x, y, z, w), and so on until a total tour is formed.

This procedure can be started with any element e_{ix} and therefore it can be used to produce many tours.

(2)   The tours resulting from stage 1 are permuted in a way similar to that used by Reiter and Sherman, in order to produce even lower-cost tours.

(3)   From the tours obtained so far the number of times that a specific link appears is counted, and if it occurs in many of the tours that have been generated, say, in over 75 per cent of the cases, as suggested by Roberts and Flores, it is then assumed to be part of the optimal tour.

(4)   The combinatorial matrix M is defined as a matrix in which

the entries in column *j* list the cities to which city *j* may branch. The ordered row index matrix is the combinatorial matrix of the complete graph. Roberts and Flores reduce the graph and thus restrict the branching possibilities to something that can be totally enumerated. This is done in the following way:

(a) Consider the ordered row index matrix as the unabridged **M** matrix.

(b) Truncate the **M** matrix so as to include only the first *r* rows, where *r* is chosen so that all links of the best of the tours from stage 2 appear as branching possibilities in the first *r* rows at least once.

(c) From the chains of cities committed to the optimal tour by the statistical study of stage 3, determine the interior cities (i.e. cities other than the two end cities of each chain) and remove them from the **M** matrix.

(d) Enumerate all the hamiltonian circuits that exist in the graph defined by the resulting **M**, and take the best one to be the conjectured optimum tour. Note that one of the enumerated hamiltonian circuits is the best tour found at the end of stage 2.

(E) The Gilmore–Gomory algorithm

Gilmore and Gomory [8] investigate the travelling salesman problem which has a particular kind of cost matrix that is of interest in certain job-sequencing problems. Their algorithm is remarkably simple. The same cost measure may be a good approximation to the actual costs in a variety of other special cases of the travelling salesman problem that may appear in distribution systems. Hence the algorithm described here may, in some cases, be very useful. The terminology of this section has, so far as it has been found possible, been kept the same as that used by Gilmore and Gomory, and the algorithm is described in terms of job sequencing, although the substitution of "city" for "job" will leave the algorithm unchanged.

Each job *i* has two numbers associated with it, A_i and B_i. To start the *i*th job the machine must be in cost state A_i (i.e. the state variable $x = A_i$), and at the completion of the *i*th job the machine cost state is automatically B_i. If the *j*th job is to follow job *i*, the machine state must be changed from B_i to A_j. The cost of this change is c_{ij}, which is assumed to have the form:

$$c_{ij} = \int_{B_i}^{A_j} f(x)\,dx \qquad \text{if } A_j \geqslant B_i \left.\vphantom{\int}\right)$$

$$\text{or} \int_{A_j}^{B_i} g(x)\,dx \qquad \text{if } B_i > A_j \left.\vphantom{\int}\right)$$

(7.11)

Thus, for example, if $f(x)$ is taken to be 1, then c_{ij} is calculated as $c_{ij} = A_j - B_i$. In general, however, the functions $f(x)$ and $g(x)$ are given and are interpreted as the costs of respectively increasing and decreasing the state variable x by a unit amount.

The following algorithm will then find the ordering of the jobs so as to minimize the total changeover cost, i.e. solve the travelling salesman problem with the cost matrix elements c_{ij} given by equation (7.11). However, we will first attend to some preliminary definitions.

We are interested in the permutation of n cities such that each city is "assigned" only to one other city. The assignment of city i to j implies that the travelling salesman goes from i to j. This permutation is characterized by the function ϕ such that

$$\phi(i) = j$$

For example, if $n = 5$ the assignment may take the following form:

From	To
1	2
2	5
3	4
4	3
5	1

The assignment here results in two subtours: $1-2-5-1$ and $3-4-3$. The values of ϕ are

$$\phi(1) = 2$$
$$\phi(2) = 5$$
$$\text{etc.}$$

We now define an operator α_{ij} which describes the interchange of cities i and j in a given permutation. This operator is written as

$$\alpha_{ij}(i) = j$$

which simply means that when we interchange i and j the point i is always replaced by j. Similarly,

$$\left.\begin{array}{l} \alpha_{ij}(j) = i \\ \alpha_{ij}(k) = k \quad \text{(for } k \neq i, j\text{)} \end{array}\right\} \tag{7.12}$$

Thus application of α_{ij} to the permutation ϕ results in a new permutation $\overline{\phi} = \alpha_{ij}\phi$ given by

$$\overline{\phi}(i) = \phi(j),$$
$$\overline{\phi}(j) = \phi(i),$$
$$\overline{\phi}(k) = \phi(k) \quad \text{for } k \neq i, j.$$

The cost of an interchange α_{ij} when applied to a permutation ϕ is measured by the improvement that it yields. If $C(\phi)$ and $C(\overline{\phi})$ define the costs of the permutations ϕ and $\overline{\phi}$ respectively, then the improvement is given by

$$\Delta C(\alpha_{ij} \mid \phi) = C(\phi) - C(\overline{\phi}) \tag{7.13}$$

where the cost of a permutation ϕ is

$$C(\phi) = \sum_{i=1}^{n} c_{ij} = \sum_{i=1}^{n} c_{i\phi(i)} \tag{7.14}$$

The algorithm is now as follows:

(a.1) Arrange the numbers B_i in descending order and renumber the jobs so that with the new numbering

$$B_i \leqslant B_{i+1} \quad i = 1, 2, \dots, n-1$$

(a.2) The renumbering adopted in (a.1) is now used to renumber the corresponding elements in the series A_i in a descending order of magnitude.

(a.3) Find the permutation for which

$$\phi(1) = q_1$$

where $A_{q_1^-}$ is the smallest in the A_i list. Similarly, find a permutation for which

$$\phi(2) = q_2$$

where A_{q_2} is the second smallest in the A_i list. Proceed in this way until all the elements in list B_i are exhausted.

(a.4) Compute the costs $\Delta C(\alpha_{i, i+1} \mid \phi)$ for $i = 1, 2, \dots, n-1$, where $\Delta C(\alpha_{i, i+1} \mid \phi)$ is given as

$$\Delta C(\alpha_{i, i+1} \mid \phi) = 0 \quad \text{if } \max(B_i, A_{\phi(i)}) \geqslant \min(B_{i+1}, A_{\phi(i+1)}),$$

otherwise $\Delta C(\alpha_{i,\,i+1}\mid\phi) = \int\limits_{\max(B_i,\,A_{\phi(i)})}^{\min(B_{i+1},\,A_{\phi(i+1)})}\left[f(x)+g(x)\right]dx$

Note that steps (a.1) to (a.4) find the minimal permutation ϕ and its associated cost. Thus, in the general case this would correspond to the solution of the assignment problem.

The minimal permutation ϕ does not necessarily form a tour, but it may consist of several subloops. Steps (b.1) to (b.3) below find the minimal spanning tree linking all subloops by considering each of them as a single node of a graph:

(b.1)   Form the graph of the n nodes with arcs connecting the ith and $\phi(i)$th nodes ($i = 1, 2, \ldots, n$).

(b.2)   If the graph is connected, go to step (c.1), otherwise select the smallest value $\Delta C(\alpha_{i,\,i+1}\mid\phi)$ such that i is in one subloop and $i+1$ in another.

(b.3)   Adjoin the arc $R_{i,\,i+1}$ to the graph using the i value selected in (b.2).

The following interchanges given in steps (c.1) to (c.3) have been shown to produce the optimal tour:

(c.1)   Divide the arcs added in step (b.3) into two groups: those $R_{i,\,i+1}$ for which $A_{\phi(i)} \geqslant B_i$ go into group 1 and all others go into group 2.

(c.2)   Arrange the indices i (which correspond to arcs $R_{i,\,i+1}$ in group 1) in descending order (say $i_1, i_2,\ldots, i_l$), and the indices j (which correspond to arcs $R_{j,\,j+1}$ in group 2) in ascending order (say $j_1, j_2, \ldots, j_m$).

(c.3)   The minimal tour is obtained by following the ith job by the job $\phi^*(i)$, where

$$\phi^*(i) = \alpha_{i_1,\,i_1+1}\,\alpha_{i_2,\,i_2+1}\cdots\alpha_{i_l,\,i_l+1}\,\alpha_{j_1,\,j_1+1}\cdots\alpha_{j_m,\,j_m+1}\phi(i)$$

$$(7.15)$$

The order of applying the operators for interchanges in equation (7.15) is from right to left (namely, we first find the value of $\alpha_{j_m,\,j_m+1}\phi(i)$, then apply the next operator, etc.)

BOUNDS FOR THE TRAVELLING SALESMAN PROBLEM

In general, only comparatively small problems (with a few tens of cities) can be solved optimally, whereas the heuristic programs which can "solve" larger problems give solutions which may or may not be near-optimal. One is then faced with the problem of deciding whether the answers given by the heuristic programs are close enough. This can only be done (since the optimal solution itself is not known) by having a sufficiently good lower bound for the cost of the optimal tour, the result of the heuristic program being itself an upper bound for the optimal cost.

Some ways of calculating lower bounds are suggested below. All of these are easy to calculate and could be computed in an amount of time which would be negligible when compared with the total solution time of the equivalent travelling salesman problem by any method.

(A) The shortest spanning tree (SST)

The travelling salesman problem can be represented by a graph of n nodes and $n(n-1)$ possible links which completely interconnect these nodes. A spanning tree of such a graph is any set of $(n-1)$ links that connect all of the n nodes. Obviously there is a very large number of spanning trees in a graph, just as there are many possible hamiltonian circuits. However, contrary to the case for the hamiltonian circuits, the shortest of the spanning trees can be determined very easily by an algorithm due to Kruskal [12].

Consider now a hamiltonian circuit from which any one branch has been removed, leaving a hamiltonian chain. A hamiltonian chain is a particular case of a spanning tree and is thus limited from below by the length of the SST. However, it is obvious that we would obtain a better bound for the travelling salesman problem if instead of removing any one branch from the optimal tour, we remove the longest one.

Now let d_{jk} be the cost between the jth city and the kth nearest of its neighbouring cities. Thus d_{j1} is the cost of the nearest city to city j, and d_{j2} is the cost of the second nearest. The longest branch in the optimal tour is at least as long as $\max_j (d_{j2})$. Thus a valid lower bound to the optimal travelling salesman tour, defined as B_{SST}, is

$$B_{SST} = C_{SST} + \max_j (d_{j2}) \qquad (7.16)$$

where C_{SST} is the cost of the SST.

(B) The assignment problem (AP)

The classical linear assignment problem can be stated as follows:

Minimize
$$z = \sum_{i=1}^{n} \sum_{j=1}^{n} c_{ij} x_{ij}$$
(7.17)

subject to:
$$\left. \begin{array}{c} \sum_{i} x_{ij} = \sum_{j} x_{ij} = 1 \\ \text{(for all } i \text{ and } j) \\ \text{and } x_{ij} = 0 \text{ or } 1 \end{array} \right\}$$
(7.18)

If the matrix $[c_{ij}]$ in equation (7.17) represents the cost matrix of the travelling salesman problem (with all diagonal elements set to infinity) then equations (7.17) and (7.18), together with the extra requirement that the solution must be a tour, will also represent the travelling salesman problem. Thus the solution to the assignment problem (which does not necessarily yield a valid tour) is a lower bound (call it B_{AP}), for the optimal travelling salesman tour.

(C) The sum of the shortest links (SL)

In a graph that depicts a travelling salesman tour, two links emanate from each node. Now the shortest and next shortest links that can emanate from city j have costs say. d_{j1} and d_{j2} respectively. Thus, a valid lower bound for the cost of the travelling salesman tour is the quantity

$$B_{SL} = \tfrac{1}{2} \sum_{j=1}^{n} (d_{j1} + d_{j2}) .$$
(7.19)

The factor $\tfrac{1}{2}$ is necessary because each city is considered twice as "gone-to" and "come-from".

(D) Improvements to the bounds

The previously derived bounds B_{SST} and B_{AP} are based on exact solutions to problems which are related to the travelling salesman problem. Thus, the shortest hamiltonian chain is the shortest spanning tree in which the number of links at any vertex (called "the degree of the vertex") does not exceed two. As already pointed out earlier, the shortest travelling-salesman tour is a solution to the assignment problem, provided the solution is a tour. Hence, the bounds B_{SST} and B_{AP} can be improved upon, if necessary, by imposing these extra constraints step by step in a "branch and bound"-like algorithm.

In this context it should be noted that the algorithm of Little *et al.* (described earlier) is a particular case in which the sum of the reducing constants forms the lower bound, and the branches are selected so as not to violate the "tour constraint" in the first place. Conversely, if the algorithms for improving B_{SST} and B_{AP}, which are described below, are carried to completion so that the "tour constraint" is satisfied, the result would be the optimal solution to the travelling salesman problem. Thus the algorithms which follow could be used not only to improve the lower bounds but (admittedly with a much greater amount of computation than required by the computation of bounds described so far) also to derive the optimal solution to the problem.

(1) *Improvement to SST bound* Let us suppose that the *SST* of the original graph is shown in Fig. 7.7 (a). The degree of vertex 4 is 3 (i.e. there are three links joining it), and therefore at least one of these links must be absent from the shortest hamiltonian chain. Thus the shortest hamiltonian chain must be a solution to at least one of the subproblems represented by nodes *B, C* and *D* of the decision tree shown in Fig. 7.8. In this figure, $\bar{e}_{14}$, $\bar{e}_{24}$, and $\bar{e}_{34}$ mean that links e_{14}, e_{24} and e_{34} respectively have been prohibited by setting their equivalent costs to infinity. The number X_A is the bound from the *SST* to the original problem, whilst X_B, X_C and X_D are the bounds to subproblems *B*, *C* and *D* respectively. Obviously $X_B, X_C, X_D \geqslant X_A$.

If the *SST* corresponding to the node with the lowest bound has a vertex with degree greater than two, branching is continued from that node. For example, let X_B be smaller than X_C and X_D, and the *SST* of node *B* be as shown in Fig. 7.7 (b). The degree of vertex 6 is 4, and hence branching is continued to nodes *E, F, G* and *H* by prohibiting the links e_{65}, e_{68}, e_{63} and e_{67} respectively.

If the branching is carried to completion, the shortest hamiltonian chain will result (hence, with only minor modifications, a solution to the travelling salesman problem can be found); if the branching is ended prematurely and the smallest of the free-node[1] bounds is substituted for the quantity C_{SST} in equation (7.16), an improved bound (B_{SST}) to the travelling salesman problem will result.

(2) *Improvement to the AP bound* Let Fig. 7.9 (a) represent the graph of the solution to the original *AP*, and let the cost be X_A. The subloop (1, 2, 1) cannot, however, exist in the travelling salesman solution, and the shortest travelling-salesman tour must therefore be a solution to at least one of the subproblems represented by nodes *B* and *C* in Fig. 7.10.

---

[1] i.e. a node from which no further branching has so far occurred.

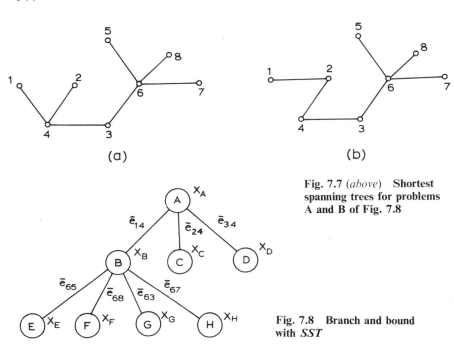

Fig. 7.7 (*above*) **Shortest spanning trees for problems A and B of Fig. 7.8**

Fig. 7.8 **Branch and bound with *SST***

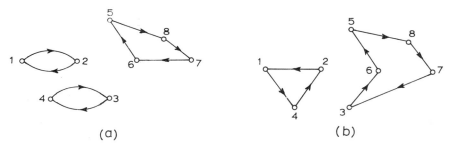

Fig. 7.9 **Solutions to assignment problems A and B of Fig. 7.10**

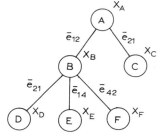

Fig. 7.10 **Branch and bound with *AP***

Branching is now continued from the node with the lowest bound, if the solution to the AP corresponding to that node contains subloops. For example, if $X_B < X_C$ and the solution to the AP corresponding to node B is as shown in Fig. 7.9(b), then the branching is to nodes D, E and F as shown in Fig. 7.10.

The algorithms of Eastman [6] and Shapiro [17] are essentially the same as this tree-search when carried to conclusion. This form of tree-search is more efficient than the Little *et al.* method, but far less flexible. When the search is ended prematurely, the lowest of the bounds on the "free" nodes is the improved B_{AP}.

COMPUTATIONAL ASPECTS

Let us now turn to the computational efficiency of the algorithms (and that of the bounds) described earlier. As published computational results of the various algorithms are given for different problems solved on a variety of computers, comparisons based on these results are very difficult. For this reason the computational results and the comparisons which follow are based on programs written by the authors and tested against each other on some published and some unpublished (randomly generated) problems. All programs were run on (and all quoted running times are for) the IBM 7094 II computer. All codes are experimental in the sense that no attempts were made to minimize running times, and it would not be difficult to improve the codes substantially. Concessions were freely made to programming expediency (e.g. no machine language). However, the relative merits of the various algorithms which are implied in the results that follow are probably essentially valid.

The usefulness of the *dynamic programming* algorithm is limited not so much by the excessive computing time that is involved, as by the vast computer storage capacity that is required. By far the largest part of the computer store is taken up by the quantities $C(S, x)$ which are calculated sequentially. Since $C(S, x)$ must be calculated for all subsets S of S_0 containing $1, 2, \ldots, (n-1)$ cities, and since each city in S must be considered as a possible end-city x, the total number of $C(S, x)$, when S contains k cities, is $k\binom{n-1}{k}$ and therefore the total number of $C(S, x)$ (for an asymmetrical problem) is given by

$$M = \sum_{k=1}^{n-1} \qquad = (n-1)\, 2^{n-2} \qquad (7.20)$$

If no auxiliary storage is used, this amount of main storage must

Table 7.1 Comparison of several travelling salesman algorithms

Algorithm		Problem (No. / Size n)										
		1 / 7	2 / 13	3 / 20	4 / 20	5 / 30	6 / 30	7 / 40	8 / 48	9 / 57	10 / 75	11 / 100
1		·01	·1									
2	2.1	<·01	·01	·10	·05	10·5	·72	19·1				
	2.2	<·01	·01	·12	·05	5·7	·61	13·5				
	2.3	<·01	·01	·12	·06	3·1	·54	8·9				
	2.4	<·01	·02	·14	·05	2·3	·56	10·7				
3			228 <·01	246 <·01		351		397	11461	12985		
4			228 <·01	246 <·01		351 ·01		397 ·68	11461 ·69	12955 2·2	608 6·8	738 10
5			228 <·01	246 <·01		351 ·01		397 60	11461 ·5	12955 1·9	608 5·0	732 10

Algorithms:

Exact

1: Dynamic programming [10]
2.1: Branch-and-bound [14] using strategy (a)
2.2: Branch-and-bound using strategy (b) with $\alpha = \cdot8$, $\beta = \cdot2$
2.3: Branch-and-bound using strategy (b) with $\alpha = \cdot65$, $\beta = \cdot35$
2.4: Branch-and-bound using strategy (b) with $\alpha = \cdot5$, $\beta = \cdot5$

Approximate

3: Algorithm of Roberts and Flores [16]
4: Algorithm of Reiter and Sherman [15]
5: 3-optimal algorithm [3, 13]

Problems:

1: Random problem (asymmetrical)
2: Held and Karp's [10] problem (symmetrical)
3: Croes' problem (symmetrical)
4: Random problem (asymmetrical)
5: Random problem (symmetrical)
6: Random problem (asymmetrical)
7: Random problem (symmetrical)
8: Held and Karp's problem (symmetrical)
9: Karg and Thompson's [11] problem (symmetrical)
10: Random problem (symmetrical)
11: Random problem (symmetrical)

For the exact algorithms the entry in the table is the time, in minutes, to solve the problem (using an IBM 7094 II). For the approximate algorithms the top entry is the cost of the best tour found and the bottom entry the time (min.) used in finding it. Algorithms 4 and 5 were started with the same random initial tours.

therefore exist. Some improvement is possible if the values of $C(S, x)$ for $m = k + 1$ are put in auxiliary storage (as soon as they are calculated from the values of $C(S, x)$ with $m = k$), and then returned to the core for the calculation of $C(S, x)$ with $m = k+2$. In this case the core storage required is the largest of the numbers $k\binom{n-1}{k}$ which occurs when $k \approx n/2$. The increase in computing time is negligible, but even the use of auxiliary storage in this manner only allows a problem with a maximum of about 14 cities to be solved on computers with a 32K storage. More extensive use of auxiliary storage facilities is not possible without very large increases in computing times.

The *branch-and-bound* algorithm of Little *et al.* also runs into storage difficulties if strategy (i) (see page 128) is used for back-branching, and therefore the figures quoted in the following tables refer to the algorithm using strategy (ii). In conjunction with this algorithm various strategies for forward-branching (i.e. finding the next node to branch to) were also tried. In these strategies the branching is made to the node $(x_1\ x_2)$ whose penalty $p_{x_1 x_2}$ is largest. The penalties are calculated as follows:

- The sum of the smallest element in row x_1 and the smallest element in column x_2 (without considering element $(x_1\ x_2)$). Call this sum $\theta'_{x_1 x_2}$.
- Similarly take the second smallest element in row x_1 and column x_2 (again excluding the element $(x_1\ x_2)$). Call the sum of these elements $\theta''_{x_1 x_2}$.

Thus in strategy (a), $p_{x_1 x_2} = \theta'_{x_1 x_2}$ (as suggested by Little *et al.*) and in strategy (b), $p_{x_1 x_2} = \alpha\theta'_{x_1 x_2} + \beta\theta''_{x_1 x_2}$, where α and β may be interpreted respectively as the probabilities of using the first and second best alternatives (when the link $(x_1\ x_2)$ is not selected for the next branching). Various values of α and β have been tried as shown in Table 7.1, and the choice of α and β appears to affect the results very significantly.

The two local optimization algorithms of Reiter and Sherman and of Lin have been found to be very similar in the quality of the tours they produce and the computing times they require. The probability that a 3-optimal tour is optimal for an n-city travelling salesman problem is claimed by Lin to be $p(n) \approx 2^{-n/10}$, and our limited experience supports his claim.

Table 7.1 shows the relative efficiency of the various algorithms, except for the Gilmore–Gomory algorithm (for special problems) which is obviously very efficient indeed in its restricted application.

Various experiments have been performed to test the lower bounds suggested in the last section. Ten travelling salesman problems with 10, 20, etc. up to 100 cities were randomly generated and "solved" using the 3-optimal method. Bounds were calculated for these problems (without any attempts to improve them), and the results are shown in Fig. 7.11. The bounds from the *SST* are seen to

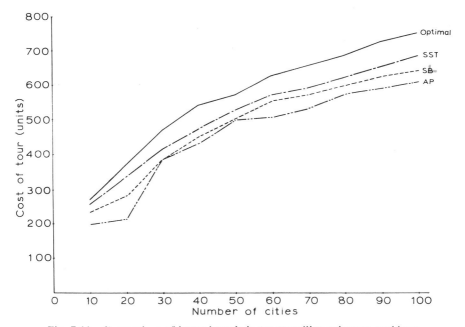

Fig. 7.11 Comparison of lower bounds in ten travelling-salesmen problems

be the best for all ten problems with an average value of about 10 per cent below the costs of the conjectured optimal tours. One should also note that for 8 out of 10 problems the bounds are within 9–11 per cent below the conjectured optimal. Next best are the bounds B_{SL} and B_{AP}, with average values of 14 per cent and 19 per cent respectively below the optimal tour costs. The computation times for obtaining the bounds for a 50-city problem are all well under 10 seconds (for the IBM 7094 II).

REFERENCES

[1] BELLMAN, R., Dynamic programming treatment of the travelling salesman problem. *J. Assoc. Comp. Mech.*, **9**, 61–3 (1962).

[2] BELLMORE, M. and NEMHAUSER, G. L., The travelling salesman problem—a survey. *Ops. Res.*, **16**, 538–58 (1968).

[3] CHRISTOFIDES, N. and EILON, S., An algorithm for the vehicle dispatching problem. *Opl. Res. Q.*, **20**, 309–18 (1969).

[4] CROES, G. A., A method for solving travelling salesman problems. *Ops. Res.*, **6**, 791–812 (1958).

[5] DANTZIG, G. B., FULKERSON, D. R., and JOHNSON, S. M., Solution of a large-scale travelling salesman problem. *Ops. Res.*, **2**, 393–410 (1954).

[6] EASTMAN, W. L., Linear programming with pattern constraints. Ph.D. Dissertation, Harvard, 1958.

[7] FLOOD, M. M., The travelling salesman problem. *Ops. Res.*, **4**, 61–75 (1956).

[8] GILMORE, P. C. and GOMORY, R. E., Sequencing a one-state variable machine—A solvable case of the travelling salesman problem. *Ops. Res.*, **12**, 655–79 (1964).

[9] GONZALES, R. H., Solution to the travelling salesman problem by dynamic programming on the hypercube. Tech. Rep. No. 18, O. R. Center, M.I.T., 1962.

[10] HELD, M. and KARP, R. M., A dynamic programming approach to sequencing problems. *S.I.A.M. Rev.*, **10**, 196–210 (1962).

[11] KARG, R. L. and THOMPSON, G. L., A heuristic approach to solving travelling salesman problems. *Mgmt. Sci.*, **10**, 225–47 (1964).

[12] KRUSKAL, J. B., On the shortest spanning subtree of a graph and the travelling salesman problem. *Proc. Amer. Math. Soc.*, **2**, 48–50 (1956).

[13] LIN, S., Computer solutions of the travelling salesman problem. *Bell Systems Tech. J.*, **44**, 2245–69 (1965).

[14] LITTLE, J. D. C., MURTY, K. G., SWEENEY, D. W., and KAREL, C., An algorithm for the travelling salesman problem. *Ops. Res.*, **11**, 979–89 (1963).

[15] REITER, S. and SHERMAN, G., Discrete optimising. *S.I.A.M. Rev.*, **13**, 864–89 (1965).

[16] ROBERTS, S. M. and FLORES, B., An engineering approach to the travelling salesman problem. *Mgmt. Sci.*, **13**, 269–88 (1966).

[17] SHAPIRO, D., Algorithms for the solution of the optimal cost travelling salesman problem. Sc.D. Thesis, Washington University, St. Louis, 1966.

Chapter 8

Expected distances in distribution problems

INTRODUCTION

In many problems in distribution management the precise location and the demands of customers are not known in advance, and yet decisions regarding the number and location of depots, or the problem of the size of the distribution fleet, have to be considered. It is then necessary to make estimates of the expected mileage that would be involved in supplying customers, so that these estimates can be fed into the distribution cost function.

The purpose of this chapter is to consider several problems concerned with the calculation of expected distances. Specifically, we shall discuss the following problems:

(1)   The expected straight-line distance between two points in a given area.
(2)   The expected rectangular distance (this term is defined later) between two points in a given area.
(3)   The expected length of a travelling salesman tour.
(4)   The expected length of vehicle routes.

EXPECTED STRAIGHT-LINE DISTANCE BETWEEN TWO POINTS

The area in which customers are located may conveniently be defined either as a circle of a given radius or as a rectangle of given dimensions. As the precise locations of the customers are unknown, we shall assume that the customers are uniformly distributed in the defined area.

A circular area

Consider a circular area of a known radius a and two points P and Q. One point may represent the depot at a given location and the other a customer randomly located in the area, so that the distance $d = PQ$ is the straight-line distance between the depot and the customer. If both points represent two customers randomly located in the area, then d is the straight-line distance between them. Consider two cases:

(a)   Point P is at a given location $(R, 0)$, inside or outside the the circle, and Q is a random point inside the circle at (r, θ) in polar co-ordinates. as shown in Fig. 8.1.

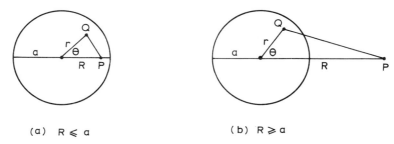

(a)   R ⩽ a   (b)   R ⩾ a

Fig. 8.1   *P* fixed. *Q* random (circular area)

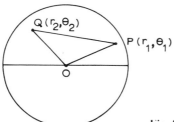

Fig. 8.2   **P and Q random (circular area)**

(b) P and Q are random points at (r_1, θ_1) and (r_2, θ_2) respectively, as shown in Fig. 8.2.

In each of these cases we wish to find $E(d)$, namely the expected distance between P and Q.

(a)   *The distance between a random point in a circle and a fixed point*   As shown in Fig. 8.1, P is the fixed point at a distance R from the centre of the circle, and Q is the random point at (r, θ). The fixed point P can either be inside the circle (in which case $R \leqslant a$) or outside (where $R \geqslant a$); denote the area of the circle by S.

The expected length of the link PQ is then given by

$$E(d) = \int_{r=0}^{a} \int_{\theta=0}^{2\pi} \sqrt{R^2 + r^2 - 2rR \cos \theta} \, \frac{r \, dr \, d\theta}{S}$$

$$= \frac{2}{\pi a^2} \int_{r=0}^{a} r \, dr \int_{\theta=0}^{\pi} \sqrt{R^2 + r^2 - 2rR \cos \theta} \, d\theta \qquad (8.1)$$

The right-hand side of equation (8.1) integrates, after some manipulation, to give:

$$E(d) = RF(-\tfrac{1}{2}, -\tfrac{1}{2}: 2: a^2 \; R^2) \qquad (8.2)$$

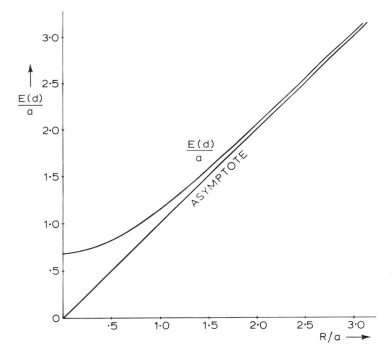

Fig. 8.3   **Expected length between a random point in a circle and a fixed point**

where F is the hypergeometric function.

In the special case when the fixed point P is at the centre of the circle (i.e. when $R = 0$), equation (8.2) reduces to

$$E(d) \bigg|_{R=0} = \frac{2}{3} a \qquad (8.3)$$

and when the fixed point P is on the periphery of the circle (i.e. when $R = a$), equation (8.2) becomes

$$E(d)\Big|_{R=a} = \frac{32a}{9\pi} \approx 1 \cdot 132a \qquad (8.4)$$

The value $E(d)/a$ is plotted in Fig. 8.3 against R/a. The asymptote drawn at $45°$ shows how, for relatively large values of R, the expected distance d approaches R.

(b)   *Two random points in a circle.*   As shown in Fig. 8.2, P and Q are two random points having polar co-ordinates (r_1, θ_1) and (r_2, θ_2) respectively. The expected length of the link PQ is then given by

$$E(d) =$$

$$\int_{r_1=0}^{a} \int_{r_2=0}^{a} \int_{\theta_1=0}^{2\pi} \int_{\theta_2=0}^{2\pi} \sqrt{r_1^2+r_2^2-2r_1r_2\cos(\theta_2-\theta_1)}\; \frac{r_1\, r_2\, dr_1\, dr_2\, d\theta_1\, d\theta_2}{S^2}$$

$$= \frac{1}{\pi^2 a^4}\int_0^a r_1\, dr_1 \int_0^a r_2\, dr_2 \int_0^{2\pi}\int_0^{2\pi} \sqrt{r_1^2+r_2^2-2r_1\,r_2\cos(\theta_2-\theta_1)}\; d\theta_1\, d\theta_2$$

$$(8.5)$$

Using symmetry considerations, the integration can be performed to yield

$$E(d) = \frac{8a}{5\{\Gamma(5/2)\}^2} = \frac{128\,a}{45\pi} \approx 0 \cdot 905\,a \qquad (8.6)$$

A rectangular area

Consider now a rectangular area measuring a by b (so that the area $S = ab$), where customers are uniformly distributed. As in the case of a circular area, let us consider the distance between two points P and Q, when

(a) P is at a fixed location outside or inside the rectangle and Q is a random point in the rectangle (as in Fig. 8.4 and 8.5);
(b) P and Q are random points in the rectangle (see Fig. 8.6).

(a) *The distance between a random point in a rectangle and a fixed point*   Let P be a fixed point with co-ordinates (x_0, y_0) outside or inside the rectangle, as shown in Fig. 8.4, and Q be a random point inside the rectangle with co-ordinates (x, y).

The expected distance between P and Q is given by

$$E(d) = \frac{1}{ab} \int\limits_{x=0}^{a} \int\limits_{y=0}^{b} \left[(x-x_0)^2 + (y-y_0)^2 \right]^{1/2} dx\, dy \qquad (8.7)$$

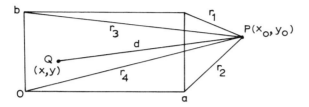

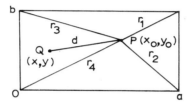

Fig. 8.4 *P* fixed, *Q* random (rectangular area)

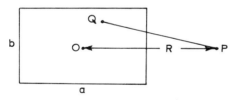

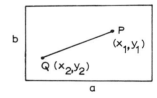

Fig. 8.5 **P at a given distance R from a rectangular area**

Fig. 8.6 **P and Q inside rectangle, and random**

and after the integration is performed the result is

$$E(d) = \frac{1}{6ab} (2ABr_1 + 2Ay_0\, r_2 + 2x_0\, Br_3 + 2x_0\, y_0\, r_4 + A^3 \ln H_1$$

$$+ B^3 \ln H_2 + x_0^3 \ln H_3 + y_0^3 \ln H_4) \qquad (8.8)$$

where
$$A = a - x_0$$
$$B = b - y_0$$

and r_1, r_2, r_3, r_4 are the distances from P to the four corners of the rectangle (see Fig. 8.4), namely

$$r_1 = \sqrt{A^2 + B^2} \qquad\qquad r_2 = \sqrt{A^2 + y_0^2}$$

$$r_3 = \sqrt{x_0^2 + B^2} \qquad\qquad r_4 = \sqrt{x_0^2 + y_0^2}$$

also
$$H_1 = \frac{B + r_1}{-y_0 + r_2} \qquad\qquad H_2 = \frac{A + r_1}{-x_0 + r_3}$$

$$H_3 = \frac{B + r_3}{-y_0 + r_4} \qquad\qquad H_4 = \frac{A + r_2}{-x_0 + r_4}$$

Consider now the following special cases.

(i) If the fixed point P is at a given distance R from the centre of a rectangle (as in Fig. 8.5), then

$$A = \tfrac{1}{2}a - R$$

$$x_0 = \tfrac{1}{2}a + R = A + 2R$$

$$y_0 = B = \tfrac{1}{2}b$$

$$r_1 = r_2 = \sqrt{A^2 + \tfrac{1}{4}b^2}$$

$$r_3 = r_4 = \sqrt{(A + 2R)^2 + \tfrac{1}{4}b^2}$$

$$H_2 = H_4$$

so that $\mathrm{E}(d)_R =$

$$\frac{1}{6ab}\left[4ABr_1 + 4(A + 2R)Br_3 + A^3 \ln H_1 + 2B^3 \ln H_2 + (A + 2R)^3 \ln H_3\right]$$

$$(8.9)$$

Values of $\mathrm{E}(d)$ for equation (8.9) are given in Table 8.1 for various values of R/a and b/a. For comparatively large values of R/a we find that R becomes a good approximation for $\mathrm{E}(d)$.

(ii) For the special case $R = 0$ (when the fixed point is in the middle of the rectangle) we have—

$$A = x_0 = \tfrac{1}{2}a$$

$$B = y_0 = \tfrac{1}{2}b$$

$$r_1 = r_2 = r_3 = r_4$$

$$H_1 = H_3 \quad \text{and} \quad H_2 = H_4$$

leading to

$$\mathrm{E}(d)\bigg|_{R=0} = \frac{1}{3}r_1 + \frac{a}{24}\left(\frac{a}{b}\ln H_1 + \frac{b^2}{a^2}\ln H_2\right) \qquad (8.10)$$

Table 8.1 Expected distance from a fixed point to a random point in a rectangle (see equation (8.9))

Shape factor b/a	$R/a = 0$	0·25	0·5	0·75	1·0	1·5	2·0	2·5	5·0	10·0
0·1	25·31	31·55	50·18	75·06	100·04	150·02	200·02	250·01	500·00	1000·00
0·2	26·04	32·24	50·63	75·26	100·18	150·11	200·08	250·06	500·03	1000·01
0·3	27·05	33·20	51·28	75·59	100·41	150·25	200·19	250·15	500·07	1000·03
0·4	28·27	34·34	52·09	76·04	100·72	150·46	200·34	250·27	500·13	1000·06
0·5	29·66	35·65	53·03	76·61	101·12	150·71	200·53	250·42	500·20	1000·10
0·6	31·18	37·08	54·10	77·28	101·61	151·03	200·76	250·60	500·30	1000·15
0·7	32·82	38·61	55·27	78·06	102·18	151·40	201·03	250·82	500·40	1000·20
0·8	34·56	40·24	56·54	78·93	102·82	151·82	201·35	251·07	500·53	1000·26
0·9	36·37	41·94	57·89	79·89	103·54	152·30	201·71	251·36	500·67	1000·33
1·0	38·26	43·71	59·32	80·93	104·34	152·83	202·10	251·67	500·83	1000·41
1·1	40·20	45·54	60·81	82·05	105·20	153·41	202·54	252·02	501·01	1000·50
1·2	42·19	47·43	62·37	83·23	106·13	154·04	203·04	252·41	501·20	1000·60
1·3	44·22	49·35	63·99	84·49	107·12	154·72	203·53	252·82	501·40	1000·70
1·4	46·29	51·32	65·65	85·80	108·16	155·45	204·09	253·27	501·63	1000·81
1·5	48·40	53·33	67·36	87·17	109·27	156·23	204·68	253·74	501·87	1000·93
1·6	50·54	55·36	69·12	88·59	110·43	157·05	205·31	254·25	502·13	1001·06
1·7	52·70	57·43	70·92	90·68	111·64	157·92	205·97	254·79	502·40	1001·20
1·8	54·89	59·52	72·75	91·58	112·90	158·83	206·68	255·36	502·68	1001·34
1·9	57·09	61·64	74·62	93·14	114·20	159·78	207·41	255·96	503·00	1001·50
2·0	59·32	63·78	76·52	94·74	115·55	160·77	208·19	256·59	503·32	1001·66

Notes: (1) The fixed point is at a distance R from the centre of the rectangle as in Fig. 8.5.
(2) In this table $a = 100$ was taken.

(iii)   When the fixed point P is in the middle of a square area $(a = b)$, the last expression is reduced to

$$E(d)\bigg|_{\substack{R=0 \\ a=b}} = \frac{a}{6}\left[\sqrt{2}+\ln\left(1+\sqrt{2}\right)\right] \approx 0\cdot383a \qquad (8.11)$$

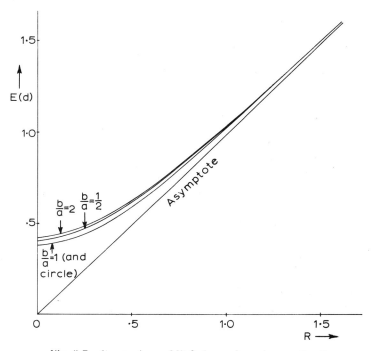

Fig. 8.7   Comparison of E(d) for various shapes of unit area

(iv)   When P is at the corner of the rectangle (such as at $x_0 = y_0 = 0$),

then $\qquad E(d)\bigg|_{\substack{x_0=0 \\ y_0=0}} = \frac{1}{6ab}\left(2abr+a^3\ln\frac{b+r}{a}+b^3\ln\frac{a+r}{b}\right) \qquad (8.12)$

where $r = \sqrt{a^2+b^2}$. For the case of a square this expression is reduced to

$$E(d)\bigg|_{\substack{x_0=y_0=0 \\ a=b}} = \frac{a}{3}\left[\sqrt{2}+\ln\left(1+\sqrt{2}\right)\right] \approx 0\cdot765a \qquad (8.13)$$

and this is precisely twice the result in equation (8.11), since the expected distance from a corner-point of a square of side-length a

must be the same as the expected distance from a centre-point of a square of side-length $2a$.

In Fig. 8.7 the effect of the shape of the area is explored. Four alternatives are considered, all having the same area $S = 1$, namely a circle, a square, a rectangle in which $a/b = \frac{1}{2}$, and a rectangle in which $a/b = 2$. In each of these cases the fixed point is located at a given distance R from the centre of the area, and the expected distance $E(d)$ is plotted against R. In the cases of the rectangles the

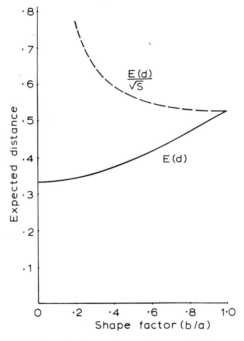

Fig. 8.8 Expected distance between two random points in a rectangle of area S measuring a ($= 1$) by b

point P is along an axis, as shown in Fig. 8.5. Clearly, the shape of the area is noticeable when R is small, but its effect becomes negligible for large values of R.

(b) *Two random points in a rectangle* (*Fig.* 8.6) The expected length of the line PQ is now given by

$$E(d) = \frac{1}{a^2 b^2} \int_0^a \int_0^a \int_0^b \int_0^b \sqrt{(x_1 - x_2)^2 + (y_1 - y_2)^2} \, dx_1 \, dx_2 \, dy_1 \, dy_2 \qquad (8.14)$$

The results of the above integration are too complex to present in a closed form, and the expected length d was therefore found by simulations for various values of a and b. The value of a is kept constant at one unit, the value of b is varied from 0 to 1, and the ratio b/a is called the "shape factor". Fig. 8.8 shows the results of the simulations.

The lower curve gives the value of $E(d)$, the expected distance between the two points, and the upper curve shows the ratio of this distance to the square root of the area. For any given rectangle of a unit area the effect of the shape factor b/a is significant when this factor is low, but becomes relatively unimportant when b/a is between 0·6 and, say, 1·6.

EXPECTED RECTANGULAR DISTANCES

In practice one is often interested not so much in the straight-line distance between two points, as in the actual road distance between them. For example, where the points lie in a city which has a rect-angular road network, the road distance can be appreciably greater than the straight-line distance.

The rectangular distance between two points P and Q is defined as one that is measured along the x and y axes, and we shall now consider the expected rectangular distance for a circular and for a rectangular area.

A circular area

(a) The rectangular distance between a fixed point P and a random point Q is shown in Fig. 8.9 where $R \geqslant a$. The rectangular distance consists of two portions,

one horizontal: $R - r \cos \theta$

one vertical: $r \sin \theta$.

Hence the expected rectangular distance d' for $R \geqslant a$ is given by

$$E(d')\Big|_{R \geqslant a} = \frac{1}{S} \int_{r=0}^{a} \int_{\theta=0}^{2\pi} (R - r \cos \theta + r \sin \theta)\, r\, dr\, d\theta$$

$$= R + \frac{2}{\pi a^2} \int_{0}^{a} r^2\, dr \int_{0}^{\pi} (\sin \theta - \cos \theta)\, d\theta \qquad (8.15)$$

Integration yields the following solution:

$$E(d')\Big|_{R \geqslant a} = R + \frac{4}{3\pi} a \approx R + 0.423a \qquad (8.16)$$

and for the special case where P is situated at $(a, 0)$.

$$E(d') \bigg|_{R=a} \approx 1\cdot423a \qquad (8.17)$$

   (b)   In Fig. 8.10 the fixed point P is inside the circle at $(R, 0)$, i.e. $R \leqslant a$. The circle is divided into two parts by a vertical chord

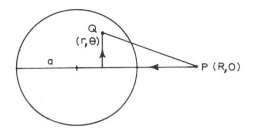

Fig. 8.9   Rectangular distance from a fixed point P to a random point Q (P outside, Q inside circle)

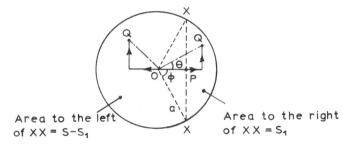

Area to the left of XX = $S-S_1$

Area to the right of XX = S_1

Fig. 8.10   Rectangular distance from a fixed point P at $(R, 0)$ to a random point Q at (r, θ) (P and Q inside circle)

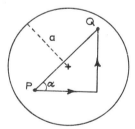

Fig. 8.11   Rectangular distance between two random points in a circle

drawn through P, with a corresponding angle at the centre of 2ϕ (from $-\phi$ to $+\phi$). When the random point Q is in the right-hand portion of the circle (namely $-\phi \leqslant \theta \leqslant \phi$), the rectangular distance is

$$r \cos \theta - R + r \sin \theta$$

and when Q is in the left-hand portion (where $\phi \leqslant \theta \leqslant 2\pi - \phi$) the rectangular distance is

$$R - r\cos\theta + r\sin\theta$$

Hence the expected rectangular distance is

$$\left. \mathrm{E}(d') \right|_{R \leqslant a} = \frac{2}{S}\left[\int_{r=0}^{a}\int_{\theta=0}^{\phi} (r\cos\theta - R + r\sin\theta)\, r\, dr\, d\theta \right.$$

$$\left. + \int_{r=0}^{a}\int_{\theta=\phi}^{\pi} (R - r\cos\theta + r\sin\theta)\, r\, dr\, d\theta \right] \tag{8.18}$$

Integration yields the following results:

$$\left. \mathrm{E}(d') \right|_{R \leqslant a} = R\left(1 - \frac{2S_1}{S}\right) + \frac{4a}{3\pi}(1 + \sin\phi) \tag{8.19}$$

where $S_1 = \int_{r=0}^{a}\int_{\theta=-\phi}^{\phi} r\, dr\, d\theta$, which is the area of that portion of the circle to the right of the dividing chord at P. Consider the following special cases:

(i) $R = a$, namely P is on the circumference of the circle; hence $S_1 = 0$ and $\phi = 0$, and then $\mathrm{E}(d') \approx 1 \cdot 423a$ as in equation (8.17).

(ii) $R = 0$, namely P is at the centre, so that $S_1 = \frac{1}{2}S$ and $\phi = \pi/2$, resulting in

$$\left. \mathrm{E}(d') \right|_{R=0} = 0 \cdot 846a \tag{8.20}$$

(c) In Fig. 8.11 the rectangular distance between two random points in the circle is shown. The horizontal portion here is $d\cos\alpha$ and the vertical portion is $d\sin\alpha$, so that the horizontal distance is given by

$$d' = (\cos\alpha + \sin\alpha)d = \lambda d$$

where d is the straight-line distance and α is the angle between the two points. λ may be regarded as a "correction" factor, which allows d' to be calculated when d is known.

Since the angle α is independent of the positions of P and Q and varies over the range 0 to $\pi/2$, the expected length of the rectangular distance PQ is the same as the straight-line distance PQ multiplied by the factor λ, where

$$\lambda = \frac{2}{\pi}\int_{0}^{\pi/2} (\cos\alpha + \sin\alpha)\, d\alpha = \frac{4}{\pi} \approx 1 \cdot 273 \tag{8.21}$$

Hence, from equation (8.6), we find the expected rectangular distance d' as

$$\mathrm{E}(d') = \frac{512}{45\pi^2}a \approx 1\cdot 153a \qquad (8.22)$$

A rectangular area

(a)   First consider a fixed point P outside the rectangle (see Fig. 8.12) at (x_0, y_0), where $x_0 \geq a$ and $0 \leq y_0 \leq b$. The expected horizontal distance is obviously $x_0 - \frac{1}{2}a$.

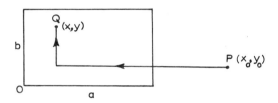

Fig. 8.12   **Rectangular distance from a fixed point P to a random point Q**
(P outside, Q inside rectangle)

The expected vertical distance is

$$\left(\frac{b-y_0}{b}\right)\left(\frac{b-y_0}{2}\right) + \frac{y_0}{b}\frac{y_0}{2} = \frac{y_0^2}{b} + \frac{b}{2} - y_0$$

so that the total rectangular distance is

$$\mathrm{E}(d')\Big|_{\substack{x_0 \geq a \\ 0 \leq y_0 \leq b}} = x_0 - y_0 - \tfrac{1}{2}(a-b) + \frac{y_0^2}{b} \qquad (8.23)$$

For the special case when P is at the corner of the rectangle ($x_0 = a$ and $y_0 = 0$), then

$$\mathrm{E}(d')\Big|_{\substack{x_0 = a \\ y_0 = 0}} = \tfrac{1}{2}(a+b) \qquad (8.24)$$

(b)   If the fixed point P is inside the rectangle ($0 \leq x_0 \leq a$ and $0 \leq y_0 \leq b$), then the total rectangular distance is similarly found to be

$$\mathrm{E}(d')\Big|_{\substack{0 \leq x_0 \leq a \\ 0 \leq y_0 \leq b}} = \frac{x_0^2}{a} + \frac{y_0^2}{b} + \tfrac{1}{2}(a+b) - (x_0 + y_0) \qquad (8.25)$$

Examine now two special cases:

(i)   The fixed point is at the corner of the rectangle, say at $x_0 = 0$ and $y_0 = 0$. The expected rectangular distance is as in (8.24).

(ii) The fixed point is in the middle of the rectangle, i.e. $x_0 = b/2$ and $y_0 = a/2$, leading to

$$\left. E(d') \right|_{\substack{x_0 = \frac{1}{2}a \\ y_0 = \frac{1}{2}b}} = \tfrac{1}{4}(a+b) \qquad (8.26)$$

(c)   The case of two random points in a rectangular area is shown in Fig. 8.13. The expected horizontal distance between the two points is calculated as follows.

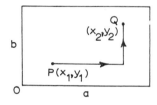

Fig. 8.13   **Rectangular distance between two random points in a rectangle**

The expected horizontal distance is obviously $a/3$ since the projections of P and Q on the x axis are uniformly distributed from 0 to a. Similarly, the expected vertical distance is $b/3$ and hence the total rectangular distance is:

$$E(d') = \tfrac{1}{3}(a+b) \qquad (8.27)$$

EXPECTED LENGTH OF A TRAVELLING SALESMAN TOUR

In this section we derive an expression for the expected length of a travelling salesman tour through a large number of points n randomly and uniformly distributed over some arbitrary area S.

The basic inequality

Consider an arbitrary region S containing the n points, and partition S into k disjoint subregions $S_1, S_2, \ldots, S_k$, so that $S = \sum_{j=1}^{k} S_j$, as shown in Fig. 8.14. The minimal length of a tour through x points distributed in some region Y will be denoted by $L(x, Y)$.

By dividing S into k disjoint subregions one can form travelling salesman tours for each individual subregion. If a link is now erased from each one of these tours and other links added to join the tours in the different subregions together, the resulting single tour has a length greater than or equal to the length of the optimal tour passing through all n points. Hence one obtains the inequality

$$L(n, S) \leqslant \sum_{j=1}^{k} \{L(n_j, S_j) + (\text{connections between subregions})\}$$

or $\quad L(n, S) \leqslant \sum_{j} \{L(n_j, S_j) + \text{dia}\,(S_j \cup S_{j+1})\}$ \hfill (8.28)

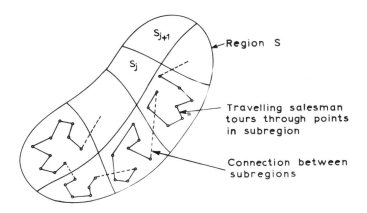

Fig. 8.14 Graphical explanation of inequality (8.28)

where n_j is the number of points in region S_j, and dia $(S_j \cup S_{j+1})$ refers to the maximum distance between any two points, one of which is in S_j and the other in S_{j+1}. The region S_{k+1} is defined to be the same as S_1.

Effect of the area S

The effect of the area S of the region on the length of the travelling salesman tour can be determined as follows. Consider an m-fold magnification of the area, which results if every point (x, y) on the periphery of the region is moved to position $(x\sqrt{m}, y\sqrt{m})$. This m-fold magnification obviously does not affect the optimal tour through the points in the region, but the length of the tour would be increased by $\sqrt{m}$ since every linear distance is increased by this factor. Hence $L(n, S)$ is proportional to the square root of S, i.e.

$$L(n, S) = Kf(n)\sqrt{S} \qquad (8.29)$$

where $f(n)$ is some function of n, and K is a constant.

The special case of a square area

Consider a square area S (of side $a = \sqrt{S}$) and divide this area into α^2 smaller squares of side-length a/α, where α^2 is a finite number. Fig. 8.15 shows such a partition into 16 smaller squares ($\alpha = 4$).

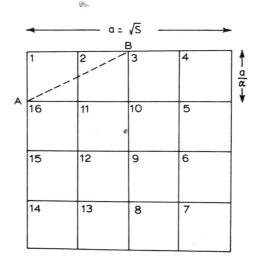

Fig. 8.15   Example of partitioning a square

If the number of points in S is n, then the number of points in each small square would (on the average) be n/α^2. Thus the length of the travelling salesman tour through the large square is, by equation (8.29),

$$L(n, S) = Kf(n)a$$

and that through each of the small squares is

$$L(n/\alpha^2, S/\alpha^2) = Kf(n/\alpha^2)\, a/\alpha \qquad (8.30)$$

If the subregions are arranged so that S_{j+1} is next to S_j as shown in Fig. 8.14, then $S_j \cup S_{j+1}$ is always a rectangle of side-lengths a/α and $2a/\alpha$. The last term, dia $(S_j \cup S_{j+1})$, in equation (8.28) is therefore the length of line AB in Fig. 8.15, which is $(a/\alpha)\sqrt{5}$.

Thus, applying inequality (8.28) to this case gives

$$L(n, S) = Kf(n)\, a \leqslant \alpha K f(n/\alpha^2)\, a + a\alpha\sqrt{5} \qquad (8.31)$$

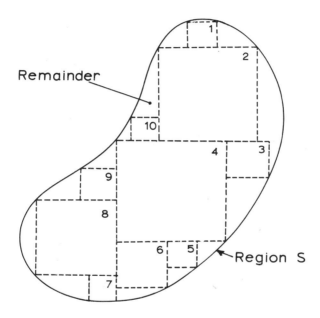

Fig. 8.16   Covering a region of area S with a finite number of square subregions

Dividing throughout by $Ka\sqrt{n}$ and rearranging, we have

$$\frac{f(n)}{\sqrt{n}} \leqslant \frac{f(n/\alpha^2)}{\sqrt{n/\alpha^2}} + \frac{\alpha\sqrt{5}}{K\sqrt{n}}$$

Taking the limit as $n \rightarrow \infty$, but leaving α^2 as a finite number, this inequality becomes

$$\lim_{\sqrt{n}\to\infty} \left(\frac{f(n)}{\sqrt{n}} \right) \leqslant \lim_{\sqrt{n/\alpha^2}\to\infty} \left(\frac{f(n/\alpha^2)}{\sqrt{n/\alpha^2}} \right) \qquad (8.32)$$

The two limits are obviously identical, and hence the equality sign applies and equation (8.32) becomes

$$f(n) = \alpha f(n/\alpha^2) \quad \text{as } n \to \infty \tag{8.33}$$

The function $f(n) = \sqrt{n}$ satisfies equation (8.33), and hence for a square area S we obtain

$$L(n, S) = K\sqrt{n}\, a \tag{8.34}$$

where the constant K is independent of a or n .

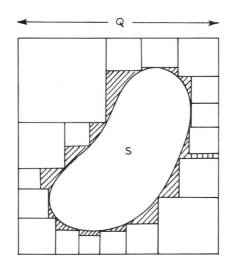

Fig. 8.17   Covering by square regions in order to obtain lower bound

The general case

We shall now show that equation (8.34) applies generally to any arbitrary area S .

(a)   *An upper bound*   Consider an area S, which is covered by a finite number of k squares, as shown in Fig. 8.16. The jth square has n_j points and its side-length is p_j. The remainder of S can be made arbitrarily small by taking a large enough k. Applying inequality (8.28) and using the result of equation (8.34), one can state that

$$L(n, S) \leqslant \sum_{j} \{K \sqrt{n_j}\, p_j + \text{dia}\,(S_j \cup S_{j+1})\} \tag{8.35}$$

If the density of points in S is denoted by ρ (where $\rho = n/S$), then the expected value of n_j will be equal to ρp_j^2. Thus, equation (8.35) becomes

$$L(n, S) \leqslant \sum_j K\sqrt{\rho}\, p_j^2 + \sum_j \text{dia}\,(S_j \cup S_{j+1}) \qquad (8.36)$$

As $n \rightarrow \infty$ the last term of equation (8.36) becomes negligible (as compared with the first), and hence (since $\sum_j p_j^2 = S$) we have

$$L(n, S) \leqslant KS\sqrt{\rho} \quad \text{as } n \rightarrow \infty \qquad (8.37)$$

(b)   *A lower bound*   Consider now the area S to be enclosed in a large enough square of side-length Q. Cover the remaining area $Q^2 - S$ by a finite number k of squares of side-lengths $q_1, q_2, \ldots$, shown in Fig. 8.17, and assume that this area is also populated with points, distributed with the same surface density ρ as the area S. Applying inequality (8.28) to the large square of side Q, and again using the results of equation (8.34), we obtain

$$L(Q^2\rho, Q^2) \leqslant \sum_j K\sqrt{\rho}\, q_j^2 + L(n, S) + \sum_j \text{dia}\,(S_j \cup S_{j+1})$$

or

$$K\sqrt{\rho}\, Q^2 \leqslant K\sqrt{\rho}\,(Q^2 - S) + L(n, S) + \sum_j \text{dia}\,(S_j \cup S_{j+1}) \qquad (8.38)$$

Again as $n \rightarrow \infty$, i.e. $(\rho \rightarrow \infty)$, the last term of equation (8.38) becomes negligible and the expression is then reduced to

$$L(n, S) \geqslant KS\sqrt{\rho} \quad \text{as } n \rightarrow \infty \qquad (8.39)$$

The upper bound given by equation (8.37) and the lower bound given by equation (8.39) coincide, and hence the equality applies; thus

$$L(n, S) = KS\sqrt{\rho}$$
$$= K\sqrt{n}\sqrt{S} \qquad (8.40)$$

This result has been verified by simulations, using the 3-optimal travelling salesman algorithm described in Chapter 7. The tour-length $L(n)$ is shown in Fig. 8.18 and 8.19, from which the value of K is obtained as 0·75. A more rigorous, but more involved, proof of equation (8.40) and its generalization to more than two dimensions are given in references [1] and [2].

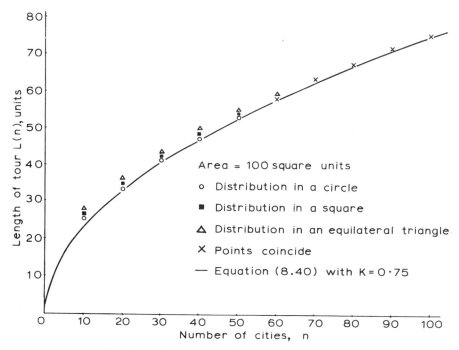

Fig. 8.18   Expected travelling salesman tour-lengths

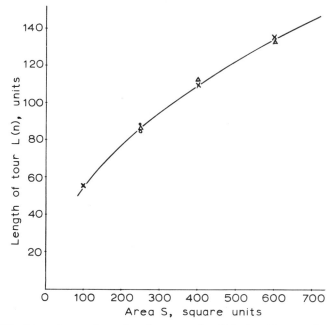

Fig. 8.19   Dependence of tour-length on area in which the cities are distributed
Legend as in Fig. 8.18; number of cities = 50

EXPECTED LENGTH OF TOUR FOR n CUSTOMERS IN A SQUARE

In many distribution problems it is useful to have estimates of the vehicle tours, when it is known that each vehicle is scheduled to supply a given number of customers. Reference to the way in which such estimates can be used in the distribution cost function has been made in Chapter 5. If we assume that n customers are to be included in the tour, and if the customers are randomly distributed in a square of known dimensions, the problem is to determine the length of the tour D_0 for a given location of the depot.

We consider the cost of a depot situated at a distance R from the centre of a square (as in Fig. 8.5, except that the case of a square instead of a rectangle is taken) and generate n customers in the square; the travelling salesman problem for this case is solved. A new set of n customers is then generated and the problem is solved again. Thus, after simulating the n-customer problem many times, the expected length of the tour can be computed.

The results are shown in Fig. 8.20 for various values of n and R. In the special case $n = 1$ the tour-length D_0 is twice the expected distance from the depot to a random point in the square, and this expected distance is also given in Table 8.1 in the row $b/a = 1$.

The approximate length of the vehicle tour D_0 for large values of n can also be derived from

$$D_0 = L(n) + 2(R - a)$$

where $L(n)$ is the expected length of the travelling salesman tour through n points, given in Fig. 8.18, and a is the side of the square.

EXPECTED LENGTH OF VEHICLE ROUTES

The measure used to represent the distance covered by a fleet of vehicles (and hence the transportation costs) is usually assumed to be either the sum D_r of the radial (straight-line) distances between the customers and the depot, or the sum of the weighted distances, the weights being taken as either the average demand of the customer over a period of time or the frequency of service that he requires.

This arbitrary definition of a measure of the transportation cost has been justified so long as we had no method that yielded the optimal vehicle routes and their total associated distance (D_0). Clarke and Wright [4] suggest an algorithm that provides near-optimal solutions for the routing problem. Using the algorithm,

Webb [6] investigates the correlation between the measure of distance, defined by D_r and the measure D_0. Webb's results are to some extent conflicting, mainly because he considers only four particular

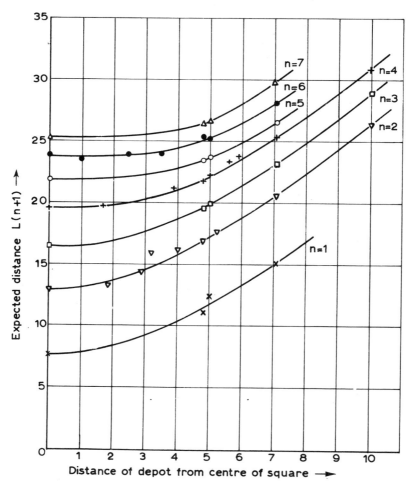

Fig. 8.20   Expected length $L(n+1)$ of a travelling salesman tour through n customers and one depot

examples, but also because he allows an important parameter ε (see below) to vary, and does not include it in the final relationship between D_0 and D_r. At least some of the variation in his results, however, is due to the fact that the Clarke and Wright algorithm sometimes departs very appreciably from the optimal solution (see Chapter 9 for further details.)

It has been noted that a critical parameter in any such correlation study is ε—the average value of the maximum number of customers that can be supplied on one route—and this parameter must be explicitly included in the equation relating D_0 with D_r. The value of ε is determined by all the constraints acting separately or together, the main constraints being the vehicle capacity and the maximum time for the duration of each route. If, for example, the capacity is the limiting constraint, and the vehicle capacity is five times the average customer demand, then $\varepsilon = 5$.

The value of ε will vary, depending on the nature of the product

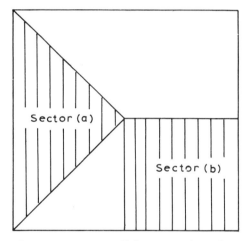

Fig. 8.21   Two extreme radial segmentations (for $m = 4$)

being distributed, e.g. for the distribution of petrol $\varepsilon = 2$ or 3, since a road tanker can only supply two or three petrol stations at a time, whereas for the distribution of, say, confectionery ε may be as much as 25. The value of ε can be readily determined by an analysis of a firm's historical data, or by simulation.

The total mileage covered by a delivery fleet to visit n' customers is made up of individual vehicle routes, which may be thought of as separate travelling salesman tours. Thus, assuming that the various routes do not intersect each other, the expected total mileage covered by the fleet is M times the expected length of one route, where M is the number of routes; and the expected length of one route is calculated by distributing $\varepsilon = n'/M$ customers in $(1/M)$th of the area. Considering the area to be a square with the depot at the centre, there are various ways in which radial segmenting of the area can be carried out, and the $(1/M)$th of the total area can be chosen to vary between the two extremes of (a) and (b) of Fig. 8.21.

However, following the results shown in Fig. 8.18, the length of the tour is not likely to be greatly affected by the shape of the segment. In fact, the length of a tour through points distributed in a sector such as (a) has been found to be only 5 per cent greater than the length of an equivalent tour in (b) in the case where $M = 4$, only 2 per cent greater in the case of $M = 8$, and even less for larger values of M. It is, therefore, sufficient to choose a "typical" sector, $(1/M)$th of the original area, in order to calculate the expected length of an individual route.

This procedure is easy to apply but, unfortunately, it produces good results only when the assumption of non-intersecting routes is valid, and this occurs only when the constraints existing in the actual distribution problem are mild. Moreover, the method is based on the assumption that the optimal vehicle routes will be in sectors as shown in Fig. 8.21, which is not always the case.

The total mileage covered by the delivery fleet in a particular problem can, instead, be calculated by using the 3-optimal algorithm for vehicle scheduling described in Chapter 9.

Experimental results

The following experiments have been performed. A square 100×100 units has been defined as the area of operations of a depot. Six sets of 10-customer, 20-customer, etc., up to 70-customer problems were generated by locating customers randomly in the square, assuming a uniform probability distribution. Each of these 42 problems was solved, using the method of Chapter 9, for values of ε of 3, 4, 7 and 10 and with the depot located first in the centre of the square (co-ordinates: 50, 50), and then at three random places. It was assumed that ε remained constant for each problem. When this method is used in a depot location problem, the value of ε may be affected through successive relocation of the depot, and this can be accounted for by recomputing the value of ε after each iteration by a new simulation.

The demands of each customer were randomly generated, assuming a normal demand distribution with a mean value of one unit.

From these experiments the following results became immediately apparent:

(i)   There is a very well defined relationship between D_0, D_r and ε.

(ii) The position of the depot does not affect the above relationship appreciably.

(iii) The standard deviation σ of the normal customer demand distribution affects the above relationship in the following way: the values of D_0 calculated by equation (8.41) below (which applies to $\sigma = 0$) must be increased by 2 per cent for $\sigma = \cdot 1$, by 4 per cent for $\sigma = \cdot 25$ and by 9 per cent for $\sigma = \cdot 5$.

The relationship between D_0, D_r and ε (with $\sigma = 0$) is given by

$$D_0 = \frac{AD_r}{\varepsilon} + B\sqrt{a}\sqrt{D_r} \qquad (8.41)$$

where A and B are constants, and a is the length of the side of the square in which the customers lie.

Multiple correlation analysis on the results of the experiments gave the numerical values of the constants as follows:

Depot location (50, 50): $A = 1\cdot 8$, $B = 1\cdot 1$;
                          correlation coefficient $= 0\cdot 997$
Depot location (81, 62): $A = 1\cdot 7$, $B = 1\cdot 05$;
                          correlation coefficient $= 0\cdot 993$
Depot location (37, 33): $A = 1\cdot 7$, $B = 1\cdot 02$;
                          correlation coefficient $= 0\cdot 990$

These results justify statements (i) and (ii) above. The standard error for the case of the depot location at the centre is 3 per cent.

Fig. 8.22 shows the relationship between D_0 and D_r graphically with ε as a parameter. It can be seen that for low values of ε the first term of equation (8.41) predominates, giving an almost linear relationship between D_0 and D_r. For any given value of D_r the second term in equation (8.41) is constant; and as ε decreases, the first term becomes relatively larger. For comparatively large values of D_r (i.e. large n') and for $\varepsilon = 1$ the first term is dominant, and if the second term were then ignored equation (8.41) would become $D_0 \approx 1\cdot 8\ D_r$ (whereas the exact relationship for this limiting case is $D_0 = 2D_r$, namely the radial distances apply). For large values of ε the second term of equation (8.41) predominates, giving the relationship

$$D_0 \approx B\sqrt{a}\sqrt{D_r} \quad \text{(for } \varepsilon \gg 1)$$

which is shown as the lowest curve in Fig. 8.22. In this limiting case all the n' customers will be supplied on a single travelling salesman tour and the expression for D_0 is equivalent to equation (8.40), with $n = n' + 1$; the extra point takes into account the depot, although for large n' the difference between n and n' may be neglected. The effect of the second term in equation (8.41) is shown by the difference between the respective ordinates of the lowest curve and any other given curve in Fig. 8.22.

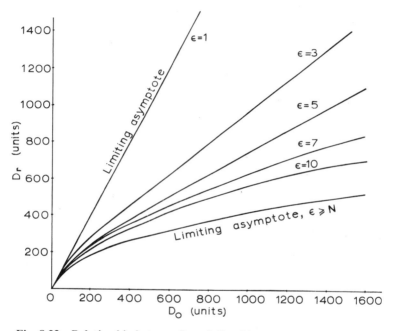

Fig. 8.22   Relationship between D_r and D_0 with ε as a parameter ($\sigma = 0$)

The value of ε used in the experiments was taken as a constant. If, instead, ε is assumed to be Poisson-distributed with a mean value $\bar{\varepsilon}$, then the expected value of D_0 is obtained from equation (8.41) as:

$$E(D_0) = A\,D_r\,E\!\left(\frac{1}{\varepsilon}\right) + B\sqrt{a}\sqrt{D_r} \tag{8.42}$$

The second term of equation (8.41) is unchanged, but in the first term $1/\bar{\varepsilon}$ is replaced by $E(1/\varepsilon)$. The values of these two factors are shown in Fig. 8.23, and it is seen that for large values of $\bar{\varepsilon}$ the first term of equation (8.42) is approximately the same as the first term of equation (8.41), but that for small values of $\bar{\varepsilon}$ the differences are appreciable.

Thus, equation (8.41) is a simple yet effective way of representing the distance that would be covered by a fleet of vehicles when supplying the customers from a depot. The quantity D_0 becomes a simple function of the radial distances D_r. Nevertheless, it can be seen from Fig. 8.21 that for reasonably small values of ε, or for large values of D_r (i.e. a very large number of customers in an area) the

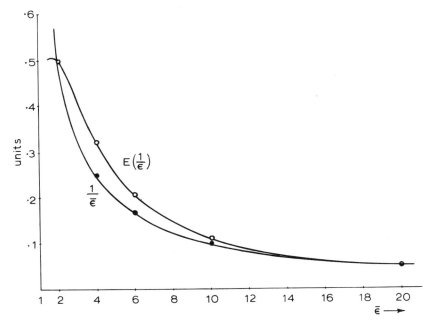

Fig. 8.23   Variation of factors $1/\bar{\varepsilon}$ and $E(1/\varepsilon)$ with Poisson variable ε

curves approximate to straight lines, and under these circumstances the depot location determined by minimizing a function of D_0 would be approximately the same as the location that would result by minimizing the same function D_r. Equation (8.41) shows that such conditions exist when

$$\frac{A D_r}{\varepsilon} \gg B \sqrt{a} \sqrt{D_r}$$

or
$$\sqrt{\frac{D_r}{a}} \gg \frac{B}{A} \varepsilon \tag{8.43}$$

With the depot approximately in the centre of the square, the expected length D_0 is given by equation (8.11) as $0 \cdot 383 \ n'a$, and hence, after substituting numerical values for the constants, condition (8.43) becomes

$$n' \gg \varepsilon^2$$

This condition is easy to check, and the more strongly it applies the more justified is the estimate of route lengths by radial distances.

REFERENCES

[1] BEARDWOOD, J., HALTON, J. H., and HAMMERSLEY, J. M., The shortest path through many points. *Proc. Camb. Phil. Soc.*, **55,** 299 (1959).

[2] CHRISTOFIDES, N., The expected length of a travelling salesman tour. Imperial College Internal Report, December 1967.

[3] CHRISTOFIDES, N., and EILON, S., Expected distances in distribution problems. *Opl. Res. Q.*, **20,** 437–43 (1969).

[4] CLARKE, G., and WRIGHT, J. W., Scheduling of vehicles from a central depot to a number of delivery points. *Ops. Res.*, **11,** 568 (1963).

[5] FAIRTHORNE, D., Distances between pairs of points in towns of simple geometrical shapes. *Second International Symposium on the Theory of Road Traffic Flow*, OECD, Paris, 1965.

[6] WEBB, M. H. J., Cost functions in the location of depots for multiple delivery journeys. *Opl. Res. Q.*, **19,** 311 (1968).

[7] WYLER, O. *Amer. Math. Monthly*, **75,** 802 (1968).

Chapter 9

Vehicle scheduling

INTRODUCTION

The problem of vehicle scheduling was originally posed by Dantzig and Ramser [4] and can be stated as follows.

A set of customers, each with a known location and a known requirement for some commodity, is to be supplied from a single depot by delivery vehicles of known capacity. The problem is to design the routes of these vehicles, subject to the following constraints:

(a) The requirements of all the customers must be met.
(b) The capacity of vehicles may not be violated, i.e. the total load allocated to each may not exceed its capacity. By "capacity" we mean a multi-dimensional quantity representing the vehicle's weight, volume, etc., capabilities.
(c) The total time (or alternatively distance) for each vehicle to complete its route may not exceed some predetermined value. (This is usually a legal or contractual condition.)
(d) There is an earliest and a latest time within which a customer can accept a delivery, and these limits must not be violated.

The objective of a solution may be stated in general terms as that of minimizing the total cost of delivery, namely the sum of costs associated with the fleet size and the cost of completing the delivery routes. Several subproblems and associated problems may be formulated:

(i) If the fleet consists of a single vehicle having a sufficiently large capacity, so that constraint (b) can be ignored, and if in addition constraints (c) and (d) are ignored, find the shortest tour to visit all customers. The problem is thus simplified to the classical travelling salesman problem discussed in Chapter 7.

(ii) If constraints (c) and (d) are ignored, find the smallest number of vehicles that would be needed. This problem of the fleet size is closely related to the classical knapsack problem and is treated in greater detail in Chapter 10.

(iii)   For a given number of vehicles compatible with the constraints, design the vehicle routes so that the total distance of the routes is minimized. This is the problem usually referred to as the vehicle-scheduling problem, and most of the past literature in the wider field of journey planning deals with this. It is this problem that we discuss in greater detail in this chapter.

(iv)   If the locations of the customers and their requirements are known for, say, every day of the week, and successive weeks are assumed to follow the same demand pattern, find (for a given truck capacity) the relative size of the company-owned delivery fleet compared with the size of the fleet that should be hired, so that the total delivery costs are minimized. This problem is treated in greater detail in Chapter 11.

Problems of journey planning are fairly common. All delivery operations of goods to or from customers involve these problems. The collection of mail from mail-boxes or the operation of school bus services are familiar examples of "deliveries" in reverse. Moreover, some problems of scheduling jobs on machines have exactly the same mathematical structure and may therefore be handled in the same way.

MATHEMATICAL FORMULATION OF THE VEHICLE SCHEDULING PROBLEM

Integer linear programming

The vehicle scheduling problem in the form stated earlier, or in a slightly different form, has been studied and formulated as a zero–one program by Balinski and Quandt [1] and by Garvin, Crandall, John and Spellman [5], but the two groups of authors give entirely different formulations.

The problem considered by Balinski and Quandt includes only constraints of type (a) and (b). They define an activity i ($i = 1, 2,...,$ m) as a potential route that a vehicle may have to operate, m being the total number of single feasible routes possible. A matrix of numbers $[\delta_{ij}]$ determines whether or not the jth customer is in activity i, depending on whether $\delta_{ij} = 1$ (in which case the customer j is included in activity i) or $\delta_{ij} = 0$ (when he is not). If the cost of each activity is known, say c_i, then their formulation becomes:

$$\text{Minimize } z = \sum_{i=1}^{m} x_i c_i \qquad (9.1)$$

where $x_i = 1$ when activity i is chosen and $x_i = 0$ when it is not,

$$\text{subject to} \quad \sum_{i=1}^{m} \delta_{ij} x_i = 1 \quad \text{for all } j = 1, 2, ..., n. \qquad (9.2)$$

Constraint (9.2) expresses the fact that one customer is supplied by one vehicle. This formulation has a number of very real limitations. First, the number of single feasible routes in a problem (and hence the number of 0–1 variables) may be a very large number indeed. If, for example, the average number of customers served by a single vehicle is h, the number of variables would be of the order of

$$m = O\left[\sum_{i=1}^{h} \binom{n}{i} \right] \qquad (9.3)$$

representing all possible groupings of n customers in ones, twos, etc.

Secondly, finding all feasible single routes is not an easy problem, if it is to be solved by enumerating all possible compositions of a single feasible route from the total number of customers. If n' is the maximum number of customers that a single vehicle can serve, then the number of route compositions that must be enumerated in order to find all the feasible single routes is given by

$$\sum_{i=1}^{n'} \binom{n}{i}$$

a number which can be very much larger (since $n' \geqslant h$) than that given by equation (9.3). Moreover, finding the cost of an activity requires the solution of a small travelling salesman problem for the customers involved in that activity.

The Garvin, Crandall, John and Spellman formulation of the problem is as follows.

Let q_k = demand of customer k;
         Q = vehicle capacity;
         c_{ij} = cost (or distance) from i to j;
         y_{ijk} = quantity shipped from i to j destined for k (suffix 0 indicates the warehouse).

One then has the following constraints:

$$\sum_{i} y_{ijk} = \sum_{r} y_{jrk} \quad \text{for all } j, k \ (j \neq k) \qquad (9.4)$$

where r is an arbitrary customer.

Constraint (9.4) expresses the fact that there is no accumulation of material at j destined for another customer k. Also,

$$\sum_i y_{ikk} = q_k \quad \text{for all } k \tag{9.5}$$

$$\sum_k \sum_j y_{0jk} = \sum_k q_k \tag{9.6}$$

Constraints (9.5) and (9.6) say, respectively, that what is accumulated at point k equals the demand of k, and what leaves the warehouse equals the total demand.

Let a variable $x_{ij} = 1$ or 0, depending on whether a vehicle visits customer j from i or not. Then,

$$\sum_i x_{ij} = \sum_r x_{jr} = 1 \quad \text{for all } j \tag{9.7}$$

i.e. only one vehicle enters and leaves j, and

$$\sum_k y_{ijk} \leqslant x_{ij} Q \quad \text{for all } i, j \, (i \neq j) \tag{9.8}$$

i.e. the capacity of the vehicles must not be violated.

The objective is then to minimize the total cost or distance travelled, i.e.

$$\text{Minimize} \quad H = \sum_i \sum_j c_{ij} x_{ij} \tag{9.9}$$

This formulation requires $n(n-1)^2$ continuous and $n(n-1)$ zero–one variables, as well as $2n^2 + 1$ constraints, and this is obviously impractical even for a problem of a dozen or so customers.

Dynamic programming

The dynamic programming formulation given for the travelling salesman problem in Chapter 7 can be readily generalized to apply to the vehicle scheduling problem as follows.

Let $C(S)$ denote the cost of the optimal route through the customers of the set S, starting and finishing at the depot. If S denotes all the customers to be supplied, then what is required is the minimum of the quantity

$$H = \sum_{j=1}^p C(S_j) \tag{9.10}$$

over all possible feasible partitions $S_j \, (j = 1, 2, \ldots, p)$ of the set S.

Let $f_k(U) = $ minimum cost achievable using k vehicles and delivering to a subset U of the set S of customers.

Then

$$f_k(U) = \min_{U^* \subset U} \left[f_{k-1}(U - U^*) + C(U^*) \right]$$

and $U \subseteq S .$ (9.11)

Equation (9.11) simply states that the best way of supplying a subset U of the customers, using k vehicles, is the cheapest of the best ways of supplying a smaller subset $U - U^*$ of customers with $k - 1$ vehicles and supplying the remaining U^* customers with another vehicle; the "cheapest" here means the least costly of all the possible ways that the U^* customers can be chosen to form the extra route.

The list of optimizing subsets U^* in equation (9.11) will be the optimum partition $S_1, S_2, \ldots, S_p$ (i.e. of the customers on routes $1, 2, \ldots, p$) which minimizes H of equation (9.10).

A comparison of the dynamic programming formulation with the 0–1 programming method of Balinski and Quandt shows great similarities. In fact, both methods require finding all feasible routes (activities or partitions) and evaluating their costs. They differ only in the method of determining which activities should be in the final solution. Thus the practical objections raised with regard to the formulation of Balinski and Quandt are equally applicable to the dynamic programming formulation of this problem.

ALGORITHMS BASED ON TRAVELLING SALESMAN SOLUTION METHODS

If the n customers and the depot of a vehicle scheduling problem are considered as a travelling salesman problem with $(n + 1)$ cities, the solution would be a tour passing through all the customers and the depot only once. In the vehicle scheduling problem, if the individual vehicle routes are combined into a single tour, this tour visits the depot as many times as there are vehicle routes. The vehicle scheduling problem may therefore be formulated as a travelling salesman problem by eliminating the real depot and replacing it by N artificial depots, all located in the same position, where N is the number of vehicles in the fleet. Travelling from one artificial depot to another is prohibited by setting the distance between any two depots to infinity, as shown in the cost matrix in Fig. 9.1, and a travelling salesman solution is now sought to this cost matrix, subject to the capacity constraints of the vehicles.

The number of artificial depots N is equal to the number of vehicles employed in the final solution, and the way it is chosen is discussed in greater detail in Chapter 10. In any case N has a lower bound determined by the vehicle capacity, namely

$$N \geqslant \sum_{i=1}^{n} q_i / Q \qquad (9.12)$$

where q_i is the demand of customer i and Q is the vehicle capacity.

The problem may now be solved for several values of N and the best solution is chosen. Usually no more than three values of N need be considered for the final solution to be obtained (starting with the lowest possible value of N, as determined by equation (9.12) and further elaborated in Chapter 10, and increasing it by one at a time).

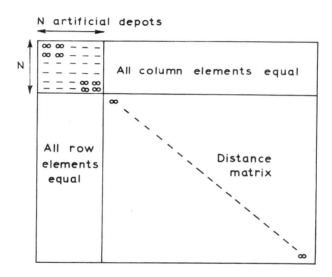

Fig. 9.1   Matrix for the vehicle scheduling algorithm

A branch-and-bound approach

A branch-and-bound algorithm for the solution of the travelling salesman problem has been described in some detail in Chapter 7, and our discussion here is restricted to the modifications that are necessary to accommodate the various constraints of the vehicle scheduling problem.

After each forward step in the tree search it is necessary to check that none of the constraints have been violated. If all the constraints set out in the introduction to this chapter exist, the order in which they are checked for feasibility is quite important, the best order depending on which constraint is most binding. If any of the constraints are violated, a backward step is taken and branching continues to a new node.

At each forward step it is important to check not only that the incoming link does not violate the constraints but also that the remaining part of the problem does not clearly become infeasible. For example, if the two links first chosen join a customer with two artificial depots, thus completing a vehicle route with only one customer served, the remaining vehicles may be incapable of supplying the remaining customers (because of insufficient capacity), but this may not be discovered until a large number of further forward branchings are made. Hence, a great deal of unnecessary tree search can be avoided if the unsolved part of the problem is checked for feasibility. This check may, of course, be very difficult to implement at each forward step, but we find that even a simple check, for example merely to ascertain at every point that the remaining vehicles have sufficient capacity to supply the remaining customers, results in a substantial saving of computing time.

Another complication which makes the branch-and-bound algorithm much less efficient in solving vehicle scheduling, compared with travelling salesman problems, is due to the heuristic rule, which determines which node to branch to next. In the travelling salesman problem we branch to the node which has the highest associated penalty (as explained in Chapter 7) and this is very successful in limiting the size of the tree that needs to be searched. In the vehicle scheduling problem, however, what seems to be a desirable link may cause a constraint to be violated and lead to further branchings. Hence, other ways of choosing the next node to branch to, and which give some consideration to the constraints of the problem, may well be more efficient than the method based on the penalties. The computational efficiency of the branch-and-bound algorithm in solving vehicle scheduling problems is shown in Table 9.2, page 194.

The *r*-optimal approach

The principle of *r*-optimality was explained in Chapter 7. Again, considering the vehicle scheduling problem as a travelling salesman problem having the cost matrix of Fig. 9.1, we can start with a random tour and generate a 2-optimal, 3-optimal or any *r*-optimal tour.

Thus, if a 3-optimal tour is to be produced from a random tour, the basic operation is to replace three links by another set of three links whose total cost is less. In the vehicle scheduling problem, however, one has to make a further check at each stage to ensure that the new set of links will not form infeasible routes. Thus, in the

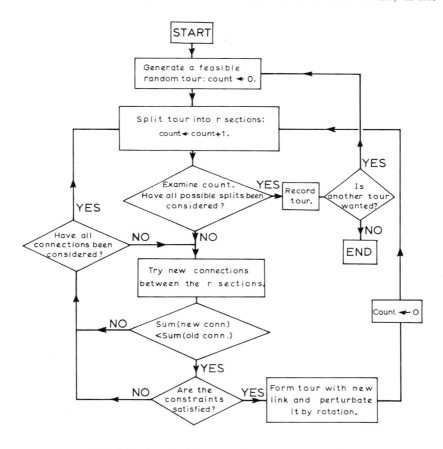

Fig. 9.2   An algorithm to produce an *r*-optimal tour

vehicle scheduling problem one would start with an initial tour which is made up of feasible routes and progressively improve it until it is 3-optimal, maintaining feasibility throughout the transformations.

The initial feasible tour may be obtained in a number of ways. One tour which is always feasible, for example, is made up of routes containing one customer each. Other feasible routes with which one can start the 3-optimal algorithm may be obtained by using any one of the approximate methods that are described later (such as Clarke and Wright's [3] savings method, the method of Hayes [7], or others).

With the cost matrix as shown in Fig. 9.1 one would (by virtue of the fact that distances between artificial depots are set to infinity, thus prohibiting any direct link between depots without intermediate customers) obtain a 3-optimal tour with the same number of vehicle routes as the initial tour. If, however, we replace the $N \times N$ top left-hand corner block of infinities in the cost matrix by one containing zeros, the same algorithm would produce a 3-optimal tour and at the same time automatically reduce the number of vehicle routes, if this leads to a saving in terms of the distance travelled. Both versions of the algorithm are useful in different circumstances, depending on the objectives. It may be worth while to mention here (this matter is discussed in further detail in Chapter 10) that the solution of the vehicle scheduling problem which minimizes the total distance travelled does not necessarily use the minimum number of vehicles required to supply the customers.

As in the travelling salesman problem, we have found that in exploring r-optimal tours, it is perfectly satisfactory to confine our considerations to 3-optimal tours, which produce very good results in a reasonable amount of computer time. In the vehicle scheduling problem, however, we found that better results can be obtained faster if from a given number of initial tours 2-optimal tours are produced first and the best ones of these are then used to produce the 3-optimal tours. Fig. 9.2 shows the procedure for determining an r-optimal tour from a random feasible initial tour.

ALGORITHMS BASED ON SAVINGS

In 1963 Clarke and Wright introduced the concept of "savings", and since then a number of methods that have been published attempt to solve the vehicle scheduling problem using techniques based on this concept.

Consider a depot which is required to supply n customers. More-over, suppose enough vehicles of sufficient capacity exist at the depot, so that each customer can be supplied individually by one vehicle that supplies that customer only. The total cost (or distance travelled) by all the vehicles is then

$$2 \sum_{j=1}^{n} c_{0j}$$

where the suffix zero represents the depot and c_{0j} is the cost of the journey from the depot to customer j. The number of vehicles used in this case is n. Now suppose two customers i and j are linked together so that they are supplied by one vehicle on one route. This linking of customers i and j eliminates one vehicle route and also reduces the cost by an amount $s_{ij} = c_{0i} + c_{0j} - c_{ij}$. The quantity s_{ij} is called the saving of link (ij) and is non-negative; obviously, the larger the saving s_{ij} the more desirable the linking of customers i and j on one route.

The algorithm of Clarke and Wright [3]

This algorithm can be described by the following procedure:

(a)   Calculate the savings s_{ij} for all pairs of customers ij.
(b)   Arrange the savings in descending order of magnitude.
(c)   Starting from the top of the list, do the following:
   (i)   If making a given link results in a feasible route according to the constraints of the problem, then add this link to the solution; if not, reject the link.
   (ii)   Try the next link in the list and repeat (i) until the list is exhausted.
(d)   The links that have been picked form the solution to the problem.

Obviously, this algorithm does not produce an optimal answer, and under certain circumstances (e.g. when the constraints of the problem are tight) the answer may differ quite appreciably from the optimum. The algorithm is very simple to apply and requires only a small amount of computer time to execute; however, some constraints are difficult to incorporate, and computer storage requirements may become excessive.

There is one main shortcoming of this algorithm that can adversely affect the quality of the answers it produces. A link once made is not removed, or indeed its desirability is considered to be independent of the other links that may be chosen, regardless of the fact that it may prohibit the future choice of many other links whose savings are only slightly less than its own, whereas another less "desirable" link may allow these other links to be picked at some future time.

The following algorithm is a slight modification of the Clarke and Wright method to partly overcome this shortcoming.

The algorithm of Tillman and Cochran [9]

This algorithm differs from the one just mentioned only in the way that the links are selected. Instead of picking the feasible link with the greatest saving at each stage, one picks that link which, when made, allows a second-best link to be made, such that the sum of the savings of the two links together is largest.

The above selection criterion, which requires looking at the effect of two choices in sequence, could be extended to looking at three or more, but the computation involved thereby would soon become quite extensive.

The method of Gaskell [6]

This method also differs from that of Clarke and Wright only in the measure of the desirability of a link. Gaskell suggests the following two alternative measures to the savings:

$$\lambda_{ij} = s_{ij}(\bar{c} + |c_{0i} - c_{0j}| - c_{ij})$$

and

$$\pi_{ij} = s_{ij} - c_{ij}$$

where $\bar{c}$ is the average value of all the c_{0i}, and s_{ij} are the savings.

These measures put a greater emphasis on the distance c_{ij} between the points i and j than on the saving s_{ij}, thereby discriminating in favour of links which are more or less radial; whereas the savings method favours links which are circumferential.

Thus, in the Clarke and Wright algorithm, instead of arranging the links in descending order based on s_{ij}, the criterion for ranking is based either on λ_{ij} or on π_{ij}; all the other steps of the algorithm remain unchanged.

A tree-search method based on the savings [8]

This method uses the savings as a criterion for branching in a decision tree-search, which at each stage gives the possibility of selecting either the best or the next-best feasible link. The method (being a tree-search) is related in principle to the branch-and-bound method described earlier, although no bounds are calculated here and no attempt is made to limit the size of the search. Instead, only a very small part of the tree is explored, and hence optimality is not guaranteed.

The method is as follows.

Consider the list of links in descending order of savings to be as follows: (i, j), (k, l), (m, n), (p, q), ... In the Clarke and Wright algorithm, link (i, j) would be selected first, then link (k, l) if feasible, then (m, n) if feasible, and so on. In the present algorithm a choice is given at the first stage to make links (i, j) or (k, l) as shown diagrammatically in Fig. 9.3. If link (i, j) is made, the next link to be made can be either (k, l) or (m, n) (provided of course that they are feasible). If, however, link (k, l) is chosen first, the next link to be

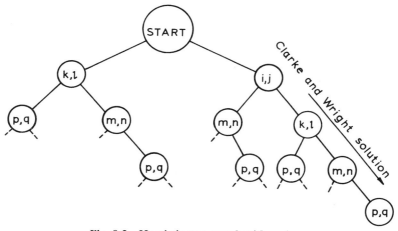

Fig. 9.3   Heuristic tree-search with savings

made may either be (m, n) or (p, q) (again provided they are feasible). This process continues until no more branchings are possible.

When the tree-search is complete, we have a number of possible routes and their costs, and the best one is selected. Note that the route represented by the right-hand chain of nodes in Fig. 9.3 is in fact the Clarke and Wright solution. The search is carried out "depth first", i.e. a branching, once made, is followed by other branchings in series forming a chain until a solution is reached, and only then are alternative branchings explored. Thus, if the search is ended prematurely, some complete tours exist, so that a solution may be chosen. One should also note that even if the whole of the tree is searched, the solution is not optimal, since only two alternatives are investigated at each stage. Three, four or more alternatives may be introduced at any one stage, but the amount of computation becomes totally impractical and much greater than that of the branch-and-bound method.

THE ALGORITHM OF HAYES [7]

This algorithm is conceptually different from all the other algorithms described earlier in that it attempts to copy the same techniques that an experienced human dispatcher uses. Most of the decisions taken by a human dispatcher are subjective in nature and hence impossible to copy exactly; however, the following procedure is suggested as a reasonable approximation.

(a)   Produce a number of outside points, i.e. points located on the periphery of the area served by the depot. The first of these points is chosen to be the customer furthest from the depot. Choose the second from the remaining customers so as to maximize the product of its distance from the depot and its distance from the first point (this would be a point diametrically opposite the first one). Successive points are also chosen so as to maximize the product of the distance to the depot and the distance to all points previously selected.

(b)   Select an outside point to start a route.

(c)   Compute a score for each unplaced point as a linear combination of the following characteristics:

    (i)   demand,

    (ii)   number of other unplaced customers in its "neighbour-hood",

    (iii)   distance from a straight line between the outside point and the depot,

    (iv)   distance from the depot,

    (v)   distance from the nearest other unplaced outside point, and

    (vi)   random element.

    For characteristics (i), (iv), (v) and (vi), the higher the magnitude of the characteristic the greater the addition to the score. The opposite holds true for characteristics (ii) and (iii).

(d)   Select the point with the highest score and allocate to the route under construction (if this is feasible).

(e)   Recompute the scores and repeat. When a route is complete choose another outside point to start a new route, and so on.

Various refinements to this procedure were suggested by Hayes, including the solution of the travelling salesman problem for each route. The method can be used to solve the problem very quickly many times with different values of the random element, and finally the best of these solutions is selected. Although the quality of the tours produced may not be as good as the other methods described earlier, the algorithm is very fast and would be particularly useful as an input device to provide feasible tours for the 3-optimal algorithm.

COMPUTATIONAL RESULTS AND CONCLUSIONS

The computational efficiency of the algorithms just described is compared by solving a number of problems. These problems are listed in Table 9.1, and details about them can be found in the Appendix to this chapter.

Table 9.1   List of problems

Problem number	Number of customers	Problem origin
1	6	Hayes [7]
2	13	Dantzig and Ramser [4]
3, 4, 5	21, 22, 29	Gaskell [6]
6	30	Clarke and Wright [3]
7	32	Gaskell [6]
8	50	Christofides and Eilon [2]
9	75	,, ,,
10	100	,, ,,

Computational experience with some algorithms is non-existent and very limited with some others. The results are shown in Table 9.2, from which it is concluded that the 3-optimal method is the best of those explored. The branch-and-bound method was tested only for problems 1 and 2 because both the computation time and memory space requirements of this method became prohibitive for the other problems. Clearly, the computational efficiency of the branch-and-bound algorithm, when applied to the vehicle scheduling problem, is substantially reduced when compared with its efficiency in solving an equivalent travelling salesman problem.

Examination of Table 9.2 shows that the 3-optimal method produces routes which are up to 10 per cent less in length than the routes

Table 9.2   Results for 10-vehicle scheduling problems

Method Problem	Distance travelled					Number of vehicles					Computation time[1] (min.)				
	A	B	C	D	E	A	B	C	D	E	A	B	C[3]	D	E[4]
1	114	119	114	—	—	2	2	2	—	—	1·5	·1	·1	—	—
2	290	290	290	—	—	4	4	4	—	—	15	·1	·1	—	—
3	—	598	585[2]	602/598	598	—	4	4	4/4	4	—	·1	·6	·2/·2	6·0
4	—	955	949	988/1015	949	—	5	5	5/6	5	—	·1	·5	·2/·2	6·0
5	—	963	875[2]	979/943	876	—	5	4	5/5	4	—	·2	·8	·2/·2	6·0
6	—	1427	1414	1434/1500	—	—	8	8	8/9	—	—	·2	·8	·2/·2	—
7	—	839	810	821/850	834	—	5	4	5/5	4	—	·2	·8	·3/·3	6·0
8	—	585	556	—	—	—	6	5	—	—	—	·6	2·0	—	—
9	—	900	876	—	—	—	10	10	—	—	—	1·3	4·0	—	—
10	—	887	863	—	—	—	8	8	—	—	—	2·5	10·0	—	—

Method: A: Branch and bound [2]
         B: The savings approach (Clarke and Wright) [3].
         C: 3-optimal method (best of 3 runs unless otherwise stated) [2]
         D: Gaskell's method (λ/π) [6].
         E: Heuristic tree search with savings [8].

[1] IBM 7090 (min.), unless otherwise stated.
[2] Best of 10 runs.
[3] Time for one run.
[4] IBM 360/30 (min.), approximate.

produced by the savings method of Clarke and Wright. Moreover, in 3 out of a total of 10 problems considered, the number of vehicles used to supply the customers was also less in the tours produced by the 3-optimal method than in the tours produced by the savings method.

It should also be noted that neither of the two methods proposed by Gaskell is consistently better than the method of Clarke and Wright, and that the heuristic tree-search technique using the savings (method E), although by its very nature it produces better results than method B, almost certainly requires a longer computation time and produces results which (at least for the problems tested) are not as good as the results of the 3-optimal method. However, as the constraints of the problem are made more and more stringent (for example, if all the constraints listed in the introduction to this chapter exist), one would expect method E to become progressively more efficient and method C progressively less efficient; hence the above conclusions on the relative merits of the two methods may not be general.

APPENDIX 9.1   DETAILS OF TEST PROBLEMS

Details of problem 1

The distance matrix is symmetrical and as shown in Table A.9.1.

Table A.9.1   Details of problem 1

	0	1	2	3	4	5	6
1	10	1					
2	20	12	2				
3	25	20	10	3			
4	25	25	11	2	4		
5	20	30	22	11	10	5	
6	10	20	30	25	20	12	6

The depot is denoted by 0. All customer demands: 1 unit. Vehicle capacity: 3 units. No distance constraint on vehicle routes.

Details of problem 2

The distance matrix is symmetrical and as shown in Table A.9.2.

Table A.9.2   Details of problem 2

	q	0	1	2	3	4	5	6	7	8	9	10	11	12
1	1200	9	1											
2	1700	14	5	2										
3	1500	21	12	7	3									
4	1400	23	22	17	10	4								
5	1700	22	21	16	21	19	5							
6	1400	25	24	23	30	28	9	6						
7	1200	32	31	26	27	25	10	7	7					
8	1900	36	35	30	37	35	16	11	10	8				
9	1800	38	37	36	43	41	22	13	16	6	9			
10	1600	42	41	36	31	29	20	17	10	6	12	10		
11	1700	50	49	44	37	31	28	25	18	14	12	8	11	
12	1100	52	51	46	39	29	30	27	20	16	20	10	10	12

The depot is denoted by 0. Column q gives customer demands. Vehicle capacity: 6000 units. No distance constraint on vehicle routes.

APPENDIX 9.1 (*cont.*)

Details of problems 3, 4 and 5

The location of customers is given by their co-ordinates. The distance matrix is calculated from the straight-line distances.

Table A.9.3   Details of problem 3

No.	x	y	q	No.	x	y	q
1	151	264	1100	12	156	217	1300
2	159	261	700	13	129	214	1300
3	130	254	800	14	146	208	300
4	128	252	1400	15	164	208	900
5	163	247	2100	16	141	206	2100
6	146	246	400	17	147	193	1000
7	161	242	800	18	164	193	900
8	142	239	100	19	129	189	2500
9	163	236	500	20	155	185	1800
10	148	232	600	21	139	182	700
11	128	231	1200				

Vehicle capacity: 6000.   Maximum route distance: 200 units.
Drop time equivalent to 10 units. Depot co-ordinates: (145, 215).

APPENDIX 9.1 (*cont.*)

Table A.9.4   Details of problem 4

No.	x	y	q	No.	x	y	q
1	295	272	125	12	267	242	300
2	301	258	84	13	259	265	250
3	309	260	60	14	315	233	500
4	217	274	500	15	329	252	150
5	218	278	300	16	318	252	100
6	282	267	175	17	329	224	250
7	242	249	350	18	267	213	120
8	230	262	150	19	275	192	600
9	249	268	1100	20	303	201	500
10	256	267	4100	21	208	217	175
11	265	257	225	22	326	181	75

Vehicle capacity: 4500. Maximum route distance: 240 units.
Drop time equivalent to 10 units. Depot co-ordinates: (266, 235).

Table A.9.5   Details of problem 5

No.	x	y	q	No.	x	y	q
1	218	382	300	16	119	357	150
2	218	358	3100	17	115	341	100
3	201	370	125	18	153	351	150
4	214	371	100	19	175	363	400
5	224	370	200	20	180	360	300
6	210	382	150	21	159	331	1500
7	104	354	150	22	188	357	100
8	126	338	450	23	152	349	300
9	119	340	300	24	215	389	500
10	129	349	100	25	212	394	800
11	126	347	950	26	188	393	300
12	125	346	125	27	207	406	100
13	116	355	150	28	184	410	150
14	126	335	150	29	207	392	1000
15	125	355	550				

Vehicle capacity: 4500. Maximum route distance: 240 units.
Drop time equivalent to 10 units. Depot co-ordinates: (162, 354).

Table A.9.6 Details of problem 6

The distance matrix is symmetrical and as shown in Table A.9.6. The depot is denoted by 0.

No.	Demand in 50-kg units (q)	0	1	2	3	4	5	6	7	8	9	10	11	12	13	14	15	16	17	18	19	20	21	22	23	24	25	26	27	28	29
0																															
1	24	41																														
2	34	38	3																													
3	11	80	54	56																												
4	15	80	54	56	3																											
5	11	97	64	67	19	16																									
6	1	92	59	62	13	10	7																								
7	3	96	56	59	16	16	11	10																							
8	29	78	39	41	54	54	53	57	48																						
9	6	98	59	62	20	17	12	13	4	39																					
10	25	87	52	50	47	46	42	8	35	45	33																				
11	6	95	58	61	15	12	8	8	4	12	6	28																			
12	25	77	38	41	30	29	34	32	25	45	21	18	26																		
13	2	93	55	53	15	12	10	14	3	24	7	15	14	14																	
14	28	91	52	53	25	25	24	19	47	47	9	36	24	6	12																
15	8	98	58	61	19	16	10	12	30	9	5	28	6	14	14	2															
16	10	96	59	62	17	14	14	8	4	36	66	41	2	4	24	65	66														
17	18	40	5	5	60	61	71	65	63	9	39	16	4	26	17	42	44	9													
18	45	73	34	37	46	46	50	46	39	31	12	18	40	28	8	28	35	22	31												
19	33	82	48	46	44	44	45	42	33	45	4	19	16	34	14	41	50	36	45	21											
20	17	55	16	19	54	44	58	55	48	22	36	18	36	8	18	36	18	45	33	35	59										
21	9	52	16	17	68	68	77	72	69	42	49	19	18	7	28	17	60	14	40	39	57	6									
22	16	76	46	46	8	9	19	15	18	40	36	19	19	24	34	16	22	36	6	44	64	5	10								
23	35	76	44	53	11	11	20	18	15	36	18	20	20	18	8	20	7	45	15	39	35	47	5	6							
24	5	72	50	53	4	4	14	14	18	9	43	16	19	18	14	20	62	35	41	50	40	34	64	47	10						
25	60	98	33	34	53	54	57	55	47	45	15	18	49	28	18	18	34	18	6	16	50	28	30	34	42	50					
26	80	98	61	61	33	30	27	30	21	6	18	19	22	34	28	46	17	19	15	44	16	44	47	34	28	35	32				
27	39	98	61	61	32	29	26	29	27	45	15	21	19	8	34	17	16	60	60	19	61	34	34	34	28	34	34	3			
28	95	93	66	68	14	12	18	20	18	71	20	54	20	7	8	16	7	14	26	44	61	79	20	15	20	15	64	39	39		
29	90	89	55	58	10	9	5	5	6	39	39	20	5	32	18	24	9	39	39	39	51	69	69	12	24	11	52	24	23	15	
30	123	68	32	33	64	64	66	57	22	55	38	34	60	47	58	60	32	26	33	21	18	66	53	60	18	51	52	76	65		

Vehicle capacity: 7 tons. No distance constraint on vehicle routes.

APPENDIX 9.1 (*cont.*)

Details of problems 7, 8, 9 and 10

The location of customers is given by their co-ordinates. The distance matrix is calculated from the straight-line distances.

Table A.9.7   Details of problem 7

No.	x	y	q	No.	x	y	q	No.	x	y	q
1	298	427	700	12	311	442	150	23	313	378	700
2	309	445	400	13	304	427	250	24	304	382	750
3	307	464	400	14	293	421	1600	25	295	402	1400
4	336	475	1200	15	296	418	450	26	283	406	4000
5	320	439	40	16	261	384	700	27	279	399	600
6	321	437	80	17	297	410	550	28	271	401	1000
7	322	437	2000	18	315	407	650	29	264	414	500
8	323	433	900	19	314	406	200	30	277	439	2500
9	324	433	600	20	321	391	400	31	290	434	1700
10	323	429	750	21	321	398	300	32	319	433	1100
11	314	435	1500	22	314	394	1300				

Vehicle capacity: 8000. Maximum route distance: 240 units.
Drop time equivalent to 10 units. Depot co-ordinates: (292, 425).

Table A.9.8   Details of problem 8

No.	x	y	q	No.	x	y	q	No.	x	y	q	No.	x	y	q
1	37	52	7	14	12	42	21	27	30	48	15	40	5	6	7
2	49	49	30	15	36	16	10	28	43	67	14	41	10	17	27
3	52	64	16	16	52	41	15	29	58	48	6	42	21	10	13
4	20	26	9	17	27	23	3	30	58	27	19	43	5	64	11
5	40	30	21	18	17	33	41	31	37	69	11	44	30	15	16
6	21	47	15	19	13	13	9	32	38	46	12	45	39	10	10
7	17	63	19	20	57	58	28	33	46	10	23	46	32	39	5
8	31	62	23	21	62	42	8	34	61	33	26	47	25	32	25
9	52	33	11	22	42	57	8	35	62	63	17	48	25	55	17
10	51	21	5	23	16	57	16	36	63	69	6	49	48	28	18
11	42	41	19	24	8	52	10	37	32	22	9	50	56	37	10
12	31	32	29	25	7	38	28	38	45	35	15				
13	5	25	23	26	27	68	7	39	59	15	14				

Depot co-ordinates: (30, 40). Customer demands (q) in 50-kg units (cwt).
Vehicle capacity: 8 tons. No distance constraint on vehicle routes.

APPENDIX 9.1 (*cont.*)

Table A.9.9 Details of problem 9

No.	x	y	q	No.	x	y	q	No.	x	y	q	No.	x	y	q
1	22	22	18	20	66	14	22	39	30	60	16	58	40	60	21
2	36	26	26	21	44	13	28	40	30	50	33	59	70	ᴧ4	24
3	21	45	11	22	26	13	12	41	12	17	15	60	64	4	13
4	45	35	30	23	11	28	6	42	15	14	1¹	61	36	6	15
5	55	20	21	24	7	43	27	43	16	19	18	62	30	20	18
6	33	34	19	25	17	64	14	44	21	48	17	63	20	30	11
7	50	50	15	26	41	46	18	45	50	30	21	64	15	5	28
8	55	45	16	27	55	34	17	46	51	42	27	65	50	70	9
9	26	59	29	28	35	16	29	47	50	15	19	66	57	72	37
10	40	66	26	29	52	26	13	48	48	21	20	67	45	42	30
11	55	65	37	30	43	26	22	49	12	38	5	68	38	33	10
12	35	51	16	31	31	76	25	50	15	56	22	69	50	4	8
13	62	35	12	32	22	53	28	51	29	39	12	70	66	8	11
14	62	57	31	33	26	29	27	52	54	38	19	71	59	5	3
15	62	ᴧ4	8	34	50	40	19	53	55	57	22	72	35	60	1
16	21	36	19	35	55	50	10	54	67	41	16	73	27	24	6
17	33	44	20	36	54	10	12	55	10	70	7	74	40	20	10
18	9	56	13	37	60	15	14	56	6	25	26	75	40	37	20
19	62	48	15	38	47	66	24	57	65	27	14				

Depot co-ordinates: (40, 40). Customer demands (q) in 50-kg units (cwt). Vehicle capacity: 7 tons. No distance constraint on vehicle routes.

APPENDIX 9.1 (*concluded*)

Table A.9.10   Details of problem 10

No.	x	y	q	No.	x	y	q	No.	x	y	q	No.	x	y	q
1	41	49	10	26	45	30	17	51	49	58	10	76	49	42	13
2	35	17	7	27	35	40	16	52	27	43	9	77	53	43	14
3	55	45	13	28	41	37	16	53	37	31	14	78	61	52	3
4	55	20	19	29	64	42	9	54	57	29	18	79	57	48	23
5	15	30	26	30	40	60	21	55	63	23	2	80	56	37	6
6	25	30	3	31	31	52	27	56	53	12	6	81	55	54	26
7	20	50	5	32	35	69	23	57	32	12	7	82	15	47	16
8	10	43	9	33	53	52	11	58	36	26	18	83	14	37	11
9	55	60	16	34	65	55	14	59	21	24	28	84	11	31	7
10	30	60	16	35	63	65	8	60	17	34	3	85	16	22	41
11	20	65	12	36	2	60	5	61	12	24	13	86	4	18	35
12	50	35	19	37	20	20	8	62	24	58	19	87	28	18	26
13	30	25	23	38	5	5	16	63	27	69	10	88	26	52	9
14	15	10	20	39	60	12	31	64	15	77	9	89	26	35	15
15	30	5	8	40	40	25	9	65	62	77	20	90	31	67	3
16	10	20	19	41	42	7	5	66	49	73	25	91	15	19	1
17	5	30	2	42	24	12	5	67	67	5	25	92	22	22	2
18	20	40	12	43	23	3	7	68	56	39	36	93	18	24	22
19	15	60	17	44	11	14	18	69	37	47	6	94	26	27	27
20	45	65	9	45	6	38	16	70	37	56	5	95	25	24	-20
21	45	20	11	46	2	48	1	71	57	68	15	96	22	27	11
22	45	10	18	47	8	56	27	72	47	16	25	97	25	21	12
23	55	5	29	48	13	52	36	73	44	17	9	98	19	21	10
24	65	35	3	49	6	68	30	74	46	13	8	99	20	26	9
25	65	20	6	50	47	47	13	75	49	11	18	100	18	18	17

Depot co-ordinates: (35, 35). Customer demands (*q*) in 50-kg units (cwt).
Vehicle capacity: 10 tons. No distance constraints on vehicle routes.

REFERENCES

[1] BALINSKI, M. L. and QUANDT, R. E., On an integer program for a delivery problem. *Ops. Res.*, **12**, 300 (1964).

[2] CHRISTOFIDES, N., and EILON, S., An algorithm for the vehicle dispatching problem. *Opl. Res. Q.*, **20**, 309 (1969).

[3] CLARKE, G. and WRIGHT, J. W., Scheduling of vehicles from a central depot to a number of delivery points. *Ops. Res.*, **11**, 568 (1963).

[4] DANTZIG, G. B., and RAMSER, J. H., The truck dispatching problem. *Mgmt. Sci.*, **6**, 80 (1959).

[5] GARVIN, W. W., CRANDALL, H. W., JOHN, J. B., and SPELLMAN, R. A., Applications of linear programming in the oil industry. *Mgmt. Sci.*, **3**, 407 (1957).

[6] GASKELL, T. J., Bases for vehicle fleet scheduling. *Opl. Res. Q.*, **18**, 281 (1967).

[7] HAYES, R. L., The delivery problem. Carnegie Institute of Technology, Graduate School of Industrial Administration, Pittsburg, Report No. MSR 106, 1967.

[8] KNOWLES, K., The use of a heuristic tree-search algorithm for vehicle routing and scheduling. *Operational Research Conference,* Exeter, England, 1967.

[9] TILLMAN, F. A. and COCHRAN, H., A heuristic approach for solving the delivery problem. *J. Ind. Engineering*, **19**, 354 (1968).

Chapter 10

Vehicle loading

INTRODUCTION

In Chapter 9 we were concerned with vehicle scheduling, namely with the problem of minimizing the total distance travelled to supply an array of customers in given locations. In this chapter we concentrate on the problem of vehicle loading, where an array of consignments has to be accommodated in vehicles of known size, and the problem is to minimize the number of vehicles required for the purpose.

Vehicle scheduling and vehicle loading are subproblems in the wider context of minimizing the total cost of distribution. A solution derived for the vehicle scheduling problem need not be compatible with the solution to the corresponding vehicle loading problem. Nevertheless, the two subproblems play a part in formulating methods for solving the total distribution problem, and there are many circumstances in which each of the subproblems becomes dominant and requires a solution of its own.

The vehicle loading problem is, in fact, a member of a larger class of general problems called the *loading problem*, which is concerned with loading or accommodating items in boxes. The "box" may be a vehicle, a ship, a warehouse, or indeed any container to which items of given capacities are to be assigned. The loading problem covers many problems which do not involve any physical loading operations, for example in cutting stock (such as in shearing bars from longer bars [3], or in cutting rectangles from larger rectangular sheets [6, 7]), or in assigning jobs of given duration to shifts (when jobs cannot be carried forward from shift to shift).

Let us now turn to the discussion of the loading problem.

THE LOADING PROBLEM

A particular type of loading problem, which is akin to the knapsack problem, may be formulated as follows. Allocate n objects or items of given magnitude $q_i (i = 1, 2, \ldots, n)$ to boxes, each box having a capacity Q, in such a way that the capacity constraints are not violated and the number of boxes required is a minimum. An assumption is made that the capacity requirements are additive, so that the capacity needed to accommodate two items of magnitude q_1 and q_2 is $q_1 + q_2$, as is the case when q_i and Q are measured in units of weight, length, money, or liquid volume.

This is only one of several types of loading problems. More generally, if an array of magnitude q_i is specified, where the value of item i is given by u_i $(i = 1, 2, \ldots, n)$, and if an array of boxes of capacity Q_j and their corresponding values v_j $(j = 1, 2, \ldots, N)$ are given, then two situations can arise (denoted as S_1 and S_2):

$S_1 : \sum_j Q_j \geqslant \sum_i q_i$ and all the items can be accommodated in the

array of boxes;

$S_2 :$ either $\sum_j Q_j \geqslant \sum_i q_i$ but not all items can be accommodated,

or $\sum_j Q_j < \sum_i q_i$.

Several objectives can be stated for the allocation of items to boxes, as suggested below (the objectives are denoted as O_1, O_2 and O_3):

O_1 : *objective based on boxes*

    (a)   Minimize the number (or value) of boxes required.
    (b)   Minimize the unused space (or its value) of the partially used boxes.

O_2 : *objective based on items*

    Minimize the number (or value) of items not accommodated in the boxes.

O_3 : *combined objective*

    Minimize the combined (weighted) value of boxes chosen and value of items not accommodated.

These situations and criteria define the following problem matrix.

	O_1	O_2	O_3
S_1	1	—	—
S_2	2	3	4

Problem 1 is a more general formulation of the problem described at the beginning of this chapter. In situation S_1, where the array of boxes has adequate capacity to accommodate all the given items, objectives O_2 and O_3 are irrelevant. Problem 2 is an extension of problem 1, except that O_1(b) becomes the relevant objective. Problem 3 is the classical multi-dimensional knapsack problem, except that there are several boxes rather than a single one. This problem can be solved by methods somewhat similar to those suggested by Gilmore and Gomory [8, 9] for problems of cutting stock. The methods of Gilmore and Gomory, which are based on dynamic programming, can also be employed to solve problem 3 in two (or more) physical dimensions, where the two dimensions are inter-related, such as in the problem of "packing" several small rectangles into a larger rectangle. It should be pointed out that the two physical dimensions problem does not strictly belong to this matrix of problems, because the additivity conditions for q_i mentioned earlier do not apply, for example in the problem of cutting rectangles. Problem 4 involves an objective O_3 which is based on a combination of objectives O_1 and O_2.

This chapter is concerned with a particular case of problem 1, where all the Q_j have the same value, say, Q. Two methods of solution are examined, and their efficiency is compared: the first method makes use of zero–one programming and the second uses a heuristic algorithm.

The methods are also tested against a problem which is more general than problem 1, in that each item is characterized not by a single magnitude q_i, but by several magnitudes $q_i(1), q_i(2), \ldots$, each representing a particular attribute, for example weight, liquid volume, money value, etc. Similarly, the boxes have corresponding capacities Q_1, Q_2, etc.

The models described in this chapter have applications in solving problems of loading vehicles (or other containers) with consignments that cannot be split, or in solving some apportioning problems where large units need to be subdivided into several smaller units of given or constrained magnitude.

In Appendix 10.1 it is also shown that the zero–one programming method can also solve the general problem 1 with boxes of differing capacities. In fact, this programming approach can be used to solve all the problems listed in the problem matrix, although this is not discussed further here.

METHOD I: THE ZERO–ONE PROGRAMMING METHOD

Let $[x_{ij}]$ denote the allocation matrix of items to boxes, so that $x_{ij} = 1$ if item i is allocated to box j $(j = 1, 2, \ldots, N)$, otherwise $x_{ij} = 0$. The total capacity taken up by all the items in box j must not exceed the capacity of the box, and this constraint is expressed for each box by

$$\sum_{i=1}^{n} q_i x_{ij} \leqslant Q \qquad (10.1)$$

where

$$Q \geqslant q_i > 0 \qquad (10.2)$$

Each item can be allocated to one box only; hence

$$\sum_{j=1}^{N} x_{ij} = 1 \quad (x_{ij} = 1 \text{ or } 0) \qquad (10.3)$$

A penalty V_j is assigned to the allocation of items to box j, and this penalty increases with j so that

$$V_{j+1} \gg V_j > 0 \qquad (10.4)$$

The total penalty function when the allocation is completed is then

$$z = \sum_{j=1}^{N} \left(V_j \sum_{i=1}^{n} x_{ij} \right) \qquad (10.5)$$

and provided V_{j+1} is sufficiently greater than V_j, the minimization of the penalty function z will ensure that the smallest number of boxes is used in the allocation process. If the largest number of items that can be loaded into a box cannot exceed p, then the penalty values in equation (10.5) can be chosen as

$$V_{j+1} > pV_j \quad \text{and} \quad V_1 = 1 \qquad (10.6)$$

The objective function to be minimized is then given in equation (10.5), subject to the conditions in expressions (10.3) and (10.6) and subject to the capacity constraints in expression (10.1). There may be additional constraints that have to be incorporated; for example, if item i_1 cannot be allocated to box j_1 this may be expressed as

$$x_{i_1 j_1} = 0 \qquad (10.7)$$

or if two items i_1 and i_2 must not be allocated to the same box then, for all j,

$$x_{i_1 j} + x_{i_2 j} \leqslant 1 \qquad (10.8)$$

The tree-search algorithm of Balas [1] can be reformulated for the solution of the loading problem, and the method suggested by Glover [10], which is found to reduce the required computer storage, can also be incorporated.

A flow diagram of the program for solving the loading problem is given in Fig. 10.1 and some explanations are given below.

An initial upper bound $\bar{z}$ is determined, either by inspection or by using the heuristic algorithm which is referred to later, and whenever a better solution is obtained, it replaces the upper bound.

Of the nN variables x_{ij} a set S is formed, consisting of k variables, to each of which the value of 0 or 1 is assigned, the other $nN - k$ variables remaining "free". Thus, the set S defines a subproblem involving $nN - k$ free variables. This subproblem is resolved either when the best values for the free variables are determined (and these values together with those in set S then form a feasible solution that minimizes z), or when no feasible solution is obtainable. In the former case, the solution is denoted by the vector $\mathbf{X}$ and is recorded for future reference. In either case, k is reduced and the computation procedure is then repeated.

When a solution $\mathbf{X}$ is not feasible, a subset T is defined. This subset consists of all the "free" variables representing nodes in the decision tree that are permissible (i.e. that will not violate the capacity constraints and the upper bound $\bar{z}$). One member of T is then transferred to S, thereby defining a new subproblem. One way to exclude whole sections of the tree at this point (sections that lead to infeasible solutions) is to resort to an LP formulation of the subproblem, allowing the variables to assume any value between 0 and 1. If the solution to this LP problem exceeds the upper bound $\bar{z}$, or if there is no solution that conforms with all the constraints of the problem, then further search of the branch may be abandoned. When T is empty, no further subproblems in the branch under consideration are possible. Various other suggestions [2, 5] that increase the efficiency of the algorithm outlined in Fig. 10.1 were used in the actual program.

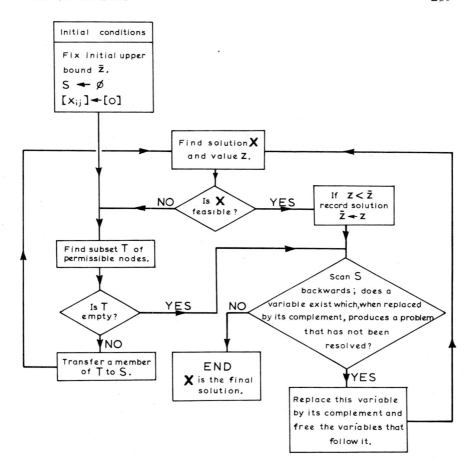

Fig. 10.1   Outline of the solution to the zero–one model

METHOD II: A HEURISTIC ALGORITHM

The heuristic algorithm for the loading · problem [4] involves comparatively little computation and yields a feasible solution N for the required number of boxes. A lower bound N_0 for N is then found from

$$\sum_{i=1}^{n} q_i / Q \leqslant N_0 < \sum_{i=1}^{n} q_i / Q + 1 \qquad (10.9)$$

N_0 being the smallest possible number of boxes dictated by the total capacity requirements of the n items. If the solution $N = N_0$ then N is optimal. If, however,

$$N > N_0 \tag{10.10}$$

then the solution N may not be optimal and a reshuffle routine is resorted to, which allows for the allocation to depart from the algorithm at one point in the procedure. Unlike the zero–one model, this algorithm does not ensure that the optimal solution is always obtained.

The procedure is as follows:

(1) Make two lists: one for boxes in ascending order of the available space in each, the other for items in descending order of magnitude.
(2) Scan the list of items to see if any single item will precisely fill the first box in the list of boxes; if so, transfer the item to the box and remove both the item and the box from their respective lists.
(3) Repeat (2) for each box in turn.
(4) Rearrange the list of boxes, if necessary, to have them in ascending order of available space.
(5) Take the first item in the list of items and allocate it to the first box that will accommodate it.
(6) Repeat (2) for the box that has been loaded by step (5).
(7) Repeat (4).
(8) Repeat (5), (6) and (7) until one of the two lists is exhausted; if the list of items is exhausted first, then the total number of boxes required is given by the fully and partially loaded boxes used by this procedure; but if the list of boxes is exhausted first, the remaining items are those that cannot be accommodated in the limited number of boxes available.

In a large number of cases it was found that the algorithm's efficient performance was not impaired when steps (2), (3) and (6) were eliminated from the procedure. The algorithm has been tested for many numerical examples, and several cases are cited below to illustrate its application.

A reshuffle routine

When the heuristic algorithm yields a solution such that $N > N_0$ then it is possible that the solution is not optimal. Under these circumstances, the following reshuffle routine may be employed:

(1) Start with the two lists and perform the first four steps outlined in the algorithm.
(2) Continue with the algorithm as before up to the point when a box is to be loaded with its second item.
(3) Instead of allocating the item to this box, reallocate it to the next available box (or the next but one, etc.).
(4) Continue allocating the items to boxes according to the algorithm, until the list of items is exhausted.
(5) Find the value of N. If now $N = N_0$, the new solution is optimal, but if $N > N_0$ then the reshuffle routine may be repeated for other alternatives in step (2).

The "reshuffling" of items in the boxes occurs at the point of departure from the algorithm, since at this point the new allocation of an item does not conform to step (5) in the algorithm. However, except for this single point of departure, the algorithm is adhered to.

During the loading process there may clearly be several alternative points of departure from the algorithm. Step (2) in the routine identifies a point at which one box in the list of boxes is to be loaded with its second item. Other possible alternatives for departure from the algorithm are:

– the point at which a second box in the list is to be loaded with its second item, or
– the point at which a box is to be loaded with its third item,

or in general: the point at which the first (or second, third, etc.) box is to be loaded with its second (or third, fourth, etc.) item. This simply means that the point of departure may be at any point on the list of items, so that the reshuffle procedure may be examined for up to $n-2$ alternative points of departure (since there are n items, but no meaningful departure from the algorithm can occur when the allocation of the first or the last item is considered); in practice the number of different alternatives is often much smaller.

The results of a large number of numerical examples suggest that the routine is effective in improving on the initial solution of the algorithm, when that solution involves $N > N_0$. Furthermore, when an optimal solution $N = N_0$ exists, the routine is generally effective in producing that solution with a comparatively small number of alternative departure points considered by the routine. It is, of course, possible that a solution $N = N_0$ exists, but that the routine fails to produce it. A more elaborate routine may then be pursued involving more than one departure point, and the iterations repeated for all possible combinations of departure points. In practice, however, the performance of the algorithm, coupled with the reshuffle routine having a single departure point, is very effective in yielding optimal solutions, so that further computations with multi-departure points may be rarely justified.

EXAMPLES TO ILLUSTRATE THE HEURISTIC LOADING ALGORITHM

Example 10.1

Items (listed in descending order of magnitude): 68, 65, 40, 39, 32, 30.

Capacity per box, $Q = 100$.

Solution: Box 1: $68 + 32 = 100$
  2:   $65 + 30 = 95$
  3:   $40 + 39 = 79$

Test: $\Sigma q_i / Q = 274/100 = 2 \cdot 74$ or $N_0 = 3$.

The solution $N = 3 = N_0$, hence this is an optimal solution.

Example 10.2

Fifty random numbers are taken to represent the magnitude of items and then arranged in descending order:

99, 99, 97, 95, 94, 90, 88, 88, 86, 75,
75, 75, 73, 73, 73, 71, 71, 68, 66, 64,
61, 60, 55, 55, 54, 53, 50, 49, 47, 45,
44, 42, 39, 39, 38, 37, 36, 35, 32, 28,
28, 23, 21, 18, 16, 12, 11, 8, 5, 3.

Capacity per box, $Q = 300$.

Solution:

Box 1: $99 + 99 + 97 + 5 = 300$
  2:   $95 + 94 + 90 + 21 = 300$
  3:   $88 + 88 + 86 + 38 = 300$
  4:   $75 + 75 + 75 + 73 = 298$
  5:   $73 + 73 + 71 + 71 + 12 = 300$
  6:   $68 + 66 + 64 + 61 + 39 = 298$
  7:   $60 + 55 + 55 + 54 + 53 + 23 = 300$
  8:   $50 + 49 + 47 + 45 + 44 + 42 + 18 + 3 = 298$
  9:   $39 + 37 + 36 + 35 + 32 + 28 + 28 + 16 + 11 + 8 = 270$

Test: $\Sigma q_i / Q = 2664/300 = 8 \cdot 9$ or $N_0 = 9$.

As $N = N_0$, this solution is optimal.

Example 10.3

Items: 60, 50, 30, 20, 20, 20.
Capacity per box, $Q = 100$.
Solution: Box 1: $60 + 30 = 90$
            2:   $50 + 20 + 20 = 90$
            3:   20

Test: $\Sigma\, q_i/Q = 200/100 = 2 = N_0$.

As $N > N_0$, this solution may not be optimal. However, when the reshuffle routine is employed, the optimal solution is obtained as follows:

Steps 1 and 2 of the algorithm result in loading the first two items to two boxes respectively, and the point of departure is then defined as that of allocating the third item. According to the algorithm, this item should be allocated to box 1 (which contains item 1); instead, the item is now allocated to box 2, so that the position after performing step 3 of the routine is:

Box 1:   60
Box 2: $50 + 30$.

Proceeding with the algorithm, the final result is

Box 1: $60 + 20 + 20 = 100$
Box 2: $50 + 30 + 20 = 100$

and now $N = 2$, which is optimal.

Example 10.4

Items: 59, 26, 15, 35, 10, 77, 22, 14, 27, 68, 17, 45, 5, 21, 94,
           19, 24, 30, 40, 46.
Capacity per box, $Q = 100$.

The heuristic method, with or without the reshuffle routine, yields the solution $N = 8$, whereas the zero–one algorithm gives $N = 7$.

MULTI-DIMENSIONAL CONSTRAINTS

The constraints in expressions (10.1) and (10.2) refer to constraints in a single dimension. In practice, problems have to be solved involving constraints in more than one dimension, for example when items have an array of values $q_i(1)$ to denote weight, an array $q_i(2)$ to denote money values, etc. In general, each item may be specified by r values, each relating to one particular dimension, and similarly each box will have r "capacity" constraints, and expressions (10.1) and (10.2) must each be repeated r times. The objective function in equation (10.5) and the conditions (10.3) and (10.6) remain unchanged.

The zero–one programming method can easily cope with the multi-dimensional problem and requires no modifications. The heuristic algorithm can be extended in several ways to handle this problem, and the following two methods are noteworthy:

(i) Consider each dimension separately and solve the problem by ordering the items in relation to that dimension, each time checking for feasibility in relation to the other dimensions. r solutions are obtained and the one with the smallest number of boxes is then selected.

(ii) Define a new "equivalent" dimension by a weighting procedure, for example by

$$q_i = \sum_{k=1}^{r} q_i(k)/Q(k) \quad \text{where } k = 1, 2, \ldots, r,$$

and then proceeding with the algorithm as if the problem were one-dimensional.

Method (ii) was found to be generally more efficient than (i).

Two-stage loading

Two-stage loading occurs when "boxes" have to be accommodated in larger boxes. The problem then becomes that of loading items into boxes and then boxes into super-boxes, and the zero–one programming method in Appendix 10.1 can readily be extended to formulate the two-stage loading problem with the object of minimizing the total weighted value.

COMPUTATIONAL RESULTS AND CONCLUSIONS FOR SINGLE-STAGE LOADING

Fifty one-dimensional problems with up to 50 items were solved by the zero–one programming method and by the heuristic algorithm. The capacity of the boxes was taken as $Q = 100$ and the magnitude of the items was randomly generated. In all these problems the only constraints (in addition to the conditions (10.2), (10.3) and (10.6) were of the box capacity type, as expressed in equation (10.1); constraints of the type described in (10.7) and (10.8) were not considered. A comparison between the results of the two methods is summarized in Table 10.1.

In every case Method I (the zero–one programming model) took longer to produce the result than Method II (the heuristic algorithm), and as the program compilation time (on an IBM 7094) in either case was about 0·5 min., the difference in net computing time was often quite appreciable.

In almost 90 per cent of the cases (44 problems out of 50) Method II yielded the optimal solution without resorting to the reshuffle routine. For the remaining six problems, Method II was effective in yielding optimal solutions in four cases by the use of the reshuffle routine, leaving only two problems out of fifty for which it failed to produce the optimum; it did, however, produce the next-best solution.

Some measure of the difficulty in devising optimal solutions to combinatorial problems, such as the loading-boxes problem, may be obtained by considering the success of random solutions. In the context of the loading problem a random solution is obtained by allocating item i in a random fashion to box j, and if the box j cannot accommodate item i because of the capacity constraints, another box is tried at random. After the list of items is exhausted, a feasible solution is obtained, and from several such solutions the best can then be selected. Random solutions were tried for the fifty problems referred to in Table 10.1, and the results are summarized in Table 10.2. Clearly, some of the randomly generated problems had a great deal of slack and must have been easy to solve, if some 60 per cent of the problems could be solved optimally by no more than three random trials. The difficult problems are represented in the lower part of Table 10.2, where the random method of solution became increasingly ineffective.

Twelve additional problems with multi-dimensions were also solved and the results are shown in Table 10.3. Of the five problems for which Method II(a) did not yield the optimum, one was solved optimally by using the reshuffle routine.

Clearly, the algorithm in Method II is not as effective in solving multi-dimensional problems as it is in handling one-dimensional ones, but even when it did not produce the optimal solution the next-best solution was obtained.

Table 10.1   Comparison of results for two methods of solution for one-dimensional problems

Problem	Number of items, n	Solution N for number of boxes			Computing time		
		Method I	Method II II(a)	II(b)	Method I	Method II II(a)	II(b)
1	10	5	5	—	1·3	·6	—
2	10	4	4	—	1·9	·6	—
3	10	4	4	—	2·5	·6	—
4	10	6	6	—	2·5	·6	—
5	10	4	4	—	1·4	·6	—
6	10	5	6	5	1·5	·6	·8
7	10	5	5	—	1·1	·6	—
8	10	6	6	—	1·9	·6	—
9	15	4	4	—	1·7	·6	—
10	15	3	3	—	1·2	·6	—
11	15	5	5	—	2·4	·6	—
12	15	5	5	—	2·0	·6	—
13	15	5	6	5	2·1	·6	·9
14	15	6	6	—	2·9	·6	—
15	15	3	3	—	1·5	·6	—
16	15	4	4	—	1·8	·6	—
17	20	6	6	—	3·0	·7	—
18	20	6	6	—	5·0	·7	—
19	20	5	5	—	3·1	·7	—
20	20	5	5	—	2·8	·7	—
21	20	6	6	—	4·6	·7	—
22	20	7	7	—	6·1	·7	—
23	20	6	6	—	4·3	·7	—
24	20	7	8	8	6·0	·7	1·0
25	25	5	5	—	3·9	·7	—
26	25	6	6	—	5·5	·7	—
27	25	5	5	—	5·1	·7	—
28	25	6	6	—	6·6	·7	—
29	25	7	7	—	9·0	·7	—
30	25	6	6	—	5·3	·7	—
31	30	5	5	—	4·2	·7	—
32	30	5	5	—	4·8	·7	—
33	30	4	4	—	3·7	·7	—
34	30	6	6	—	8·8	·7	—
35	30	7	8	8	13·2	·7	1·2
36	35	4	4	—	6·0	·7	—
37	35	4	4	—	7·1	·7	—
38	35	3	3	—	4·3	·7	—
39	35	3	3	—	4·1	·7	—
40	35	4	4	—	5·9	·8	—
41	40	3	3	—	6·2	·8	—
42	40	4	4	—	8·1	·8	—
43	40	3	3	—	5·3	·8	—
44	40	4	4	—	7·2	·8	—
45	40	4	5	4	6·6	·8	1·0
46	50	3	3	—	5·9	·8	—
47	50	3	3	—	6·1	·8	—
48	50	3	3	—	7·8	·8	—
49	50	3	3	—	5·0	·8	—
50	50	3	4	3	4·1	·8	1·0

Method I: The zero–one programming method
Method II: The heuristic algorithm [10]
  II(a):   Method II without the reshuffle routine
  II(b):   Method II including the reshuffle routine

The computing time refers to the time (in min.) required on an IBM 7094, including about 0·5 min. of program compilation time.

Table 10.2   Random solutions to 50 one-dimensional problems

Number of trials	Number of problems for which optimal solution was obtained
1	24
2	27
3	30
4	30
5	31
10	36
15	39
20	40
25	41
40	42
70	44
100	45

Table 10.3   Multi-dimensional problems

Problem	Number of items n	Number of dimensions	Solution N for number of boxes			Computing time		
			Method I	Method II II(a)	II(b)	Method I	Method II II(a)	II(b)
1	10	2	4	4	—	1·5	·6	—
2	10	4	3	3	—	1·5	·6	—
3	10	6	5	6	6	1·6	·7	1·0
4	20	2	6	6	—	2·9	·7	—
5	20	4	5	5	—	2·9	·8	—
6	20	6	6	7	7	3·0	·9	1·1
7	30	2	5	5	—	8·2	·7	—
8	30	4	6	7	7	8·1	·8	1·2
9	30	6	5	6	6	4·4	1·0	1·4
10	40	2	4	4	—	7·3	·8	—
11	40	4	4	4	—	7·0	·9	—
12	40	6	4	5	4	5·8	1·0	1·6

APPENDIX 10.1 LOADING BOXES OF DIFFERENT CAPACITIES

A large number of boxes N is given, and what is required is the minimum number of boxes that can hold all the n items, namely the attainment of objective $O_1(a)$.

Let $[x_{ij}]$ be the allocation matrix as defined previously;

> $y_j = 1$ if box j is loaded with any one object:
> $\quad = 0$ if box j is completely empty;
> $L =$ any large number greater than n.

The problem, then, can be formulated as follows:

Minimize
$$z = \sum_{j=1}^{N} y_j \tag{A.10.1}$$

subject to
$$\sum_j x_{ij} = 1 \qquad \text{(for all } i = 1, 2, \ldots, n) \tag{A.10.2}$$

$$\sum_i x_{ij} q_i \leqslant Q_j \quad \text{(for all } j = 1, 2, \ldots, N) \tag{A.10.3}$$

$$\sum_i x_{ij} \leqslant L y_j \quad \text{(for all } j = 1, 2, \ldots, N) \tag{A.10.4}$$

Constraint (A.10.4) simply ensures that no items are accommodated in a box whose $y_j = 0$.

Thus the case of dissimilar boxes requires the introduction of the variables y_j because the boxes cannot be penalized as in the case of boxes of equal capacity. Moreover, N must now be the total number of boxes, all of which will have to be considered, whereas previously an upper bound on the number of boxes was sufficient.

It is possible, of course, to formulate the problem with boxes of equal size as a special case of the problem discussed in this Appendix, but the number of variables will then be greater (because of the introduction of the y_j's) and the problem will take longer to solve.

The loading problem for objective $O_1(b)$ can be treated in a similar manner.

REFERENCES

[1] BALAS, E., An additive algorithm for solving linear programs with zero–one variables. *Ops. Res.*, **13**, 517–46 (1965).
[2] BALAS, E., Discrete programming by the filter method. *Ops. Res.*, **15**, 915–57 (1967).
[3] EILON, S., Optimizing the shearing of steel bars. *J. Mech. Eng. Sci.*, **2**, 129–42 (1960).
[4] EILON, S. and CHRISTOFIDES, N., The loading problem. Imperial College Report, 1968.
[5] FLEISCHMANN, B., Computational experience with the algorithm of Balas. *Ops. Res.*, **15**, 153–4 (1967).
[6] GILMORE, P. C., and GOMORY, R. E., A linear programming approach to the cutting stock problem: Part I. *Ops. Res.*, **9**, 849–59 (1961).
[7] GILMORE, P. C. and GOMORY, R. E., A linear programming approach to the cutting stock problem: Part II. *Ops. Res.*, **11**, 863–88 (1963).
[8] GILMORE, P. C. and GOMORY, R. E., Multistage cutting stock problems of two and more dimensions. *Ops. Res.*, **13**, 94–120 (1965).
[9] GILMORE, P. C. and GOMORY, R. E., The theory and computation of knapsack functions. *Ops. Res.*, **14**, 1045–74 (1966).
[10] GLOVER, F., A multiphase–dual algorithm for the zero–one integer programming problem. *Ops. Res.*, **13**, 879–919 (1965).

Chapter 11

Vehicle fleet size

INTRODUCTION

In the previous two chapters we considered the following problems:

    (a)   Minimize the mileage that a given fleet of vehicles has to travel in order to supply known customer demands,

and   (b)   Find the least number of vehicles of a given capacity needed to supply the customers, without regard to the mileage that the vehicles have to cover.

Solutions to these problems are essential preliminaries to finding the optimal size of a vehicle fleet and the way in which it should be operated so as to minimize total delivery costs.

Any distributor operating his own vehicle fleet, and whose customers' demands vary from period to period over a given cycle[1], needs to decide on the number and capacity of vehicles to have in his own fleet and on the number and capacity of vehicles that he should hire on an *ad hoc* basis. The demand cycle can be typically one week (with customer-demand varying from day to day) or in some distribution systems (where deliveries are made weekly) the cycle may span several months or even a year.

Two facets of the general problem of finding the optimal fleet size are considered in this chapter, depending on the initial assumptions regarding the vehicles that are available to make up the fleet.

The first problem to be analysed assumes that all the vehicles are of the same predetermined capacity; the optimal fleet size is then found by minimizing the total costs, which include both the fixed and the variable charges for both company-owned and hired vehicles. Determining the vehicle capacity in the first instance is usually not a difficult problem. We can derive, for example, the minimum total

---

[1] A period is defined as an interval of time during which a single delivery to customers may be made.

delivery costs for several alternative values of vehicle capacity and choose that capacity which yields the minimum minimorum. However, there are usually other considerations to be taken into account in choosing vehicle capacity, such as the nature of the product which is to be distributed, possible difficulties of access to various customers because of narrow roads or gates, and so on, so that the decision regarding the capacity of vehicles in the fleet can often be isolated as a separate issue.

In the second problem considered here we relax the condition that all the vehicles must be of the same capacity, and vehicles may now be of any capacity below a certain maximum size, which is again determined by the characteristics of the particular distribution system. This problem does not consider the routing of the various vehicles directly but uses some statistical information derived from simulations to find the optimal constitution of the vehicle fleet.

Review of the literature

Very little appears to have been published on the problem of optimal fleet size. Wyatt [2] considers the variation of total demand over a cycle and shows quite simply that in order to minimize costs the proportion of the time for which extra capacity should be hired is given by $f/(g_1 - g_2)$, where f is the fixed cost per unit capacity per day for company-owned vehicles (actually he considers the problem of hiring barges, not vehicles), g_2 is the variable cost per unit capacity per day for company-owned vehicles, and g_1 is the total cost per unit capacity per day for hired vehicles.

His approach does not take account of the routing of vehicles (which must obviously affect both the values of g_1 and g_2), or of the various constraints that these routes must satisfy and which may well affect the solution.

Gould [1] considers essentially the same problem as that considered by Wyatt, but extends the method to handle non-homogeneous fleets. The method proposed by Gould formulates the problem in linear programming terms, but again nothing is said of routing and route constraints. In fact, Gould's method applies only when one load is carried by a vehicle at any one time, with the result that his problem falls into the category of "loading" problems considered in Chapter 10. The author states that the model can be extended to cover more complex situations such as supplying two or more customers on one vehicle route, but that it then becomes far too big a matrix to solve.

ASSUMPTIONS AND OBJECTIVE

If the number of customers and customer demand vary from period to period (see the example in Fig. 11.1), then the optimal solution for the routes and for the number of vehicles required to supply the customer may also vary from period to period. Even for any given period the optimal solution for the number of vehicles required is not synonymous with the solution for minimizing total mileage, as can be seen from the example in Table 11.1 and Fig. 11.2. Although in this latter example two vehicles are sufficient to satisfy the demand, the total straight-line distance of the optimal routes for two vehicles (Fig. 11.2a) is 337, whereas for three vehicles (Fig. 11.2b) it is 263 (note that the addition of a fourth vehicle will not reduce the distance further, but will in fact increase it).

Thus, the solution to adopt must depend not just on the size of the vehicle fleet nor just on the distance, but on the cost of both. Furthermore, if customer demand varies from period to period, and if in any given period the number of required vehicles exceeds the number of available vehicles in the fleet, it becomes necessary to rely on hired vehicles, the cost of which must also be accounted for in the total cost function.

We make the following assumptions:

(1)   The customers (number and location) and their demands are known for each period in the cycle and remain unchanged from cycle to cycle.
(2)   Each company vehicle carries a fixed cost α per period. This cost includes depreciation, wages of the driver and mate, licence, insurance, and any other costs which are not mileage-dependent. The fleet consists of N vehicles.
(3)   The variable cost β describes the cost per mile for a company-owned vehicle and covers such items as fuel and oil, maintenance, tyres, and any other costs that can be shown to be mileage-dependent.
(4)   Similarly, each hired vehicle carries a fixed cost α' per period, and
(5)   The variable cost for a hired vehicle is β' per mile.

Usually $\alpha' > \alpha$ and $\beta' > \beta$.

The objective is to determine the value of N (the size of the vehicle fleet) such that the total of fixed and variable costs over the cycle is minimized.

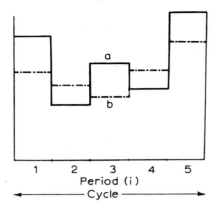

Fig. 11.1   Variation of customer demand and numbers over a cycle

(a) customer demand
(b) number of customers

Table 11.1   Example of five customers

Customer	Demand	Co-ordinates	
		x	y
1	75	10	90
2	10	5	80
3	30	10	10
4	60	90	20
5	25	95	35
Depot:		50	50

Vehicle capacity: 100

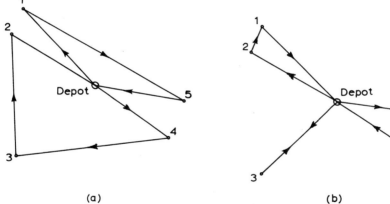

Fig. 11.2   Example of minimizing the number of vehicles versus minimizing route distances

(a) shortest routes using the minimum number of vehicles
(b) shortest routes possible using three vehicles

THE COST FUNCTION

Consider the ith period, in which the company vehicles travel a total distance of d_i miles (assuming that miles are taken as the basic unit of distance). In the same period N_i' vehicles are hired, and these travel a total distance of d_i'.

The cost to the company for the ith period arising from its own vehicles is

$$c_i = \alpha N + \beta d_i \qquad (11.1)$$

where the fleet size N is assumed to remain constant throughout the cycle, and the cost arising from the hiring of extra vehicles is

$$c'_i = \alpha' N'_i + \beta' d'_i \qquad (11.2)$$

These two linear cost functions are illustrated in Fig. 11.3.

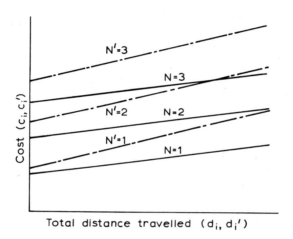

Fig. 11.3   Assumed cost functions

——— owned vehicles
— · — hired vehicles

The total cost for period i is

$$C_i = c_i + c'_i = \alpha N + \beta d_i + \alpha' N'_i + \beta' d'_i \qquad (11.3)$$

and the total cost over the whole cycle which consists of p periods is therefore given by

$$C = \sum_{i=1}^{p} C_i$$

$$= \alpha p N + \beta \sum_i d_i + \alpha' \sum_i N'_i + \beta' \sum_i d'_i \qquad (11.4)$$

Assignment of vehicles to routes

In any given period, the routes that are assigned to the hired vehicles must be carefully considered on the basis of the relative costs of operating company-owned or hired vehicles.

If the matrix of demands and routes in period i requires a total of v_i vehicles, and if the company fleet size is N, then the difference $N_i' = v_i - N$ is the number of vehicles to be hired for the period under consideration (where $N_i' \geqslant 0$). The total cost C_i for this period i is given in equation (11.3). The only unknowns in this expression are the two distances d_i and d_i' to be travelled by the company-owned and by the hired vehicles respectively. The total distance to be travelled by all the vehicles is $D_i = d_i + d_i'$ which is the length of the optimal tour using a total of v_i vehicles.

In order to minimize C_i for any given value of v_i the part of the function $\beta d_i + \beta' d_i'$ must be minimized. Since, usually, $\beta' > \beta$, it follows that for any given distance it is cheaper to operate company vehicles than hired ones.

The procedure adopted here is the following. The individual routes forming the distance-optimal tour using v_i vehicles are arranged in descending order. The company vehicles are assigned to the longer routes until the whole fleet is utilized. If $v_i > N$ the extra N_i' hired vehicles are then assigned to the remaining routes. It should be noted that strictly this procedure does not necessarily lead to a minimum of the function C_i for the period in question. It may, for example, be possible to find another set of v_i routes which is not optimal (and whose total mileage is longer than that of the routes considered previously), but whose "shorter" routes, to which the hired vehicles are assigned, are even shorter than the "shorter" routes of the distance-optimal tour. If such a set of routes is possible, it may be cheaper to operate these routes rather than the routes of the distance-minimizing tour, for then the extra cost of travelling a greater overall mileage may be more than offset by the assigning of hired vehicles to shorter routes. Although it is possible for such a situation to arise, it is not very likely to occur in practice, and if it does, the potential saving that would result by operating these routes, rather than the minimum-distance routes, would be rather small. The reason for this is that the "longer" routes of the distance-minimal tour are likely to be determined by the limits imposed by the various capacity, distance, and other constraints and cannot therefore be made much longer; and this result implies that the "shorter" routes cannot be made much shorter. Moreover, even if a set of routes is found of which the N_i' shorter ones are of smaller total length than the N_i' shorter routes in the distance-optimal tour, the total length of this new set of routes must not be very much greater than the length of the distance-optimal tour, otherwise the cost saving in $\beta' d_i'$ may be lower than the resultant increase in βd_i.

Out of a total of 20 randomly generated vehicle-scheduling problems with realistic constraints and values for the cost parameters α, β, α' and β' we have found that it was impossible to produce any cost saving by using distance-nonoptimal rather than the minimum-distance routes.

Method of solution

Consider period i in which a number of routes require a total of v_i vehicles, which must cover a total distance of at least D_i miles in order to supply the demands of all the customers during this period.

Let us now define two other solutions to the problem:

> v_{i1} is the smallest number of vehicles with which customer demands can be met, and this number corresponds to a total mileage D_{i1}.
>
> v_{i2} is the number of vehicles required to achieve the shortest total corresponding distance, denoted by D_{i2}.

As mentioned earlier, v_{i2} cannot be smaller than v_{i1} or v_i, and by definition v_{i1} cannot be larger than v_i, hence

$$v_{i2} \geqslant v_i \geqslant v_{i1}$$

and similarly

$$D_{i2} \leqslant D_i \leqslant D_{i1}$$

Clearly, the solution to the problem must lie between v_{i1} and v_{i2}, since no value of v_i below v_{i1} is feasible, while values above v_{i2} will only lead to increases both in fleet size and mileage and therefore result in higher total costs.

For any given array of customers and their demands the values for v_{i1} and v_{i2} can be found by using the methods suggested in the previous two chapters. Three situations may arise:

(1) $N < v_{i1}$
(2) $v_{i1} \leqslant N \leqslant v_{i2}$
(3) $N \geqslant v_{i2}$

Let us now analyse each of these situations.

(1) $N < v_{i1}$

The company fleet is not sufficient to supply the customers, and vehicles must be hired; the question is, how many? The smallest possible number is $v_{i1} - N$ and the largest possible number that must be investigated is $v_{i2} - N$. Since the best possible routes employing v_i ($v_{i1} \leqslant v_i \leqslant v_{i2}$) vehicles are known (they can be calculated from Chapters 9 and 10), all that is necessary is to allocate the hired vehicles to routes according to the procedure described earlier and calculate and compare the costs for alternative values of N_i' between the limits mentioned above. The number of vehicles hired and the routes that are operated in period i are then those that yield the minimum cost for this period.

(2) $v_{i1} \leqslant N \leqslant v_{i2}$

In this case the tours requiring v_{i1}, $v_{i1} + 1$, etc., up to N vehicles may be operated without any hiring of extra vehicles. However, the solution of not hiring any vehicles need not necessarily produce a minimum cost, and tours requiring more than N vehicles (up to v_{i2}) and the hiring of the remainder, must also be investigated. Again, the total costs for various values of v_i can be compared and those routes which produce the minimum cost are then chosen.

(3) $N \geqslant v_{i2}$

In this case (and provided the assumptions that $\alpha' > \alpha$ and $\beta' > \beta$ are valid), no hiring is necessary and those routes which produce the minimum cost for this period are again chosen.

Having thus found the best routes to be operated during each period and the number of vehicles to be hired (if any), the total cost function C over the whole cycle can be calculated from equation (11.4). This cost function can be calculated for all possible values of the company fleet N, and that number of vehicles which produces the minimum cost is then adopted. The values of N must range between an upper limit of $\max_i v_{i2}$ (i.e. the largest possible number of vehicles that may have to be used in any one period) and a lower bound of $\min_i v_{i1}$ (i.e. the smallest possible number of vehicles that can supply at least one period). One should note that the upper bound is absolute and independent of the values of the cost parameters, whereas the lower bound is relative and applies only when $\alpha' > \alpha$ and $\beta' > \beta$, because then (given any set of routes, one for each period) it is always cheaper to operate these routes with company-owned vehicles rather than with hired ones. If the above relation between the cost parameters does not hold and if there are no guide-lines for determining the lower bound for N, then values down to $N = 0$ may have to be investigated. The procedure for finding the optimal

Table 11.2   Locations and demands of 30 customers

Customers	Location x	Location y	Demands for period 1	2	3	4	5	Total over cycle
1	60	29	27	0	20	0	20	67
2	55	3	50	0	50	60	50	210
3	5	75	65	0	0	65	65	195
4	12	5	0	20	25	0	22	67
5	66	9	22	0	0	26	17	65
6	18	57	0	15	18	0	15	48
7	44	77	33	0	20	0	28	81
8	99	24	10	0	0	10	10	30
9	53	55	0	20	41	0	37	98
10	61	63	15	0	15	0	15	45
11	32	61	0	10	18	0	12	40
12	55	95	0	25	32	0	35	92
13	75	27	47	0	26	0	37	110
14	49	4	12	0	0	27	14	53
15	8	38	59	0	0	13	65	137
16	45	11	65	0	0	50	65	180
17	71	89	5	0	8	0	10	23
18	28	96	17	0	0	19	15	51
19	76	77	0	20	45	0	50	115
20	25	40	30	0	0	28	25	83
21	53	42	26	0	0	31	30	87
22	78	64	43	0	29	0	33	105
23	77	52	0	23	35	0	28	86
24	39	44	0	26	40	0	34	100
25	5	67	50	0	25	0	50	125
26	92	8	70	0	0	40	60	170
27	22	34	12	0	0	9	5	26
28	93	38	0	15	22	0	12	49
29	42	19	10	0	0	10	10	30
30	94	80	15	10	15	10	10	60
Total demands			683	184	484	398	879	
No. of customers			21	10	18	14	30	

value of N is to start with, say, the upper bound (namely put $N = v_{i2}$), calculate the corresponding cost C, and repeat for new values of N, reducing it by one vehicle at a time, until the minimum for C is found; or alternatively until the lower bound is reached (namely $N = v_{i1}$).

A NUMERICAL EXAMPLE

A detailed numerical example will serve to illustrate the proposed method for determining the optimal fleet size. In this example a day is taken as the "period" and a working week (i.e. five days) as the cycle. The number, location. and demand of customers varies from day to day, but the pattern is the same from week to week.

Table 11.2 shows the location and demand of each customer for each period. The locations are given in terms of x and y co-ordinates (as in Table 11.1) and lie within an imaginary 100×100 km square with the depot at the centre. A total of 93 deliveries must be made during the whole week, but the maximum number for any one day is 30. The demands given in the table may be taken as being in, say, 50-kg units (or cwt) of some commodity, and the capacity of the vehicles constituting the fleet is 5 tons. The maximum length of a vehicle route is not allowed to exceed 200 km, and the allowance for drop-time is neglected.

Five different sets of cost parameters are investigated (given in Table 11.3) and the problem is solved for each. From the resulting

Table 11.3   Cost parameters

Code	α	β	α'	β'
I	10	·05	10	·1
II	10	·05	20	·1
III	10	·05	10	·4
IV	10	·05	15	·4
V	10	·05	15	·5

answers it will be possible to draw conclusions about the sensitivity of the model to these cost parameters.

The minimum number of vehicles per period

The minimum number of vehicles that are necessary to supply all the customers in each period can be found by solving the cor-

Table 11.4   Minimum fleet size requirements

Period 1: 7 vehicles

Vehicle	Customers	Load
1	10, 21, 15	100
2	5, 14, 16	99
3	27, 29, 2, 1	99
4	22, 13	90
5	17, 30, 8, 26	100
6	25, 18, 7	100
7	3, 20	95

Period 2: 2 vehicles

Vehicle	Customers	Load
1	12, 19, 30, 28, 23	93
2	24, 4, 6, 11, 9	91

Period 3: 5 vehicles

Vehicle	Customers	Load
1	7, 17, 30, 10, 9	99
2	19, 28, 13	93
3	11, 6, 24, 1	96
4	2, 4, 25	100
5	12, 22, 23	96

Period 4: 5 vehicles

Vehicle	Customers	Load
1	2, 14, 29	97
2	3, 18	84
3	21	31
4	30, 8, 26, 5	86
5	20, 15, 27, 16	100

Period 5: 9 vehicles

Vehicle	Customers	Load
1	26, 8, 28, 10	97
2	18, 3, 6	95
3	21, 16	95
4	9, 25, 11	99
5	2, 29, 27, 24	99
6	22, 23, 13	98
7	7, 17, 30, 19	98
8	20, 4, 14, 5, 1	98
9	15, 12	100

responding loading problems, using one of the methods described in Chapter 10, yielding the following results:

$$v_{11} = 7 \qquad v_{41} = 5$$
$$v_{21} = 2 \qquad v_{51} = 9$$
$$v_{31} = 5$$

The detailed results are summarized in Table 11.4.

The shortest tours

Having calculated the minimum number of vehicles for each

Table 11.5 Calculation of shortest tours

	Period 1	Period 2	Period 3	Period 4	Period 5
$v_{i1} =$	7: 916	2*: 331	5: 695	5*: 573	9: 1,146
	8*: 858	3: 336	6*: 600	6: 622	10*: 1,046
	9: 875		7: 605		11: 1,055

* This is the value of v_{i2} which yields the shortest D_{i2}.

Table 11.6 The shortest routes for periods 1, 3 and 5

Route	Period 1	Period 3	Period 5
1	25, 18, 7	4, 2, 1	21, 5, 8, 28, 23
2	13, 1, 21	19, 30, 17, 12	9
3	5, 2, 14, 27	13, 28, 23	25, 6, 24
4	22, 30, 17, 10	24	30, 17, 12, 18, 7
5	3	10, 22, 9	2, 14, 4, 27
6	29, 16	7, 25, 6, 11	13, 26
7	15, 20		10, 19, 22
8	26, 8		3, 11
9			1, 16, 29
10			20, 15

Table 11.7 Individual route distances

Period		1	2	3	4	5	6	7	8	9	10
1	M	127	108	127	101	200	136	117			
	S	136	70	133	121	102	79	86	131		
2	M	180	151								
	S	180	151								
3	M	133	133	107	200	122					
	S	150	141	102	24	65	118				
4	M	102	132	16	196	127					
	S	102	132	16	196	127					
5	M	148	135	79	102	125	101	135	160	161	
	S	142	10	100	172	149	117	81	102	86	86

period, we can now apply the 3-optimal algorithm of Chapter 9 to determine the near-optimal routes. We can find the minimum number of routes required, v_{i1}, and the corresponding total distance involved. We can then investigate fleet size of $v_{i1} + 1$, $v_{i1} + 2$, etc., until the absolute shortest tour is obtained, and the number of vehicles corresponding to that is v_{i2}. The results for all five periods are shown in Table 11.5. The first figure in each column corresponds to the number of vehicles and the second to the total length of the routes using that number of vehicles. The first row in the table gives the values of v_{i1} and the corresponding distances D_{i1}. It can be seen from

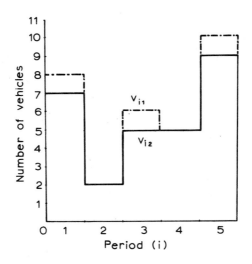

Fig. 11.4   Variation of v_{i1} and v_{i2} with the period i

v_{i1} = minimum number of vehicles (in period i)
v_{i2} = number of vehicles to give shortest tour

Table 11.5 that in periods 2 and 4 the shortest routes use the minimum number of vehicles required for these periods (i.e. $v_{i1} = v_{i2}$); for periods 1, 3 and 5 the shortest routes use the minimum number plus one (i.e. $v_{i2} = v_{i1} + 1$). The optimal routes using the minimum number of vehicles visit customers in the same order as that shown in Table 11.4. The absolute shortest routes for periods 1, 3 and 5 are shown in Table 11.6, whereas, as mentioned above, those for periods 2 and 4 are the same as those shown in Table 11.4.

Table 11.7 gives the lengths of the individual route distances of the tours using v_{i1} up to v_{i2} vehicles, and contains all the information necessary to continue to the next stage of solution. In this table, M refers to the tour using the minimum number of vehicles v_{i1}, and S refers to the shortest tour using v_{i2} vehicles.

Optimal fleet-size calculation

The variations of v_{i1} and v_{i2} over the cycle are shown in Fig. 11.4. From this figure it is seen that the optimal fleet size may be anywhere between a lower limit of 2 and an upper limit of 10 vehicles.

Calculating now the total cost over the cycle, for $N = 2, 3, \ldots, 10$, the optimal value of N can be determined. The results for the various cases of Table 11.3 are shown in Table 11.8.

Table 11.8   Optimal fleet sizes and routes

Cost code	Optimum fleet size	Total cost over cycle	Tours
I	5	505	M, M, M, M, M
II	6	559	⎫
III	7	594	⎬ M, M, S, M, M
IV	8	602	⎫
V	9	610	⎬ S, M, S, M, M

In this table the M and S again refer to the 3-optimal tours using the minimum of vehicles v_{i1} and those with a fleet size of v_{i2}, respectively. There are five tours, one for each period. Thus, for example, with cost structure IV (see Table 11.3) the optimal fleet size is $N = 8$ vehicles at a cost of 602 per cycle, and the tours to be operated are:

Period 1: The route pattern shown in the first column of Table 11.6;
Period 2: The route pattern shown in Table 11.4;
Period 3: The route pattern shown in the second column of Table 11.6;
Period 4: The route pattern shown in Table 11.4;
Period 5: The route pattern shown in Table 11.4.

Comparing the results for cost structures I and II in Table 11.8, we note that doubling the value of α' (i.e. the fixed hiring charge per vehicle) only increases the total cycle costs by about 11 per cent and the optimal fleet size increases from 5 to 6 vehicles, so that a different set of routes must be operated in period 3. Comparing the results for cost structures I and III shows that total costs increase by about 18 per cent for a four-fold increase of the distance-dependent hiring charges, but the optimal fleet size now increases by 2 vehicles, from 5 to 7. It is interesting to note that the routes to be operated under cost structure III are the same as those to be operated under cost structure II.

Note that under cost structure IV (with $\alpha' = 1 \cdot 5\alpha$ and $\beta' = 8\beta$) the optimum fleet size is 8 vehicles with one vehicle to be hired in only one period (period 5), and that under cost structure V (with $\alpha' = 1 \cdot 5\alpha$ and $\beta' = 10\beta$), no hiring at all is necessary and the optimal fleet size is 9 vehicles.

THE OPTIMAL COMPOSITION OF A FLEET

So far we have analysed the use of a fleet with vehicles of equal given capacity, but if vehicles of various capacities can be considered, the problem becomes that of determining the optimal composition of the fleet for the cycle, coupled with the problem of hiring vehicles of an appropriate size and in the required number when demand exceeds the available capacity.

We now make the following assumptions and observations.

(1)   Once again, it is assumed that customer demands in each period are known, and that each period in one cycle is identical with the corresponding period in the next cycle. Let the total demand in period i be W_i (where $i = 1, 2, \ldots, p$).

(2)   There are m different types of vehicles which can be considered for the fleet. A vehicle of type j (where $j = 1, 2, \ldots, m$) has a capacity Q_j. If x_j vehicles of type j are selected for the fleet, then the total capacity of the fleet is given by

$$T = \sum_{j=1}^{m} x_j Q_j \tag{11.5}$$

(3)   The cost per vehicle per period is assumed to depend on vehicle capacity. An increase in its capacity means that the vehicle can generally supply more customers in one route. Thus, in any given problem the distance travelled by a vehicle depends on its capacity and to some extent on the composition of the rest of the fleet, but it is assumed that the latter effect is negligible, particularly as the fixed-cost element in the cost function is often quite substantial. It

is, therefore, assumed that the cost per vehicle of capacity Q_j is e_j per period and that this cost is known for all the m vehicle types. In a study of the fleet operations of a large distribution firm in Britain we found that

$$e = a + b\sqrt{Q}$$

where a and b are constants, but the precise relationship between e and Q is not germane to our discussion. The assumption made here is merely that—based on an analysis of historical data or on

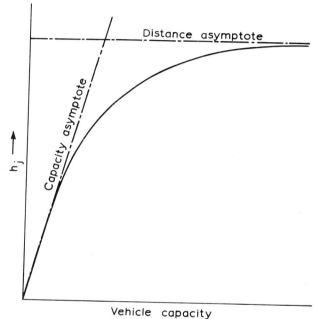

Fig. 11.5 Average of the maximum number of customers that can be served by a vehicle on a single route (derived by simulation)

simulation—an array of costs e_j can be determined, so that the inclusion of a vehicle of type j in the fleet incurs a cost of e_j per period, irrespective of the composition of the fleet and of customer demands in that period.

(4) There are m' types of vehicles available for hire, and it is assumed that a vehicle of type j (where $j = 1, 2, \ldots, m'$) has a capacity Q'_j and incurs a cost of e'_j per period. If x'_{ij} is the number of hired vehicles of type j in period i, then the capacity of the hired vehicles in that period is

$$T'_i = \sum_{j=1}^{m'} x'_{ij} Q'_j \qquad (11.6)$$

(5)   Let us further assume that a company vehicle of type j can supply h_j customers per period, while a hired vehicle can supply h'_j customers. These data may again be determined either from historical records or by simulation (see an example in Fig. 11.5).

The problem of determining the optimal composition of the fleet may now be formulated as follows. Find the value of the variables x_j and x'_{ij} so as to minimize the total cost for the cycle. The cost for period i is

$$C_i = \sum_{j=1}^{m} e_j x_j + \sum_{j=1}^{m'} e'_j x'_{ij} \qquad (11.7)$$

and the cost per the whole cycle is

$$C = \sum_{i=1}^{p} C_i = p \sum_{j=1}^{m} e_j x_j + \sum_{i=1}^{p} \sum_{j=1}^{m'} e'_j x'_{ij} \qquad (11.8)$$

The constraints are as follows:

Capacity constraints – the total capacity of the fleet and of the hired vehicles must be adequate to meet the demand:

$$T_i + T'_i \geqslant W_i \qquad (11.9)$$

Customer constraints – the total number of customers that the vehicles can supply must be at least as high as the number of customers requiring service in period i (let this number be n_i):

$$h_j x_j + \sum_{j=1}^{m'} h'_j x'_{ij} \geqslant n_i \qquad (11.10)$$

This is, therefore, an allocation problem in integer programming, since the values of x_j and x'_{ij} must be integer values, and also

$$x_j, \ x'_{ij} \geqslant 0$$

The solution to this programming problem provides the optimal composition of the company fleet and also specifies the number and type of vehicles to be hired in each period.

REFERENCES

[1] GOULD, J., The size and composition of a road transport fleet. *Opl. Res. Q.*, **20**, 81–92 (1969).
[2] WYATT, J. K., Optimal fleet size. Letter to the Editor, *Opl. Res. Q.*, **12**, 187–8 (1961).

AUTHOR INDEX

SUBJECT INDEX